Approaches to Teaching Balzac's *Old Goriot*

Aproaches to Teaching World Literature

Joseph Gibaldi, series editor

For a complete listing of titles, see the last pages of this book.

Approaches to Teaching Balzac's *Old Goriot*

Edited by

Michal Peled Ginsburg

The Modern Language Association of America
New York 2000

Library of Congress Cataloging-in-Publication Data

Approaches to teaching Balzac's Old Goriot / edited by Michal Peled Ginsburg.
p. cm. — (Approaches to teaching world literature ; 68)
Includes bibliographical references and index.
ISBN 0-87352-759-3 (cloth) — ISBN 0-87352-760-7 (pbk.)
1. Balzac, Honoré de, 1799–1850. Père Goriot. I. Ginsburg, Michal Peled, 1947–
II. Series.
PQ2168 .A77 2000 00-060952
ISSN 1059-1133

Cover illustration of the paperback edition: *Le Père Goriot*, a portrait by Charles Huard from
Œuvres complètes de Honoré de Balzac (Paris: Conard, 1912), vol. 6.

The essay by James H. Reid is adapted in part from James H. Reid,
Narration and Description in the French Realist Novel: The Temporality of Lying and Forgetting
(Cambridge: Cambridge UP, 1993). Used by permission of Cambridge University Press.

Published by The Modern Language Association of America
26 Broadway, New York, New York 10004-1789
www.mla.org

CONTENTS

PREFACE TO THE SERIES

In *The Art of Teaching* Gilbert Highet wrote, "Bad teaching wastes a great deal of effort, and spoils many lives which might have been full of energy and happiness." All too many teachers have failed in their work, Highet argued, simply "because they have not thought about it." We hope that the Approaches to Teaching World Literature series, sponsored by the Modern Language Association's Publications Committee, will not only improve the craft—as well as the art—of teaching but also encourage serious and continuing discussion of the aims and methods of teaching literature.

The principal objective of the series is to collect within each volume different points of view on teaching a specific literary work, a literary tradition, or a writer widely taught at the undergraduate level. The preparation of each volume begins with a wide-ranging survey of instructors, thus enabling us to include in the volume the philosophies and approaches, thoughts and methods of scores of experienced teachers. The result is a sourcebook of material, information, and ideas on teaching the subject of the volume to undergraduates.

The series is intended to serve nonspecialists as well as specialists, inexperienced as well as experienced teachers, graduate students who wish to learn effective ways of teaching as well as senior professors who wish to compare their own approaches with the approaches of colleagues in other schools. Of course, no volume in the series can ever substitute for erudition, intelligence, creativity, and sensitivity in teaching. We hope merely that each book will point readers in useful directions; at most each will offer only a first step in the long journey to successful teaching.

Joseph Gibaldi
Series Editor

PREFACE TO THE VOLUME

In my experience of teaching the European novel to American undergraduates two things never fail to surprise me. The first is the extent to which, in the late twentieth century, students' expectations when reading a novel still conform, by and large, to norms and criteria established by the nineteenth-century realist novel. It seems as if the set of beliefs that gets expressed in realist writing is still very much with us, in spite of changes both in our world and in our understanding of the world. If this is so, then teaching the realist novel of the nineteenth century can contribute not only to an understanding of what is by now a quite remote past but also, and what is as important, to a critical understanding of our own culture.

The second thing that surprises me is the extent to which Balzac, the epitome of realism in the French tradition, does not strike American students as realistic in the least. Insofar as this is the result of a difference in reality—a difference between social life in France of the early nineteenth century and America of the late twentieth—it suggests how useful reading Balzac can be for understanding postrevolutionary French society. Indeed, Balzac's novels provide us with a uniquely complicated historical perspective: written mainly during the July Monarchy, they anticipate social and economic developments that became manifest during the Second Empire; their action usually takes place during the Restoration, but the life of the characters is repeatedly shown to have been shaped by the events of the Revolution and Empire. Insofar as students' reaction depends on their different sense of what counts as realistic, it brings home—to us and to them—how one's sense of what is realistic is culturally bound. Again, the historical glance at the past is accompanied by a critical reflection on the present.

In saying this I do not mean to suggest that Balzac's oeuvre should be reduced to realism in a narrow way. Not only did Balzac write many novels that are in some sense nonrealistic (fantastic, romantic, philosophical, etc.) but also, as many critics have shown, even his so-called realist texts point to a crisis of realistic representation. And yet, whereas Flaubert's status as a realist has undergone a dramatic revision (so that we now think of Flaubert as the precursor of the modern novel, a kin spirit to Mallarmé), Balzac's has not. No matter how much recent readings of Balzac have made us aware of the impasses of realistic representation, they have not weakened our conviction that if realism actually exists, Balzac practices it. It is Balzac's status as the quintessential novelist of the bourgeois nineteenth century (a century dominated by the ideology of realism) that continues to deserve our attention.

Determining what of Balzac's enormous oeuvre one should teach (or teach first) is not easy. Though the editor of the Gallimard Folio series edition of *Père*

Goriot states categorically that "a reader who has never read a line of Balzac need not hesitate even a second: one must start with *Le Père Goriot*"(7; my trans.), he immediately qualifies his assertion by suggesting that the grounds on which one may want to claim centrality for *Père Goriot* are not thematic but rather structural (or formal): the novel provides entrée into much of the *Comédie humaine* by virtue of the large proportion of its characters who reappear in other texts. Some of them, such as Nucingen, Bianchon, de Marsay, and Rastignac, appear many times—respectively in thirty, twenty-eight, twenty-six, and twenty-four other novels (8). In all other respects *Père Goriot* is but one among many entryways to the complex world of the *Comédie humaine*.

This is a crucial point that bears repeating: if we take seriously Balzac's contention (in the *avant-propos* to the *Comédie humaine*) to be the secretary of society and to give a novelistic equivalent of the civil registry, no single work in the *Comédie humaine* can be taken as a synecdoche for the whole. Balzac himself made this point when he said, apologetically, that though *Père Goriot* is a "monstrously sad" work, "it was necessary, in order to give a complete picture [pour être complet], to show the moral sewer of Paris" (qtd. in van Rossum-Guyon, "*Le Père Goriot*" xxix–xxx; my trans.). The "moral sewer" of Paris, no matter how important and fascinating, is not the whole history or the whole story, and we cannot be done with Balzac by reading just one novel.

The choice of *Père Goriot* as the novel that represents Balzac in the Approaches to Teaching World Literature series should be considered, then, as a more or less contingent one. It may be that the "moral sewer" of *Père Goriot* makes a better read than the melancholy aridity of *Eugénie Grandet*, that the story of education and disillusionment *Père Goriot* tells is shorter, and more accessible, than that of Lucien de Rubempré told in *Illusions perdues*, and so on. Insisting on the contingency involved in choosing this particular work does not diminish its power and importance but rather alerts students to the multifacetedness of the social world represented by Balzac and can help encourage them to read more of the *Comédie humaine*.

Still, in the hundred-and-fifty-odd years since *Père Goriot*'s publication the novel has acquired a special status, partially perhaps through being repeatedly taught (probably for the contingent reasons mentioned above). Already in Flaubert's time Rastignac's success story was somewhat of a cliché—it is as such that Deslauriers, in *L'Education sentimentale*, evokes it when he advises Frédéric to cultivate the rich and influential Mme Dambreuse. The status of *Père Goriot* as the paradigmatic Balzacian text has been related not only to the story it tells but also to the way it represents the world: Erich Auerbach's choice, in *Mimesis*, of the description of Mme Vauquer's boardinghouse as exemplary of Balzac's writing greatly contributed to this view. And just as authors, from Emile Zola to Alain Robbe-Grillet, tried to find ways of writing that differed from Balzac's, critics in the last couple of decades have tried to show the centrality of what up to then were considered marginal Balzacian texts. The result of this gradual move away from (a certain understanding of) the Balzacian text is that, though *Père Goriot* is still regularly taught and frequently visited by critics (in Mark Waggoner's *Bibliography of Balzac Criticism, 1930–1990*, *Old Goriot* has more entries than any other Balzac text), it has not, on the whole, received the kind of critical attention that other Balzacian texts (such as the fantastic and philosophical *Peau de chagrin* and the allegorical *Chef-d'œuvre inconnu*) have recently received. One purpose of the present volume is to show that *Père Goriot*, in spite of its status as the obvious Balzac novel, can be read in many new and different ways. By offering fresh interpretations that reflect on and revise the critical tradition, the volume intends to give the reader a sense of what this (for better or for worse) canonical text may mean at the beginning of the twenty-first century.

I would like to thank the contributors to the volume for their cooperation and patience, Stirling Haig and Dean de la Motte for letting me benefit from their experience as Approaches editors, Joseph Gibaldi for his continuous support of the project, and Larry Schehr for his help and jokes. A Northwestern University Research Grant facilitated research for the annotated map Père Goriot*'s Paris*; I would like to thank Vinay Swamy for his help with this research.

Part One

MATERIALS

Editions and Translations

French Editions

The majority of survey respondents who teach *Père Goriot* in French do not show strong attachment to one particular edition. The criteria they mention as determining their choice are availability and cost. Four inexpensive editions are currently available: the Garnier-Flammarion (Citron), Livre de Poche (van Rossum-Guyon), Pocket (Gengembre; Lire et voir les classiques series), and Gallimard (Bodin; Folio series). All four use the text of the Furne edition of 1843, with the corrections Balzac made on his personal copy; two (Pocket and Gallimard Folio) reproduce the 1835 Werdet edition's division of the novel into four parts (which the Furne edition eliminates).

The Garnier-Flammarion edition is introduced by Philippe Berthier. The text is preceded by two prefaces by Balzac (written for the first and second editions) and is followed by notes, a short selection of excerpts from critics, a bibliography, and a chronology of the life of Balzac.

The Livre de Poche edition includes a preface by Françoise van Rossum-Guyon with a short rejoinder by the novelist Michel Butor. The text is followed by an appendix that includes the two prefaces by Balzac, a commentary by Nicole Mozet (a discussion of various aspects of the novel, some excerpts from other Balzac novels, a chronology of the life of Balzac, and a bibliography), and notes.

The Pocket edition has a preface by Gérard Gengembre. Short textual notes by Gengembre are given at the bottom of the page. An iconographic dossier, compiled by Sylvie Marcovitch, includes images of places mentioned in the novel and representations of the characters. A historical and literary dossier, compiled by Gengembre, includes a chronology of Balzac's life, the two prefaces, a passage Balzac eliminated from the final edition, excerpts from other Balzac novels, a bibliography, and a filmography.

The Gallimard Folio edition (used in this volume unless otherwise indicated) includes a preface by Félicien Marceau. The text is followed by a biography of Balzac, a collection of documents (the two prefaces, extracts from other prefaces and from the correspondence, and the passage eliminated from the final edition), and extensive notes.

Besides these four editions, respondents mentioned the Classiques Garnier edition by Pierre-Georges Castex (which is very costly); Peter Lock's edition published by St. Martin's; and Horatio Smith's edition, published by Scribner.

English Editions

All respondents who teach *Old Goriot* in English admit, unenthusiastically, that they use the Marion Ayton Crawford translation, published by Penguin (the edition used in this volume unless otherwise indicated). All agree that the translation is not very good but say they cannot come up with an alternative. One respondent, making virtue of necessity, mentions that when using the Crawford translation she has to repeatedly point out to students "the desexualization of Balzac's text," which leads to interesting discussions. Other respondents also mention directing students' attention to inaccuracies in translation as a way of bringing to the fore linguistic, literary, and cultural issues.

The new (1998) Norton Critical Edition has a short introduction by Peter Brooks, notes at the bottom of the page, a good selection of responses and twentieth-century criticism, a chronology of Balzac's life, and a bibliography. It also includes a partial map of Paris in 1820. The translation by Burton Raffel the edition reproduces is much more lively than that by Crawford but very often unnecessarily inaccurate. Thus the opening of the novel has "Madame Vauquer (whose maiden name was Conflans, no less) is an old woman [. . .]" (5) for "Madame Vauquer, née de Conflans, est une vieille femme [. . .]" (21).

Courses and Teaching

For the most part, *Père Goriot* is being taught in French, in French department courses. It is also taught in English in comparative literature courses (The Novel and Social Change, the Realist Novel in Europe, a course on narrative), humanities courses, English department courses (Literature of the City), and history courses (Modern France, 1789 to the Present; Urban Culture in Modern Europe). It should be noted, however, that all but one of the survey respondents come from literary studies, so we don't have sufficient information to determine how often and in what ways Balzac's novel is used in history courses, for example.

Within French departments the novel is taught in a variety of courses: upper- and lower-division courses, courses for majors and nonmajors, required and elective courses. It is taught very often in survey courses on French literature, the nineteenth and twentieth centuries, nineteenth-century literature, the nineteenth-century novel, and nineteenth-century literature and culture.

The novel is also often taught in courses on realism or Romanticism or both (in both French and comparative literature departments). It is taught in a variety of special-topic courses (mostly for seniors or graduate students): a single-author course on Balzac, a course on sociological approaches to modern fiction, and courses on transgression and literature and on reading bodies. The novel is most frequently taught (both in French and in English, both within the French department and as an interdisciplinary course) in special-topic courses on Paris (especially Paris of the nineteenth century).

Instructors who teach in English or to graduate students or who use excerpts spend as little as one week on the novel. Others spend as much as one semester; most spend two to three weeks. Given the predominance of survey courses, it is not surprising that the novel is frequently paired with French works that precede or follow it (most often *Madame Bovary, Le Rouge et le noir, René, Germinal;* less often *Lorenzaccio, Les Fleurs du mal, L'Education sentimental, L'Assomoir, Bel Ami, Swann's Way*). Other pairings include George Sand's *Indiana* (to help students think about what happens to female protagonists in the realist bildungsroman), Victor Hugo's *Notre-Dame de Paris* (for Parisian geography) and Delphine Gay de Girardin's *La Canne de M. de Balzac* (see Waller's essay in this volume). In terms of other Balzac texts, respondents mentioned teaching the novel together with the "Avant-propos" to the *Comédie humaine,* with *Gobseck,* and with *Les Secrets de la princesse de Cadignan*—"its near opposite" (on the last two see respectively the essays by Le Calvez and by Lacour in this volume). For a list of possible texts (both French and non-French) to include in a course that features *Old Goriot,* see Porter's essay in this volume.

Instructors choose the novel for a variety of reasons: "it is dramatic and a good read," both accessible and engaging; it is the right length—but complex enough to sustain interest and discussion; it is the "archetypal Balzacian novel" or, at least, the most famous; it straddles Romanticism and realism. The novel is chosen for its importance to an understanding of nineteenth-century realism (and realism's ideological interests)—it is "a textbook for important realist codes"; for its importance to an understanding of the nineteenth-century novel in general; and for its "portrait of a society in competitive flux." It is considered "the perfect novel for postrevolutionary and Restoration social life"; a good starting point for a discussion of the role of the city in the nineteenth century; a good example of the "conflict between the individual and social values"; and a good representative of the novel of education.

The main difficulty for teaching the novel in French is its vocabulary, and this difficulty is mostly felt in the long and detailed descriptions. Financial terms and issues, which are crucial to the plot, are also complicated and hard to understand. In both French and English, getting into the novel poses a problem because of the lengthy exposition. One proposed solution is to prepare students by giving them in advance a brief idea (citing the "Avant-propos" to the *Comédie humaine*) of Balzac's understanding of the relation between milieu, on the one hand, and character and action, on the other.

In terms of contents, students have a particularly hard time understanding or relating to the sexual mores taken for granted by the novel (marriage as a business transaction, extramarital relationships). They also have trouble comprehending the complexity of class structure and don't normally have sufficient knowledge of the novel's sociohistorical context. Specific cultural references (e.g., the wordplay involving the suffix *-rama*) need to be explained. As to melodrama, some instructors say it appeals to students, while other instructors say it poses difficulty (one proposed solution is to compare the novel to Westerns or soap operas). Respondents also mention that Balzac's gender characterization and cynicism can turn the students off.

Students like the "detective story" aspect of the novel, the sense of a real plot, and characters who are clearly drawn and who seem at times "bigger than life." They find it easy to identify with Rastignac (which explains why convincing them of his bad faith is a difficult task). While Vautrin seems to "go over well," some instructors report that students have a hard time relating to Goriot (primarily, probably, because he is old and they are young). One respondent states that students find the moral issues the novel raises interesting and relevant; another, that they appreciate the portrayal of city life in the nineteenth century and of its relation to social life. Many instructors are of the opinion that, in spite of the different social context, "most of the novel is easily interpretable into modern terms: questions of ambition, money, love, the desire to control society." If the instructor wishes to focus on these broad issues, pastiches and parodies are proposed as an excellent way of getting the students to modernize the text.

Instructors find that the novel poses several challenges to their teaching: explaining to the students the irony of the narrator (or his positioning); getting them beyond liking and disliking or judging characters (probably a problem with teaching any novel, maybe even any literary text); getting them to see the text's "subtlety in cultural codes" or, more modestly, getting them to understand another culture in all its difference.

The most common assignments are papers of various lengths and natures: interpretative papers on assigned topics; research papers on either literary or historical topics; and papers linking the novel to a theoretical text (e.g., asking students to think about how a few pages from Michel Foucault on the panopticon relate to the treatment of seeing in the novel or how a few pages from Roland Barthes's *S/Z* relate to the treatment of plot). Quite a few respondents mention asking students to do close readings of passages they or the instructor select; these can be done individually or in groups. Another assignment is asking students to map the novel's plot (for more on this type of assignment, see the essay by Marcus and Schwartz in this volume).

Background Reading

Many respondents feel that in teaching *Père Goriot* in French, especially in lower-division courses, assigning secondary sources is either unnecessary or unrealistic. For students in other courses, and for instructors themselves, the most pressing need seems to be that of sociohistorical background. Suggested readings include: John Lough and Muriel Lough, *An Introduction to Nineteenth Century France,* particularly addressed to a British reader; F. W. J. Hemmings,

Culture and Society in France, 1789–1848; and Gordon Wright, *France in Modern Times: From the Enlightenment to the Present.* For a broad background, E. J. Hobsbawm's *The Age of Revolution: Europe, 1789–1848* is suggested. For the history of Paris during the Restoration and July Monarchy, one might read the relevant chapters in Johannes Willms, *Paris: Capital of Europe.* The fourth volume of *A History of Private Life,* edited by Michelle Perrot, offers a useful complement to public history. Especially pertinent may be the third chapter, which opens with a cross-sectional drawing of an apartment house (where the different floors reflect class divisions).

Two books that combine historical background with thematic reading are David Bellos, *Honoré de Balzac:* Old Goriot, and Martin Kanes, Père Goriot: *Anatomy of a Troubled World.* The Norton edition of the novel also includes a variety of background material.

In French, the volume *Le Dix-Neuvième Siècle,* edited by Henri Mitterand with a historical introduction by Pierre Nora, in the series Littérature: textes et documents, combines historical and literary analysis. On student life in Paris in the first half of the nineteenth century, one can consult Jean-Claude Caron, *Générations romantiques: les étudiants de Paris et le Quartier Latin, 1814–1851.* Note, however, that much of the information about student life and conditions in this book comes from Balzac's novels. As Oscar Wilde put it, "The Nineteenth Century, as we know it, is largely an invention of Balzac's" (32). Gérard Gengembre's volume on *Père Goriot* provides an excellent selection of interpretative essays on the novel. Pierre Barbéris's Le Père Goriot *de Balzac: écriture, structure, signification* is also a useful tool.

The choice of literary-critical works, either for students or for the instructor, depends of course on the particular approach one adopts in teaching the novel. However, several books have been mentioned by many respondents and seem therefore to be of general interest. They are those of Erich Auerbach, Roland Barthes, Janet Beizer, Peter Brooks (*Imagination* and *Reading*), Georg Lukács ("*Writer*"), Franco Moretti (*Atlas* and *Way*), Sandy Petrey, Christopher Prendergast (*Balzac* and *Paris*), and Richard Terdiman.

Audiovisual Materials

Three kinds of visual materials seem to be commonly used: illustrations from a variety of editions of the novel, pictorial representations of Paris, and maps of Paris. One source for old illustrations is a special issue of *L'Année balzacienne* devoted to the novel (1986). The illustrations can be used in conjunction with caricatures from the period and linked to a discussion of the descriptions of the characters in the novel. As for representations of Paris, they include slides of contemporary Paris as well as pictorial representations of Paris of the nineteenth century. For the use of maps, see the essay by Sharon Marcus and Vanessa Schwartz in this volume.

Only two films were mentioned by respondents: one instructor uses selections from *Les Enfants du paradis* to give students an idea of mid-nineteenth-century Paris; the other shows the video *Paris in the Time of Balzac*. However, the filmography at the end of the Pocket edition of the novel lists the following films—yet to be exploited:

Karrierre in Paris. Dir. Georg C. Klaren and Hans G. Rudolph. 1951. (German)
Le Père Goriot. Dir. Travers Vale. 1915. (American)
Le Père Goriot. Dir. Mario Corsi. 1919. (Italian)
Le Père Goriot. Dir. Jacques de Baroncelli. Perf. Gabriel Signoret (Goriot). 1922. (French)
Le Père Goriot. Dir. Robert Vernay. Perf. Pierre Larquey (Goriot). 1944. (French)
Le Père Goriot. Adapt. Jean-Louis Bory. Perf. Charles Vanel (Goriot), Bruno Garcin (Rastignac), Nadine Alari (Mme de Beauséant). Prod. Guy Jorré. INA, 1972.
Paris at Midnight. Dir. E. Mason Hopper. 1926. (American)

The filmography contains two films inspired by the figure of Vautrin:
Le Galérien. Dir. Paul Wegener. 1926. (German)
Vautrin. Dir. Pierre Billon. Adapt. Pierre Benoît. Perf. Michel Simon. 1943. (French)

Père Goriot's Paris: An Annotated Map

To enable the reader to move easily between text and map (see pp. 10–11), two lists of Parisian sites are provided. The first contains all the sites indicated on the map in numerical order (which is also the order in which they appear in the text). The second list provides brief information about all sites mentioned in the novel and is arranged alphabetically. The number following the name of the site refers to the site's location on the map; this number is followed by the coordinates of the square in which the site is located. Larger areas are not numbered; only their coordinates on the map are given. Areas that lie outside the scope of the map are also listed. The numbers in parentheses are page references, first to the French edition (Gallimard Folio) then to the English translation (Penguin). Where page numbers refer to only one edition, the edition is indicated in brackets.

List of Sites Mentioned in Père Goriot

1. Rue Neuve-Sainte-Geneviève
2. Ruc de l'Arbalète
3. Val-de-Grâce
4. Panthéon
5. Bourbe
6. Salpêtrière
7. Jardin des Plantes (Jardin du Roi)
8. Boulevard Italien (des Italiens), Café des Anglais
9. Ecole Polytechnique
10. Palais-Royal, Galeries de Bois
11. Petite Jeannette
12. Bourse (Stock Exchange)
13. Estrapade
14. Ecole de Droit (School of Law, Faculté)
15. Collège de France
16. Opéra-Comique
17. Champs-Elysées
18. Odéon
19. Prado
20. Italiens (Théâtre-Italien, Bouffons)
21. Saint-Etienne-du-Mont
22. Rue Dauphine
23. Rue des Grès
24. Rue du Helder
25. Palais-de-Justice
26. Rue de Grenelle
27. Rue Saint-Dominique
28. Opéra
29. Elysée
30. Rue Saint-Lazare
31. Rue de la Jussienne
32. Halle-aux-Blés (Halle, Corn Exchange)
33. Rue Oblin
34. Rue Saint-Jacques
35. Rue des Saints-Pères
36. Cadran-Bleu
37. Ambigu-Comique
38. Tuileries
39. Variétés
40. Jardin du Luxembourg
41. Théâtre-Français

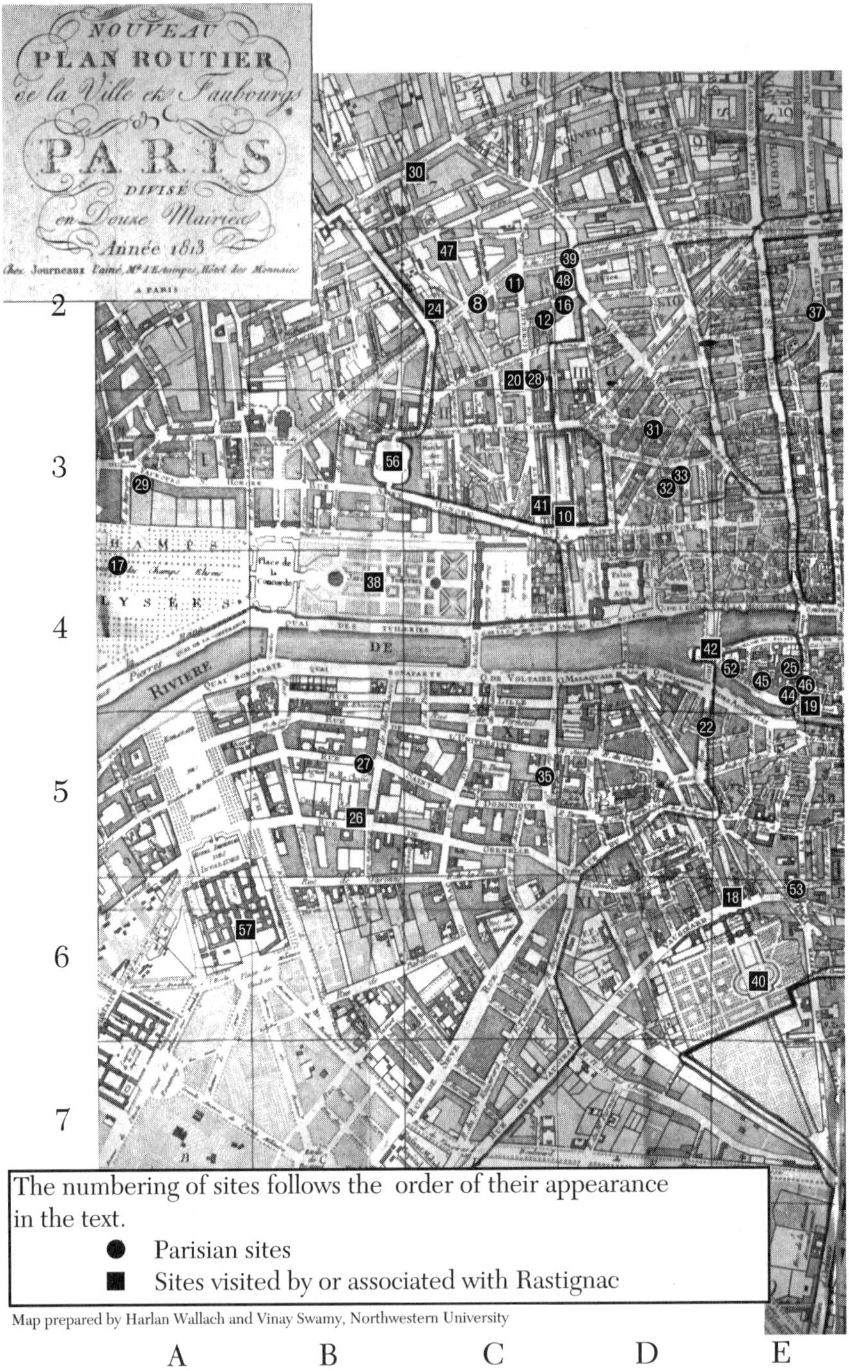

The numbering of sites follows the order of their appearance in the text.

● Parisian sites

■ Sites visited by or associated with Rastignac

Map prepared by Harlan Wallach and Vinay Swamy, Northwestern University

Père Goriot's Paris: An Annotated Map

42. Pont-Neuf
43. Rue de Buffon
44. Rue de Jérusalem
45. Petite Rue Sainte-Anne
46. Sainte-Chapelle
47. Rue d'Artois
48. Passage des Panoramas
49. Père-Lachaise
50. Gaîté
51. Hôpital Cochin (Hospice Cochin)
52. Quai des Orfèvres
53. Place Sorbonne, Flicoteaux
54. Place de Grève
55. Sainte-Pélagie
56. Place Vendôme
57. Invalides

Notes on Sites

Ambigu-Comique 37; E2. A popular theater on the boulevard Saint-Martin specializing in melodrama (156; 132)

Bois (Bois de Boulogne). A fashionable promenade on the west side of the Right Bank (60; 59)

Bouffons 20; C2. See Italiens. (60, 100, 102, 111, 202; 59, 91, 92, 99, 169)

Boulevard Italien (des Italiens) 8; C2. A hot spot of elegant and fashionable life, the boulevard owes its name to the troop of *comédiens italiens* who had their theater there in the second half of the eighteenth century. (34; 37)

Bourbe 5; E7. A lying-in hospital on the street by the same name (today, boulevard de Port-Royal) (32; 35)

Bourse (Stock Exchange) 12; C2. Between 1818 and 1826 (the year in which its current building was completed), the Bourse was located on the rue Feydeau. (50, 76; 50, 71)

Cadran-Bleu 36; F2. A famous restaurant on the boulevard du Temple (156; 132)

Café des Anglais 8; C2. On the boulevard des Italiens; one of the most expensive and most famous restaurants of the boulevards (275; 229)

Catacombes (Catacombs) From 1784, the bones from the cemetery of the Innocents and from other cemeteries were deposited in the ancient quarries and tunnels beneath the southern part of the city. (23; 28)

Champs-Elysées 17; A4. The name given at the beginning of the eighteenth century to the fashionable promenade starting at the Tuileries (previously called Cours-la-Reine). During the eighteenth century the Champs-Elysées was extended to the west several times. In the first decades of the nineteenth century there were only a few buildings around it (no cafés, shops, etc.). (56, 164, 233; 56, 139, 195)

Chaussée-d'Antin B1, B2, C1, C2. A newer part of Paris where the rich bourgeoisie lived (61, 99, 171, 189, 286; 60, 89, 145, 159, 238)

Choisy A village southeast of Paris (43; 44)

Collège de France 15; F5. Created in 1530 as an institution of higher learning independent of the Sorbonne, its lectures are free and open to the public. Many of the most prestigious scholars have taught there. (56; 55)

Corn Exchange 32; D3. See Halle-aux-Blés.

Ecole de Droit (School of Law, Faculté) 14; F6. The law school of the University of Paris, built by Soufflot in 1771 and situated in the place du Panthéon (58, 186; 57, 156, 245)

Ecole Polytechnique 9; F6. A military and engineering school created in 1794 and situated on the rue Descartes (43; 44)

Elysée 29; A3. Previously called the Elysée-Bourbon; under the Revolution it first housed the Imprimerie Nationale and then became a public dancing hall. Napoleon lived there from time to time and there signed his abdication. Louis XVIII gave the Elysée to the duc de Berry (son of the future Charles X and heir to the throne), who lived there until his assassination in February 1820. (107; 97)

Estrapade (Rue de l'Estrapade) 13; F6. (51; 51)

Faculté 14; F6. See Ecole de Droit. (56 [Gallimard])

Faubourg Saint-Germain B5, C5. The area on the Left Bank between the Invalides, rue de Varenne, rue du Bac, and the Seine; in the eighteenth century this area became the preferred quarter of the high aristocracy, who built large mansions there. (59, 61, 99, 124, 148, 189, 292; 58, 60, 89, 110, 126, 159, 243)

Faubourg Saint-Marceau F6, F7, F8, G6, G7, G8. The area on both sides of the rue Mouffetard, from Saint-Médard to the Gobelins; an area of extreme poverty and squalor (21, 110; 99)

Faubourg Saint-Marcel F6, F7, G6, G7, H6. Defined in the novel as the area between the Salpêtrière and the Bourbe (see these entries), it partially overlaps with faubourg Saint-Marceau. (32; 27, 35)

Flicoteaux 53; E6. A popular student restaurant on the place Sorbonne, known for its very cheap prices (270; 225)

Gaîté 50; F2. A popular theater on the boulevard du Temple specializing in pantomimes, farces, and harlequinades (252; 210)

Galeries de Bois 10; D3. Built in the eighteenth century in the gardens of the Palais Royal, housed fashionable boutiques. See also Palais Royal. (45; 46)

Gentilly Situated southeast of the Paris city limits on the Bièvre (43; 44)

Halle-aux-Blés (Halle, Corn Exchange) 32; D3. Built in 1767, it was the wholesale market for grain and flour. (126, 128; 111, 113)

Hôpital Cochin (Hospice Cochin) 51; F8. Built in 1780, it served the poor of Paris. (259, 315, 337; 279).

Invalides 57; A6. On the Left Bank. Built by Louis XIV to house old and disabled soldiers (367; 304)

Italiens (Théâtre-Italien, Bouffons) 20; C2. A meeting place for fashionable Paris, it was also the place for serious music lovers. Between 1819 and 1825 it was situated on the rue Louvois, next to the Opéra (on rue de Richelieu), and the two institutions performed on alternate nights to avoid competing. (103, 169, 177, 179, 185, 201, 314, 316; 93, 143, 149, 151, 156, 169, 236, 261, 263)

Jardin des Plantes 7; H5. Initially a garden of medicinal plants, it was expanded in the eighteenth century (especially under the directorship of Buffon) into a large botanical garden and museum of natural history. From the beginning the garden was also a place of instruction in natural history, free and open to the public. The courses given there by Saint-Hilaire, Lamarck, Cuvier, and others brought the garden great fame. (33, 78, 188, 220; 37, 73, 158, 184)

Jardin du Luxembourg 40; E6. A large park at the edge of the Quartier Latin, much frequented by students as well as the working class (186, 259; 156, 215)

Jardin du Roi 7; H5. See Jardin des Plantes. (251; 209)

Latin Quarter See Quartier Latin.

Longchamps In the Bois de Boulogne (152; 129)

Marais E3, E4, F3, F4, G3, G4. At the beginning of the seventeenth century, the preferred place of residence of the aristocracy. By the beginning of the nineteenth century, the aristocrats had long since moved out, first to the faubourg Saint-Honoré and then to the faubourg Saint-Germain. (45; 46)

Montmartre The hill of Montmartre, in the north, was just outside the city limits in the first half of the nineteenth century. (22; 27)

Montrouge South of the city limits (22; 27)

Odéon 18; E6. Situated on the Left Bank, this is the theater associated with the

Romantic school and regularly attended by students. During Carnival time, the most important student ball took place here. (59; 58)

Opéra 28; C2. The Opéra changed its name and location several times during the eighteenth and nineteenth centuries (between 1793 and 1820 it was located on the rue de Richelieu). During the Empire, Restoration, and July Monarchy the Opéra remained an important gathering place of high society, who went there mainly to see and be seen. (100, 111; 91, 99)

Opéra-Comique 16; D2. Between 1801 and 1829 it was located in the Salle Feydeau. Though according to an imperial decree the Opéra-Comique's repertoire could include any comedy or drama containing songs and ensemble pieces—a repertoire quite similar to that of the Opéra—in its heyday, during the first thirty years of the nineteenth century, the Opéra-Comique performed mostly light, accessible music and attracted a middle-class audience. (56; 55)

Palais-de-Justice 25; E4. Located on the Ile de la Cité, it was first the king's palace, then the seat of the Parlement (the supreme court of justice), and finally the seat of the judiciary. (77; 72)

Palais-Royal 10; D3. Built by Richelieu, who gave it as a gift to the king, it became in 1692 the possession of the members of the house of Orléans. Its gardens were open to the public, and there Camille Desmoulins improvised the demonstration that preluded the storming of the Bastille. The Galeries de Bois, built in 1791 by Phillippe Egalité, became the preferred meeting place of libertines, gamblers, and prostitutes. (45, 85, 195, 202; 46, 78, 163, 164, 170)

Panthéon 4; F6. Built by Soufflot, originally as a church dedicated to Sainte-Geneviève, it became during the Revolution a shrine to the "great men of the homeland." In 1806 it was turned back into a church and remained a church during the rest of the Empire and the Restoration. Throughout the nineteenth century it was a favorite site for students' political demonstrations. (23; 28)

Passage des Panoramas 48; D2. One of many shopping arcades built in Paris in the early nineteenth century and by far the most famous. Opening onto the boulevard Montmartre with its cafés, dance halls, and theaters, the Passage attracted a mixed crowd of strollers. (235; 196)

Père-Lachaise 49. A cemetery in northeast Paris built on the former site of a nursing home belonging to the Jesuit order and directed by Père La Chaise, the confessor of Louis XIV. The cemetery's location on a high hill overlooking the city made Père-Lachaise a favorite place for walks. (238, 249, 266, 297, 364, 366; 199, 207, 222, 247, 301, 304)

Petite Jeannette 11; C2. A fashionable store at the corner of the rue Richelieu and the boulevard des Italiens (45; 46)

Petite Rue Sainte-Anne 45; E4. The site of the offices of the Paris detective police (the Sûreté). The street no longer exists today. (227, 249, 264; 190, 208, 220)

Place de Grève 54; F4. Nowadays place de l'Hôtel-de-ville, on the bank (*grève*) of the Seine. Place de Grève was a meeting place for the unemployed as well as a location of popular celebrations. During the Old Regime it was a site of executions, during the Revolution a guillotine operated there, and place de Grève remained a place of public punishment until 1830. (250, 300; 208, 249)

Place Sorbonne 53; E6. At the center of the Quartier Latin, the site of the Sorbonne, the oldest part of the University of Paris (270; 225)

Place Vendôme 56; B3. On the Right Bank, formerly place Louis-le-Grand. Built at the end of the seventeenth century, place Vendôme had at its center an equestrian statue of Louis XIV, destroyed during the Revolution. Napoleon erected a column there commemorating the battle of Austerlitz. The statue at the top of the column changed several times during the nineteenth century according to changes in regime. (367; 304)

Pont-Neuf 42; D4. Built at the end of the sixteenth century, this bridge crosses the two branches of the Seine at the westernmost point of the Ile de la Cité. (202; 170)

Prado 19; E4. A dance hall during the winter season attended by a socially diverse, though generally lower-class, public (59; 57)

Quai des Orfèvres 52; E4. Near the Palais-de-Justice, between the Pont-Saint-Michel and the Pont-Neuf (267; 222)

Quartier Latin (Latin Quarter, pays latin) E5, E6, F5, F6. For centuries the name given to the area surrounding the University of Paris; the students' quarter. Delimited by the place Maubert to the northeast, the Panthéon to the southeast, place Saint-André-des-Arts and place de l'Odéon to the northwest, and the Jardin du Luxembourg to the southwest. Like the rest of the Left Bank, this area was not significantly transformed in the nineteenth century. (21, 44; 27, 45)

Rue d'Artois 47; C2. See Chaussée-d'Antin. (232, 235, 260, 276, 278, 294, 295, 332; 194, 196, 216, 230, 231, 244, 245, 275)

Rue Dauphine 22; D5. Since renamed rue Thionville. (69; 65)

Rue de Buffon 43; H6. (220, 251; 184, 209)

Rue de Grenelle 26; B5. See faubourg Saint-Germain. (97, 116; 88, 104)

Rue de Jérusalem 44; E4. The site of the *préfecture de police;* it no longer exists. (220; 184)

Rue de la Jussienne 31; D3. In the quartier des Halles (125, 340, 341; 111, 281, 282)

Rue de l'Arbalète 2; F7. (22; 28)

Rue des Grès 23; F6. (69, 73, 75, 76; 65, 69, 70, 71)

Rue des Saints-Pères 35; C5. (140; 120)

Rue du Helder 24; C2. See Chaussée-d'Antin. (61, 70, 73, 85, 351; 59, 66, 69, 79, 291)

Rue Neuve-Sainte-Geneviève 1; F6. Present-day rue Tournefort. (21, 22, 23, 25, 54, 55, 118, 177, 203, 206, 294, 302, 355, 365; 27, 28, 29, 30, 53, 54, 149, 170, 173, 244, 250, 294, 303)

Rue Oblin 33; D3. In the quartier des Halles (128; 113)

Rue Saint-Dominique 27; B5. See faubourg Saint-Germain. (97; 88)

Rue Saint-Jacques 34; E5. (140; 120)

Rue Saint-Lazare 30; C1. See Chaussée-d'Antin. (116, 192, 232; 104, 161, 194)

Sainte-Chapelle 46; E4. Part of the complex of the Palais-de-Justice (227; 190)

Sainte-Pélagie 55; G6. Originally a convent, after the Revolution it became a debtors' prison. (307, 255)

Saint-Etienne-du-Mont 21; F6. On the montagne Sainte-Geneviève. It was completed in 1610, replacing a thirteenth-century church on the same site. (66, 70, 365; 63, 67, 303)

Salpêtrière 6; I6. Built by Louis XIV as a hospice for the poor and housing primarily old women, it served also for the detention of prostitutes and the mentally ill. (32; 35)

School of Law 14; F6. See Ecole de Droit.

Seine (140, 367; 120, 304)

Soissy Situated southeast of the city limits (43; 44)

Stock Exchange 12; C2. See Bourse.

Théâtre-Français 41; C3. Situated on the Right Bank near the Palais Royal, the Théâtre-Français produced primarily the classical repertoire and was much frequented by students. (195; 163)

Tuileries 38; B4. A palace built by Marie de Médicis, who also constructed a park there in the Italian style. In the seventeenth century Le Nôtre turned the park into a garden in the French style. The garden was open to the public and became very popular in the eighteenth century. (165; 140)

Val-de-Grâce 3; F7. An old abbey that became a hospital in 1795 (23, 66; 28, 63)

Vallée des Gobelins G7. At the edge of the faubourg Saint-Marceau. A famous wool-dying plant was located there. (44; 45)

Variétés 39; D2. A theater situated on the boulevard Montmartre specializing in vaudeville and farce (169; 143)

Works Used in Preparing the Map and Notes

Barbier, Patrick. *Opera in Paris, 1800–1850.* Trans. Robert Luoma. Portland: Amadeus, 1995.

Calligani's New Paris Guide. Paris: Brière, 1874.

Caron, Jean-Claude. *Générations romantiques: les étudiants de Paris et le Quartier Latin, 1814–1851.* Paris: Colin, 1991.

Favier, Jean. *Paris: deux mille ans d'histoire.* Paris: Fayard, 1997.

Guichardet, Jeannine. *Balzac archéologue de Paris.* Paris: SEDES, 1986.

Lavedan, Pierre. *Histoire de Paris.* Paris: PUF, 1977.

Le Clère, Marcel, ed. *Paris de la préhistoire à nos jours.* Saint-Jean-d'Angély: Bordessoules, 1985.

Lefrançois, Philippe. *Paris à travers les siècles.* 10 vols. Paris: Calman-Lévy, 1951.

Lurine, Louis. *Les Rues de Paris: Paris ancien et moderne.* Paris: Kugelmann, 1844.

Pillement, Georges. *Paris inconnu.* Paris: Michel, 1981.

Stéphane, Bernard. *Dictionaire des noms de rues.* Paris: Mengès, 1986.

Willms, Johannes. *Paris: Capital of Europe: From the Revolution to the Belle Epoque.* Trans. Eveline L. Kanes. New York: Holmes, 1997.

Part Two

APPROACHES

Introduction

The eighteen essays in this volume are divided into three sections: "Contexts," "Theoretical Approaches," and "Specific Courses."

In the first section, the novel is studied in relation to the different contexts that determine it. Eric Le Calvez's essay places *Père Goriot* in the context of Balzac's *Comédie humaine* and demonstrates a macrotextual reading by juxtaposing the novel with another Balzacian text, *Gobseck*. Claudia Brodsky Lacour studies the tension in the novel between description and narration and questions the grounds on which one may call this novel a bildungsroman. Ruth Amossy's essay describes the relationships in the novel between fathers and sons and places *Père Goriot* in the context of postrevolutionary France and the "drama of paternity." Dean de la Motte discusses the narrative foregrounding of popular culture, understood as commodified culture, in Balzac's novel. James Reid's essay is also concerned with the opposition between description and narration but uses this opposition to show the different ways in which the narrator of *Père Goriot* constructs contemporary social reality and social relations. David Ellison's essay investigates the system of moral values in *Père Goriot* and shows the novel to be situated between the opposed moral universes of Immanuel Kant and Friedrich Nietzsche. Finally, David Bell's essay demonstrates how the new social reality created by modern urban life requires a new kind of education—a topographic one.

The second section, "Theoretical Approaches," starts with an essay by Gerald Prince on the role of the narrator. Margaret Waller's essay juxtaposes Balzac's novel with Delphine Gay de Girardin's parodic novella *La Canne de M. de Balzac* (published in 1836), to produce a feminist reading that foregrounds questions of vision, knowledge, power, and gender. The essay by Dorothy Kelly combines a psychoanalytic reading of the text with a questioning of language inspired by deconstruction. Two essays reading the novel from a queer perspective follow: Lawrence Schehr analyzes how homosexuality, especially Vautrin's, is encoded in Balzac's novel; Michael Lucey studies homosexuality against the background of the novel's portrayal of the family. John T. Booker's essay studies the theme of vision in relation to Rastignac's social education. Eric Bordas's essay closes this section with a linguistic, stylistic, and narratological investigation of the vexed question of Balzac's style.

Four essays discussing the novel in terms of particular courses constitute the third, and final, section. Catherine Nesci shows how the realistic description of Paris in *Père Goriot* can be used in a course on French culture. Laurence Porter shares with readers his insights into teaching novels in both French and comparative literature courses and shows the role *Père Goriot* can play in such courses. Janet Beizer discusses the common tendency to oppose the nineteenth-century novel (and its representative, Balzac) to the modern novel of the twentieth century and suggests how *Père Goriot* can be used to undermine such binarism. Finally Sharon Marcus and Vanessa Schwartz show how mapping *Old Goriot* can be used in courses dealing with literature, urban studies, and history.

As this short summary may already indicate, some issues and topics come up more than once in the volume. The question of education is discussed by Lacour, Bell, and Booker; the relation of narration to description is the focus of the essays by Lacour and Reid; the status of the family is analyzed by Amossy and Lucey; the crisis of paternity in postrevolutionary France is at the center of the essays by Amossy, Kelly, and Beizer; the relation of words to the world is of concern to Reid and Kelly; both Waller and Booker discuss the question of vision; the experience of the city is studied by Bell, Nesci, and Marcus and Schwartz. This partial overlap can be read as an indication of the main concerns of critics of the novel today; and since these critics adopt different theoretical approaches, this overlap highlights the fact that these issues are not simply there, in the text, but are always read, refracted, and constructed through a particular point of view.

NOTE

In the essays that follow, parenthetical page references follow translations, providing page numbers first for the French and then for the English. The two sets of page references are often given even when the French original is not quoted. In block quotations, the numbers for the French text follow the French; those for the English text follow the translation. Unless otherwise noted, all quotations from the French are taken from the Gallimard Folio edition, preface by Félicien Marceau, notes by Thierry Bodin (1971); unfortunately, different reprints of this edition, while identical in all other respects, have slightly divergent pagination (discrepancy of 1 to 3 pages). Quotations from the English text are taken from the Penguin edition, translated by Marion Ayton Crawford (1951).

CONTEXTS

Le Père Goriot and *La Comédie humaine*: From Text to Macrotext

Eric Le Calvez

Balzac consistently endeavored to link his narratives in order to unify his huge work in progress, which would eventually become *La Comédie humaine.* In this respect, the writing of *Le Père Goriot* marks a watershed in Balzacian creation, confirming the goal that had been preoccupying the writer for some time. Toward the end of 1834, when Balzac is writing *Le Père Goriot,* he finds the most important and productive device for the future of *La Comédie humaine*: recurring characters. In his forewords, Balzac insists repeatedly on the importance of this novelistic technique, in such a way that it should not be ignored. Any Balzacian narrative, therefore, must be studied, when possible, in two dependent ways: the study of an isolated text calls for the study of its interaction with what I call its macrotext, that is, related texts from *La Comédie humaine.* From a pedagogical standpoint, setting the text in parallel with its macrotext is essential, for this juxtaposition reveals to students hidden aspects of Balzacian creation. Because of the very nature of textuality, each text appears self-contained; each comprises a recognizable universe where students set landmarks. But as soon as the novel is paralleled with other narratives, new perspectives appear and reveal the immensity of the Balzacian world, bring to light or question scenes or events, and endow the characters with a multifaceted dimension (see Pugh).

The teacher who wants to illustrate this aspect of Balzacian technique encounters two problems. The first has to do with the genesis of the technique. It must be clear to students that Balzac's intentions consist not of writing sequels to his novels but rather of constructing the multiple facets of a large distorting mirror that is re-formed progressively and a posteriori. Through numerous corrections and various editions, the writer builds his universe, changing little by little names, portraits, and even details of preexisting characters' biographies. Moreover, it should be emphasized that the shaping of this macrotext shows moments that complete one another only more or less, in a way that Balzac never intended to be chronological (see Vachon).

The second problem has to do with macrotextual study itself. Many Balzacian echoes function as limited allusions. It is therefore quite possible to restrict the study of *Le Père Goriot* to these allusions. Characters recur: a character may appear in one text as a mere silhouette and in another as a complete or even main character. *Le Père Goriot* contains some of the most frequently recurring characters in *La Comédie humaine:* Rastignac, Bianchon, and Baron and Mme de Nucingen. Other characters, such as Mlle Michonneau and Poiret, are granted more limited allusions but can still be found in other works. The characters' recurrence also implies a more extended network of allusions. Plots refer to one another: the story of Mme de Beauséant, who disappears in Normandy (*Goriot* 332; 275), is concluded in *La Femme abandonnée;* the relationship of Mme de Langeais and Montriveau (*Goriot* 107, 334; 96, 277) is treated in *La Duchesse de Langeais;* the story of Taillefer evoked by Vautrin (*Goriot* 157; 133) is narrated in "L'Auberge rouge"; the means by which Rastignac will establish his fortune through Nucingen (*Goriot* 177–78; 150) are revealed in *La Maison Nucingen;* Vautrin's future evolution is developed in *Illusions perdues* and *Splendeurs et misères des courtisanes* (see Moss). But students do not need to read other works from *La Comédie humaine* to be able to understand the device of recurrence. They can be given brief summaries of other texts or even excerpts from significant scenes that show additional aspects of characters that appear in *Le Père Goriot.* Students usually become receptive to an effect of recognition, which is a first step into the macrotext but also a major component of the pleasure of the Balzacian text.

Yet, such a general study cannot illustrate the complexity of the constraints that the device of recurring characters imposes on Balzac's technique (and, even more so, on students). The macrotextual study must more precisely parallel *Le Père Goriot* with another text or other texts from *La Comédie humaine. Gobseck,* a short story that can be read in a couple of hours, is a viable choice (photocopies of relevant scenes or passages might also be sufficient).[1] Moreover, contrary to the plots of *La Femme abandonnée* or *Illusions perdues,* where the echo is diachronic (i.e., in the chronology of *La Comédie humaine*), the plots of *Le Père Goriot* and *Gobseck* are almost contemporaneous.[2] Studying these two texts makes it possible for students to grasp some of the main principles that constitute the *Comédie humaine* effect, which works on more than one level of complexity.

Textual Echoes

On the simplest level are the echoes found in almost all Balzacian narratives (such as those mentioned above). The student understands here that the effect is a matter of mere allusions, for the characters' recurrence depends on the components of each text and plot. For instance, Gobseck and Derville, main characters in *Gobseck,* are reduced to their names in *Le Père Goriot;* conversely, Delphine de Nucingen, a main character in the novel, is not even named in the short story, where it is simply noted that Goriot has two daughters (*Gobseck* 101; 233).

At the beginning of *Gobseck,* countess de Restaud is presented as a daughter of Goriot who years ago behaved so horribly to her father that she caused much gossip among the aristocracy (74; 188). This notation refers to the past, that is to say, to the plot of *Le Père Goriot* that illustrates it. Furthermore, it corresponds to various judgments made in the novel by other characters about the countess (110, 260; 99, 216). From one narrative to another, numerous notations correspond in the same way. Derville is qualified in *Gobseck* as "un homme de haute probité" 'a man of the highest honor' (75; 190), and Goriot sees him as "un honnête homme" 'an honest man' (*Goriot* 298; 247). In *Gobseck,* the usurer is called "papa Gobseck" by his clients (80; 198); this is also how he is named by Vautrin and Goriot (*Goriot* 76, 323; 71, 268). Moreover, the topology of the two stories is homogeneous: Gobseck lives in the rue des Grès in both the short story (78; 194) and the novel (76; 71), and the two narratives state that Anastasie de Restaud lives in the rue du Helder (*Goriot* 73; 69; *Gobseck* 83; 204). Beyond names of places and characters, the texts also use identical terms that become reflecting elements. At the end of *Gobseck,* count de Born declares that "Mme de Beauséant recevait Mme de Restaud" 'Mme de Beauséant received Mme de Restaud,' and vicomtesse de Grandlieu replies: "Oh! dans ses raouts" 'Yes, but only at her raouts' (128; 280), alluding to the fact that Anastasie de Restaud is merely tolerated by the Parisian aristocracy. Indeed, it is in a *raout* at Mme de Beauséant's that Rastignac sees Anastasie for the very first time: "Eugène s'était contenté de distinguer [. . .] dans ce *raout,* une de ces femmes que doit adorer tout d'abord un jeune homme" 'He had contented himself with singling out from among the crowd [. . .] with which this *raout* was packed, one of those women at whose feet a young man must fall from the very first' (*Goriot* 60; 58; my emphasis).

Additional Information and Diegetic Gaps

One should not believe, however, that the macrotext always functions in such a simple and homogeneous way. It should be stressed that each work in *La Comédie humaine* contains a complex plot, a complexity that stems mostly from the large number of characters. No two works share the same main character or the same perspective; the differences account for some diegetic anomalies.

Indeed, a Balzacian character may seem to be a block in the narrative that represents it, but this block becomes far less rigid when it is examined from a different perspective offered, in another narrative, by a different character. For instance, in *Le Père Goriot* and *Gobseck,* Anastasie de Restaud appears before Rastignac and the usurer, respectively, shortly after she wakes up. Although the two contexts are alike, the two texts differ, despite numerous similarities. Both Gobseck and Rastignac find the countess pretty (*Gobseck* 84; 206; *Goriot* 88; 81); she is "coiffée *négligemment*" '[h]er hair was *carelessly* done up' in *Goriot* (88; 81), and in *Gobseck* "ses cheveux noirs s'échappaient en grosses boucles d'un joli madras *négligemment* noué sur sa tête" 'her black hair fell in heavy curls from a silk handkerchief *carelessly* knotted round her head' (85; 206; my emphasis). In *Goriot* she is "coquettement vêtue d'un peignoir en cachemire blanc" 'coquettishly dressed in a fine woolen wrap' (88; 81), and in *Gobseck* "elle avait jeté à la hâte sur ses épaules nues un châle de cachemire" 'she had flung a [. . .] shawl round her shoulders so hastily that her shape could be guessed in all its nudity' (84; 206). Both texts insist on the countess's sensuality. However, students should be aware that the interactions between the characters are different in the two scenes.

A real novice, Rastignac reveals his inexperience of the Parisian world to the servants, who laugh at him (*Goriot* 85–86; 79–80), and he is conquered by the superiority and the luxury of the countess (89, 95; 81, 87). This superficial luxury has no effect on Gobseck, who proves himself superior to Anastasie (86; 208). Moreover, for Rastignac the countess personifies the mystery of Parisian women, especially since he understands neither her business nor her relationship with Maxime de Trailles (*Goriot* 93; 85). In contrast, Gobseck understands all the hidden mysteries of Parisian society (*Gobseck* 89; 213).

Like Anastasie, Count de Restaud looks different from different perspectives. For Goriot, the count is obviously a monster (322; 267), and he appears cold and inflexible in the scene where Rastignac searches for Anastasie (352–53; 292–93). But in *Gobseck* the usurer and Derville find him very likable given Mme de Restaud's shocking behavior. Furthermore, Restaud is sick in *Gobseck,* a fact not mentioned in *Le Père Goriot,* where all information on the count is filtered through his wife's discourse or is given from the point of view of Rastignac, who is not in close contact with the couple.

Such dissimilarities between the narratives stem first from variations of point of view. Each character's image changes or, rather, is the synthesis of the diverse images implied by changes in perspective. A character's image in one narrative is therefore questioned by the images of that character in other narratives, which act as distorting mirrors.

Variations of narration add to these variations of point of view; narrative voices and knowledge are different in different texts, which has diverse macrotextual consequences. In *Le Père Goriot,* there is one narrator who speaks in the third person; but in *Gobseck,* which contains several embedded narratives (as is often the case with Balzac), there are multiple narrators. At a first level, a third-person narrator recounts a late party at the Grandlieus; at a second level, Derville as a first-person narrator tells his own story, but also that of Gobseck and that of the Restauds, and his narrative contains at several occasions the story that Gobseck tells himself in the first person. These effects of changing voice or vision imply textual peculiarities that can be described as uncertainties of the macrotext.

In *Le Père Goriot,* we are told briefly that Goriot deals with Gobseck; he at first pays one of Anastasie's overdue notes (69–70; 65–66) and ultimately sells his own lifetime annuity (322; 268). These dealings are not mentioned in *Gobseck,* where Goriot's name is pronounced only in relation to his daughter's behavior. However, a brief allusion is made in *Gobseck* to Goriot's being a client of Derville's (96; 226). In *Le Père Goriot,* Derville is mentioned several times by Goriot but only in the context of Delphine de Nucingen's vain attempts to recover her fortune from her husband (see 233, 236, 281, 296; 194, 197, 234, 245). This plot is not dealt with in *Gobseck,* and, as we have seen, Delphine de Nucingen is absent from the short story.

The narratives therefore display diverse fragments of a life. In *La Comédie humaine,* the life of a Balzacian character is the result of a juxtaposition of fragments. Only through the correlation of these different narratives can this essential principle be brought to light. But there is more. In *Gobseck,* Derville recounts his meeting with de Trailles and mentions Goriot: "J'avais beaucoup entendu parler de ce personnage [de Trailles] par ce pauvre père Goriot, l'un de mes clients" 'I had heard a great deal of that personage [de Trailles] from poor Père Goriot, who was one of my clients' (96; 226). According to the chronology of *Gobseck,* we are in 1819 or 1820.[3] The date corresponds roughly with the chronology of *Le Père Goriot,* since the attorney begins to intervene in Delphine de Nucingen's favor in 1820. However, Derville uses the pluperfect in *Gobseck;* his relations with Goriot must then be anterior to the scene in question, although this is the first mention of the attorney in *Le Père Goriot.* The macrotext therefore seems to contain a chronological uncertainty, or even one of Balzac's mistakes (which are not rare, after all, in *La Comédie humaine*). However, when the text of *Le Père Goriot* is considered closely, the chronological inaccuracy is cleared up, since Goriot replies to his daughter when she tells him about her financial problems, "je vais aller trouver Derville, un avoué" 'I'll get hold of Derville tomorrow, he's a lawyer' (204; 171). The construction of the sentence in the French text ("Derville, un avoué," rather than "un avoué," i.e., an anonymous one) presupposes a prior acquaintance of the two men, which implies that Goriot has been a client of Derville's for a long time. Remarkably, neither narrative gives this information literally, yet the merging of allusions offers a possible trajectory that refers to a nonexistent (that is, never written) *hors-texte.*

The student therefore perceives that Balzacian gaps are not really internal; in fact, each narrative is homogeneous and logical. Narratives seem to contain textual lacunae only when they are considered in parallel. One reaches this paradoxical situation: an examination of the macrotext allows us to fill narrative gaps that are revealed as gaps only through the macrotext. Each narrative seems, afterwards, to be formed by fragments, to be constituted by the pieces of a vast puzzle that do not quite fit together yet correspond perfectly, offering the reader many different and complex perspectives to sort out.

Macrotextual Interweaving

Sometimes the textual gaps brought to light by macrotextual interferences are filled by elements that mirror one another from one text to the other. Not only is the information scattered through the stories juxtaposed and paralleled but it is also interwoven.

The narrative of *Le Père Goriot* does not show the episode where Anastasie de Restaud sells the diamonds to Gobseck in order to pay the overdue notes of her lover, Maxime de Trailles; this episode is reported in the direct speech of the countess, who once again seeks money from her father. Mere allusions in *Le Père Goriot* are well developed in *Gobseck,* although in different representational modes.

In *Le Père Goriot,* Anastasie explains her situation to her father:

> [Maxime] m'a dit qu'il devait cent mille francs! [. . .] J'ai porté chez cet usurier que vous connaissez, un homme fabriqué par l'enfer, que rien ne peut attendrir, ce monsieur Gobseck, les diamants de famille auxquels tient tant monsieur de Restaud [. . .]. Les diamants n'ont pas été vendus cent mille francs. (303, 304, 307)

> He told me that he owed a hundred thousand francs! [. . .] I went to that money-lender you know, Monsieur Gobseck, a man created in Hell with a heart nothing could ever soften, and I took him the family diamonds Monsieur de Restaud thinks so much of [. . .]. The diamonds did not fetch a hundred thousand francs [. . .]. (252–53, 255)

In *Gobseck,* the episode takes first the form of a scene narrated by Derville. Gobseck asks Maxime, "Combien vous faut-il?" 'How much do you want?' and Maxime responds, "Cent mille francs" 'One hundred thousand francs' (103; 236). Then, in the following scene, Restaud confronts Gobseck: "Vous venez d'acheter à vil prix des diamants de famille qui n'appartenaient pas à ma femme [. . .]. Elle n'avait pas le droit de disposer de ces diamants" 'You have just bought family diamonds which do not belong to my wife [. . .]. She has no legal right to dispose of those diamonds' (106; 242–43). In the first scene, Derville explains to Gobseck that "[c]ette femme étant en puissance de mari, le réméré sera nul" '[t]his woman being *femme couverte,* the deed of redemption would be null,' and Gobseck concurs: "Il a raison [. . .]. Tout est changé. Quatre-vingt mille francs comptant, et vous me laisserez les diamants" 'He is right [. . .]. The terms are changed. Eighty thousand francs down, and you [Anastasie] leave the diamonds with me' (103; 238).

However, the diamond episode does not end here, nor does the interaction between the two narratives. Anastasie later tells Goriot that Restaud found out everything and showed her the diamonds he repurchased from the usurer (*Goriot* 304–05; 253). It is never revealed, neither in *Le Père Goriot* nor in *Gobseck*, who informed Restaud about his wife's theft (this is another gap that the macrotext, in this case, does not fill). Nevertheless, once again the narrative of *Gobseck* sheds some light on Mme de Restaud's discourse, since the diamond scene is concluded by another scene in the short story (105–08; 241–46): the very same morning, Restaud comes to the usurer to recover the diamonds and accepts Derville's offer to purchase back the diamonds at the price of 85,000 francs.

The character's discourse in *Le Père Goriot* is therefore illustrated and amplified by Derville's narrative in *Gobseck*, and the two texts interpenetrate; their juxtaposition unveils these interweaving devices. However, quite often the interweaving process appears as a large spiderweb. Each thread leads to another inextricably linked to the first, showing the students possible paths that are invisible beforehand.

Indeed, in *Le Père Goriot*, the sale of the diamonds has another consequence for Mme de Restaud's future, in that Restaud learns the truth about his fatherhood (he has only one son, Ernest) and forces his wife to yield her fortune to him (305–06; 253–54). What could appear as petty revenge when reading *Le Père Goriot* is explained by another system of interference between the two narratives. To perceive the full effect of such interweaving, one must refer to the scene in *Gobseck* where the count buys back the diamonds:

> "Monsieur, dit gravement Gobseck, avez-vous beaucoup d'enfants?" [. . .] Le mari ne répondit pas. "Eh bien, reprit Gobseck en comprenant le douloureux silence du comte, je sais votre histoire par cœur. [. . .] Peut-être voudriez-vous sauver votre fortune, la réserver à un ou deux de vos enfants." (107)
>
> "Monsieur," said Gobseck, gravely, "have you many children?" [. . .] The husband did not answer. "Well," resumed Gobseck, understanding that painful silence, "I know your history by heart. [. . .] You may wish to save your fortune, and secure it to one, or, perhaps, two of your children." (245)

In other words, Gobseck, with his omniscient gaze, understands a familial issue that Restaud, at this point, only suspects. Gobseck prompts Restaud to take Mme de Restaud's fortune in order to ensure Ernest's future (once he is certain that the two other children are illegitimate); that is, he motivates the scene of the other narrative. This is the option that Restaud chooses when he goes to Derville's to verify Gobseck's integrity. Derville will be his attorney so that Ernest's fortune will remain protected after Restaud's death (108–09; 247–49).

However, Derville is here the narrator of the short story; and neither does he witness the scenes nor is he omniscient: "On dit qu'elle résista longtemps à donner sa signature [. . .] et néanmoins le comte l'obtint" 'It is said that she resisted affixing her signature [. . .] and nevertheless, the count obtained it' (113; 255). This explains why Mme de Restaud, who does not want at first to give her signature, cannot go to her dying father's bedside in *Le Père Goriot* (macrotextual consequences of seemingly scattered information are extensive). Once she does manage to escape, she has given up her fortune (*Goriot* 361; 299). The representative lacuna that is a consequence of the narrator's lack of knowledge in *Gobseck* is in fact filled in *Le Père Goriot* (353; 292–93).

Contrary to the previous example, the text of *Le Père Goriot* illustrates certain elements contained in *Gobseck,* some reported in the countess's direct speech, others in the form of a scene viewed by Rastignac. Reciprocally, if one understands, when reading *Le Père Goriot,* the motivations of Mme de Restaud, the text of *Gobseck* sheds a new light on the atrociousness of the character and, furthermore, accentuates the negative side of the countess. The short story also explains the cause of the diamond episode, completes and even concludes it.[4]

Although it is quite possible to read and teach any one of Balzac's novels without paying attention to its macrotext, the macrotextual study is an important aspect of any course on Balzac. In this respect, *Le Père Goriot* offers a good pedagogical challenge. Through the macrotextual study of the novel, students come to see that the text in fact belongs to a broader whole (as intended by the writer) that might not be visible at first. Furthermore, they understand how the novel is integrated into this whole through a wide system of allusions, of occasionally problematic recurrences, and of infinite textual interweaving. At the beginning students may be resistant to the complexity of Balzac's technique, for they are in general used to reading isolated novels, confusing characters with real people. However, with a close examination of parallel scenes or passages, and with the teacher's clear and progressive presentation of the diverse techniques used by the author, such resistance is soon replaced by a strong curiosity about the work of Balzac. Once students possess the method necessary to understand and analyze the way interrelations function, they are able to apply the method themselves and become sensitive to a certain pleasure of reading the text and the macrotext; they try to recapture this pleasure by reading other texts, other novels, and thus they enrich their knowledge of Balzac's work. At a time when literature is far from being a student's main pastime or interest, this consequence is in itself an important benefit. Moreover, the goal of any literature course should be to show students how a text operates through an examination of its literary techniques, and the macrotextual study corresponds perfectly to this requirement. Such an approach reveals diverse effects of realist illusion and textual processes of characterization. Students find that Balzacian characters can no longer be viewed as real persons: they are granted multiform images, dimensions that bypass the very limits of the texts, for, as study reveals, the macrotext often refers to a nonexistent (but paradoxically perceptible) *hors-texte.* Thus, the characters seem to live almost eternal, quasi-autonomous lives. This explains why Balzacian characters produce such a powerful effect of reality, or life, on the reader. At the same time, this approach modifies the students' way of reading and analyzing a text and allows them to avoid falling victim to the illusion the text creates. Finally, they are enabled to perceive literary characters as they really are: textual constructions.

NOTES

[1]In this essay, quotations from the French text of *Gobseck* are taken from *Gobseck [and] Une Double Famille.* Quotations in English are from the translation by Katherine Prescott Wormeley. Parenthetical references provide page numbers first for the French and then for the English.

[2]In fact, the narrative of *Le Père Goriot* extends from November of 1819 (55; 54) to February of 1820 (282; 235), whereas the narrative of *Gobseck* is shorter but covers a wider time frame: the first level takes place at Mme de Grandlieu's during the winter of 1829 to 1830 (73; 187); a long analepsis narrated by Derville takes the narrative back to 1816 (78; 194); the other episodes, narrated by Derville or, in an embedded way, by Gobseck himself, are dated 1818 to 1819 (Derville purchases his study [92; 217]), 1820 (the sale of the diamonds [96; 229]), and 1824 (Restaud's death), the narrative coming back to the first narrative level with Gobseck's death (1830). From now on, I use narratological terms such as analepsis, diegesis, and so on in their Genettian senses (see Genette, *Narrative Discourse*).

[3]Derville purchases his study from 1818 to 1819 (*Gobseck* 92; 217); the luncheon where he meets de Trailles takes place one year later (96; 224).

[4]The narrative gap in *Le Père Goriot* that constitutes the conclusion of the plot concerning Anastasie (she no longer appears after her father's death) is filled in *Gobseck,* the chronology of which extends beyond that of the novel; despite her crime (she burns the will as soon as her husband dies, almost ruining her children [122; 270]), Gobseck's integrity allows the preservation of the Restaud estate (127; 279).

Narrate or Educate: *Le Père Goriot* and the Realist Bildungsroman

Claudia Brodsky Lacour

In teaching *Le Père Goriot* and Balzac's novels in general, we work with and against their classification as "realist." Traditionally and to this day, "realism," when applied as a descriptive category to the novel, tends to swallow that literary genre whole. Interpretations whose interest lies in the political, philosophical, psychological, or even philological specificity of individual works come to rest on a reification of Stendhal's famously unstable definition ("Le roman: c'est un miroir qu'on promène le long d'un chemin" 'The novel: It is a mirror that one walks along a road' [288, my trans.]), treating the novel, its deep or surface structure, as a reflection of or substitute for historical reality. Students to whom the reality of nineteenth-century France may appear (at best) mythical, or quaint—and in any case decidedly unidentifiable with the world in which they live—may readily identify instead with the perpetually contemporary plot of the bildungsroman, in which a central, typically youthful character takes part in a course of action that, regardless of its concrete outcome, leaves the character with a residue of wisdom about whatever reality the novel represents. Any attempt to describe *Le Père Goriot*—widely considered the prototype of the realist bildungsroman in France—as a novel in which education in the ways of life is *not* achieved through the narrated actions of the plot, will naturally encounter resistance from those who would rightly question why we then link the novel to the project of education at all.

Yet it may be possible, indeed it may be imperative, for us to tie the idea of education to precisely such a novel as *Le Père Goriot,* one that thwarts the typical notion of the bildungsroman, in teaching students who have literally come of age with the notion of "self-marketing"—that indescribable course of action equated with maturity and modern-day "realism" by young people whose suggested role models resemble no fictional character more than Rastignac. In calling attention to the oppositional power of Balzac's descriptive realism, we may teach students to recognize that an exclusive focus on ascending the ladder of self-promotion can remove the self so instrumentalized, along with the very prospect of wisdom, from view. For extensive descriptions not only serve as backdrops to action in this particular novel; to a remarkable degree, they motivate *and* critique its plot. Their analysis thus compels us to recognize the relation between past objects—the objects of past actions—and object-directed action undertaken in the present. In this way, the realism of *Le Père Goriot* can thus teach students what Rastignac does not learn from le père Goriot: that in such recognition mature reflection on any course of action, and even education, may lie.

Probably no novel in modern history is better known for its commemoration of decor than *Le Père Goriot,* an exemplary tale of human edification in which external trappings are expressly rendered more meaningful than the intrinsic characters of the people who inhabit them. The description of the Maison Vauquer with which the novel opens, now a locus classicus of discussions of the compelling effects of metonymy in realist prose, achieves with great specificity of narrative detail the sense of a seamless, apparently shapeless connection between categorically different things. As if in imitation of his own expansive description of the audience for which his story is meant ("l'œuvre accomplie, peut-être aura-t-on versé quelques larmes *intra muros* et *extra*" '[. . .] perhaps some tears may be shed over it in the reading—*intra muros* et *extra*' [21; 27])—the narrator passes from a description of the neighborhood surrounding the Maison Vauquer to the outside and then the inside of the house—its common rooms and contents—before proceeding to represent a single element of those contents: their proprietor. The physical appearance of Mme Vauquer is inventoried in decrepit, yet always connective, detail:

> Son jupon de laine tricotée, qui dépasse sa première jupe faite avec une vieille robe, et dont la ouate s'échappe par les fentes de l'étoffe lézardée, résume le salon, la salle à manger, le jardinet, annonce la cuisine et fait pressentir les pensionnaires. (29)

> Her knitted woollen petticoat dipping below the refurbished old dress which forms her skirt, its wadding escaping from rents in the ripped material, expresses the essence of the sitting-room, the dining-room and the little garden, makes you realize what the kitchen must be like, and foreshadows the boarders. (33)

while her personal history and present motives, rendered in tautological and reported clichés, remain detached from the present scene, in the shadows: "madame Vauquer resemble à toutes les femmes qui ont eu des malheurs. [. . .] Qu'avait été monsieur Vauquer? Elle ne s'expliquait jamais sur le défunt. Comment avait-il perdu sa fortune? Dans les malheurs, répondait-elle" 'Madame Vauquer [. . .] resembles all *women who have had a peck of troubles.* [. . .] What had Monsieur Vauquer been? She never entered into explanations about her late husband. How had he lost his money? "Mishap and misfortune," was her answer' (29; 33). Prefaced by the worn particulars of their clothing, the introduction of the individual boarders follows, indeed, is said explicitly to "repeat" ("se répétait-il"), the same detailed yet disorienting pattern of interrelation that characterizes the "spectacle" about them, as if the tawdry contents of the *quartier*, building, and rooms had spread to the human bodies within them by dint of an inevitable contagion:

> Aussi le spectacle désolant que présentait l'intérieur de cette maison se répétait-il dans le costume de ses habitués, également délabrés. Les hommes portaient des redingotes dont la couleur était devenue problématique,

> des chaussures comme il s'en jette au coin des bornes dans les quartiers élégants, du linge élimé, des vêtements qui n'avaient plus que l'âme. Les femmes avaient des robes passées, reteintes, déteintes, de vieilles dentelles raccommodées, des gants glacés, par l'usage, des collerettes toujours rousses et des fichus éraillés. Si tels étaient les habits, presque tous montraient des corps solidement charpentés, des constitutions qui avaient résisté aux tempêtes de la vie, des faces froides, dures, effacées comme celles des écus démonétisés. (32)

> Moreover the depressing spectacle the interior of the house presented was matched by the clothing of its inmates, who were every bit as dilapidated. The men wore coats whose original colour was unimaginable, shoes like those left abandoned in the gutters in smart districts, frayed linen, clothes which were only the shadow of their former selves. The women had old-fashioned dresses, dyed and faded and redyed again, darned old lace, gloves shiny with long use, collars which were always discoloured and frills frayed at the edges. But although their clothes were of such a kind, they nearly all possessed solidly built bodies, constitutions which had withstood the storms of life. [Their] cold, hard faces were worn, like those on coins withdrawn from circulation [. . .]. (35–36)

While the names and backgrounds of the *pensionnaires* were introduced, in the paragraph directly preceding this one, according to the precise sum each pays for lodging, the bodily description of the boarders given here, beginning with their attire, likens them to coins whose specific monetary value is "effaced" ("effacées"). Used up but still present, their faces worn down to a hardness that subsists, and whose distinction owes to a resistance to—rather than individuation by—inclement forces ("the storms of life"), the inhabitants of the Maison Vauquer might well reside therein as furniture. "*All is true,*" the narrator states at the opening of the novel, calling his work a "drama" (rather than a "fiction" or "romance"), whose "elements" may be recognized in one's "own household" ("chez soi") or "in [one's] heart perhaps" ("dans son cœur peut-être"; 22; 27, 28). True to this oscillation between hearth and heart, the same hyperbolic mode is employed a few paragraphs later to describe neither dramatic characters and actions nor their internal recognition by the reader but rather the furnished salon in which the boarders gather: "Rien n'est plus triste à voir que ce salon meublé de fauteuils et de chaises en étoffe de crin à raies alternativement mates et luisantes" 'Nothing could be more depressing than the sight of this sitting-room, with its various chairs upholstered in a haircloth of alternately dull and shiny stripes' (26; 30).

A novel that ends by setting the scene for one of the longest and most theatrical monologues in the *Comédie humaine* begins by stating that nothing is sadder to see than a room containing specimens of worn-out, striped upholstery. The drama of Goriot dying, its violent mental schism between lie and truth a benchmark in modern tragic representation, is already qualified at the outset of the novel as somehow surpassed by the sight of old furniture. "*All is true*"—"[r]ien n'est plus triste à voir [. . .]"—or, as Mme Vauquer reportedly states of herself, "elle avait souffert tout ce qu'il est possible de souffrir" 'she had suffered all that a woman could' (29; 33). How can the reader of this novel of education account for such dramatic disparity between what it states to be true and the truths (and lies) it represents? What occurs in the novel that can make conflicting hyperbole, mutually discrediting professions and representations of an absolute fidelity to reality, make sense?

If we look at its narrative structure, we find the novel's mode of representing the real to be remarkably consistent. For *Le Père Goriot* is limited in its mimetic scope to a few interior scenes: in addition to the Maison Vauquer are the *hôtel* of Mme de Beauséant, those of Goriot's daughters, and, finally, the apartment for Rastignac in the rue d'Artois, furnished to resemble Delphine's and paid for by Goriot. What the reader reads in these limited settings is what Rastignac sees in them, that is, the fixtures of "cette vie constamment élégante" 'this life of constant elegance' (168; my trans.) where, as the narrator states of dining at the table of M. de Beauséant, one enjoys "un double luxe, celui du contenant et celui du contenu" 'a double luxury: delicious food [. . .] served in splendid vessels' (168; 142). Indeed, that content may be the Goriot daughters themselves, for Rastignac indistinguishable in their person from the elegance of their *parures*. "Ma vie à moi, est dans mes deux filles" 'My life is lived through my two girls' (181; 153), says Goriot of the women he will literally die to dress in gold. "La vie est dans les meubles" '[. . .] what is a house without its furniture [. . .]?,' says Mme Vauquer toward the close of the novel, literally confusing her departing boarders with furnishings by throwing into relief the metaphor of substance contained within an idiomatic verbal expression ("démeublée"): "Qu'est-ce que la vie sans mes pensionnaires? Rien du tout. Voilà ma maison démeublée de ses hommes. La vie est dans les meubles" 'What is life without my boarders? Nothing! Nothing at all! It's like taking the furniture out of a house; what is a house without its furniture, and what is a boarding-house without its men?' (285; 237).[1] Extending from her already figurative coupling of "hommes" with "démeublée," the ambiguous use of "furniture" in Mme Vauquer's concise definition of life at the denouement of a novel supposed to be a lesson in life only exposes the truth that Balzac's descriptive realism has impressed on us all along: that life is not located in the living themselves.

This peculiar truth was a source of dispute in two of the most significant accounts of modern realism in the twentieth century, those of Georg Lukács (as exemplified in his essay "Narrate or Describe") and Erich Auerbach (in *Mimesis*), which stress, respectively, the diachronically transformative and synchronically prescriptive effects of description in the novel. Yet, while analytically at odds, the two views share a common approach to the function of description itself. Whether read as the "base" for revealing action to come (Lukács 131) or the recursive inclusion of action within an already unified, "immediately apprehended state of things" (Auerbach 471)—as the vehicle of future "concrete human experience" (Lukács 131) or of "memory-pictures" of a past we "may never have experienced" (Auerbach 471)—objective description appears at one with narration in both these seminal interpretations of Balzac. The combined wealth of drama *and* description in *Le Père Goriot* makes the novel paradigmatic of that union for both critics as well, offering each of their opposing views its most economical and gripping representation.

The main story line of *Le Père Goriot* is indeed economical, straightforward and to the point, and if only because the story seems so easy to summarize, in contrast to the detailed descriptions supposed to converge with it, its actual presentation may be well worth considering closely. One need not have read the novel carefully to know that *Le Père Goriot* is a Parisian story of concealed identities—those of a self-sacrificing father and the daughters who use and shun him—discovered by a young man from the provinces whose lack of wealth, surfeit of ambition, and distant aristocratic connections combine to make him privy to the real relationships among the Goriots. Yet, in terms of the specific development of the novel, this view of its story is inaccurate, for the relationships between Mme de Restaud, Mme de Nucingen, and their father are revealed roughly one-tenth of the way into the text, when Goriot states flatly that the woman "dressed as fine as a goddess" who came to visit him is his daughter (51; 51).

The fact that the pensioners believe Goriot is lying implies there is all the more reason for us to suspect he is telling the truth. Indeed, when Mme Vauquer spells out for us the improbability of what Goriot states ("Si le père Goriot avait des filles aussi riches que paraissaient l'être toutes les dames qui sont venues le voir, il ne serait pas dans ma maison, au troisième, à quarante-cinq francs par mois, et n'irait pas vêtu comme un pauvre" 'If old Goriot had daughters as rich as all the ladies who came to see him appeared to be, he would not be in my house, on the third floor, paying forty-five francs a month, and he would not be going about dressed like a beggar') and the narrator underscores her observations with ironic, third-person report immediately thereafter ("Rien ne pouvait démentir ces inductions" 'These conclusions could not be gainsaid' [55; 54]) we can be certain that, in squarely Aristotelian fashion, it is precisely such improbable events that the novel intends to represent. Thus, roughly thirty pages into *Le Père Goriot*—still in the context of the narrator's introductory description of the *maison*, its surroundings and contents—the main mystery of the novel is revealed to the reader. A mere twenty pages later, after Rastignac has already witnessed an even more improbable event—Goriot molding an old silver tureen into refashionable ingots with his bare hands—that mystery will be explained individually to him by Balzac's authorial alter ego, Vautrin, who, after concluding that Goriot is being ruined by the comtesse de Restaud, adds summarily: "Il ne faut pas coudre deux idées pour voir clair là-dedans" 'You don't even need to put two and two together for that to be plain as a pikestaff' (76; 72).

Yet even Vautrin willfully misinterprets what he observes, failing to see as clearly as all that. Like the other pensioners, he neglects to listen to Goriot himself, and it will be another thirty pages before Goriot's paternity, having been stated openly some fifty pages earlier, is "revealed" to Rastignac by Rastignac's own distant relative, Mme de Beauséant. The drama of that scene of revelation appears as overstated as its occurrence seems delayed. To Rastignac's comment that he mentioned Goriot's name to the Restauds after seeing the old man secretly take leave of Anastasie, Mme de Beauséant replies, "Mais, enfant que vous êtes [. . .] madame de Restaud est une demoiselle Goriot" 'But, child that you are, [. . .] Madame de Restaud was a Mademoiselle Goriot' (110; 99). When the secret of the family is elaborated further by the visiting duchesse de Langeais, Rastignac and the narrator both comment melodramatically: " 'Ah! c'est son père,' reprit l'étudiant en faisant un geste d'horreur" '"Oh, is he her father?" said the student, horror-stricken' (110; 99).

The forced quality of this moment of recognition is commensurate with that of the ignorance it formally dispels: Rastignac's "horror," at once named and performed by a conventional "gesture" ("geste"), enacts a theatrical, artificial response to a truth already current for some time. For Rastignac himself just identified Goriot to Mme de Beauséant as "ce malheureux [. . .] *que nous appelons le père Goriot*" 'a poor wretch [. . .] *whom we call old Goriot*' (110; 99; my emphasis), and it was by calling Goriot "le père Goriot" that Rastignac provoked the ire of the comte de Restaud (95; 86). Thanks to an idiomatic expression of familiarity peculiar to French, Goriot had indeed been referred to as "father Goriot" from the first day of his decided economic decline (49; 49–50).[2] The central mystery of *Le Père Goriot,* one may finally say without exaggeration, is in fact stated and solved before the novel begins—in the novel's title—and whatever suspense this story of discovered paternity maintains owes only to the force of common preconception, just as the shock of discovery registered physically by Rastignac is both explained and belied by the familiar words he has just used: "ce malheureux [. . .] que nous appelons le père Goriot."

As for the romance with Parisian society in which Rastignac engages, appealing to female relatives for its financing in a familial sexual pattern already familiar to the reader from the voracious *filles* Goriot, there is little drama to relate that truly unfolds, that cannot instead be foretold. One need never have read another narrative by Balzac (or any of a dozen other great realist novelists) to know that beneath the exquisite appearance that dazzles the student, Mme de Restaud conceals an insatiable, ultimately murderous, corruption or that her sister, Mme de Nucingen, chosen strategically to be Rastignac's lover, will merely prove Mme de Restaud's rival, not her better.

The celebrated words with which the narrative ends in supposed testimony to this social romance—Rastignac's apostrophe of the beau monde from the heights of the Père Lachaise: "ces mots grandioses: 'A nous deux maintenant!' " 'and said with superb defiance, "It's war between us now!" '—are followed by what the last sentence of the novel calls a "first act of defiance" ("premier acte du défi"), Balzac's indication that both novel and act will prove part of a chain: "Et pour premier acte du défi qu'il portrait à la Société, Rastignac alla dîner chez madame de Nucingen" 'And by way of throwing down the gauntlet to Society, Rastignac went to dine with Madame de Nucingen' (367; 304). Yet, one need not have read Balzac's master novella of the same period, *Les Secrets de la princesse de Cadignan* (1839), to know that one may outdo the beau monde by joining it for dinner with the purpose of defending one's apparently "unrealistic" love against staged disillusionment—that one does well to dine in society in order not to live by it but rather to leave it behind (as the Princesse and D'Arthez do at the extraordinary close of *Les Secrets*)[3]—but that, otherwise, dining with wolves is no act of defiance at all. Not only does the notion of defiance through direct compliance ring hollow at the end of the novel, but it also rejoins, through Rastignac, Goriot to his daughters; it marries, rather than opposes, high society and the Père Lachaise. Regarding Paris from the cemetery that surrounds him, Rastignac unites the living with the dead, rendering the future, which should begin "now," vain, a version of continuity without vital interest. Pierre Barbéris's observation that burying Goriot "frees" Rastignac (204, 372) might be more meaningfully reversed: upon Goriot's death Eugène buries himself, in a plot of measured calculation that will sever him forever from the very actions he himself performs.

Just as Rastignac's passion for "father Goriot" will prove the only fortuitous event in Rastignac's ascendence in the *Comédie humaine*, it remains the only unpredictable and thus truly generative event in this novel's plot. Even Mme de Beauséant's withdrawal from society after the marriage of her lover remains motivated by the same social rules that force her to preside over a ball at the very "moment of her downfall" (329; 273). The rules of a world she is said to have "domina jusqu'à son dernier moment" 'till the last moment dominated' (329; 273) predetermine the mode of her Pyrrhic victory as the achievement of illegibility: "Personne ne pouvait lire dans son âme" 'No one could read her heart [. . .]' (330; 273). By successfully masking and denying her internal life, making herself appear as impassive as a statue—"Vous eussiez dit d'une Niobé de marbre" '[S]he looked like a marble Niobe' (330; 273)—Clara de Beauséant effectively "buries" herself (332; 275) in the center of fashionable Paris before doing so, as stated, by withdrawing to the depths of Normandy. Revealing the rue de Grenelle to resemble a burial ground even before Goriot is interred at Père Lachaise, Mme de Beauséant makes Rastignac's invocation of Paris from the land of the dead seem something of a redundancy, a threat to dominate, by joining forces with ("A nous deux"), the only apparently living.

While Rastignac's and the narrator's descriptions of Mme de Beauséant's final soiree are conspicuously peopled by literary allusions to ancient models (331, 335; 275, 278), the immediate *narrative* model for Rastignac's self-described consignment to "hell" (335; 278) lies disturbingly close at hand, in Balzac's distinctly modern *Colonel Chabert* (1832). Although at first reading this traditionally marginal novella may appear nearly opposite to the central, canonical novel it precedes by two years, we may come closer to understanding the construction of *Le Père Goriot* and the trajectory of the entire *Comédie humaine*—including the longer, core works, *Illusions perdues* (1843) and *Splendeurs et misères des courtisanes* (1847), in which a cynically successful Rastignac will reappear—if we view the earlier text as fundamental to Balzac's conception of narrative itself.

Le Père Goriot seems to invert the plot of *Le Colonel Chabert*: the officially deceased colonel, having literally risen, limb by limb, from the bodies under which he was buried at the Napoleonic battle of Eylau, returns to Paris only to be shunned by the high society of the French Restoration to which his remarried wife, who now refuses to acknowledge him, belongs; Rastignac, having buried another man in Père Lachaise, testifies to the new beginning of his own life in society, "now." Yet even though death and life, the end and beginning of experience, seem to be the symmetrically inverted themes of these two works, narratively speaking *Old Goriot* extends the death-come-to-life of *Chabert*: by returning to society Rastignac unknowingly sets the stage for a drama whose protagonist (himself) we can, to paraphrase Chabert's words, "well call dead" (*Colonel Chabert* [Barbéris] 33). Indeed Rastignac's return will be even less promising than Chabert's. For unlike the elder colonel, who, prematurely declared dead, defies the society that will not recognize him as living just as he outlived certain death in battle, in his "first act of defiance" young Rastignac renders the difference between death and life—the difference the colonel insists on and suffers to know—nearly nil.

It is a demand to remember that difference that brings Rastignac momentarily to his senses at the opening of *Splendeurs et misères des courtisanes* when he glimpses Lucien de Rubempré, the novelistic reincarnation of his own (social) reincarnation after the death of Goriot and Vautrin's new actor in the plot of social advancement. The demand is issued, fittingly enough, by Trompe-la-Mort, Cheat-Death himself, Vautrin transfigured to resemble the Spanish priest and political emissary he has murdered. The occasion of the demand, just as appropriately, is a masked ball at the Opéra, and Rastignac's immediate sensation on recognizing its doubly masked source is one of violent disorientation: "le vertige." Dragged to the window by "a hand of iron he could not throw off" ("une main de fer, qu'il lui fut impossible de secouer"; 55; my trans.), Rastignac hears his past retold:

> "Jeune coq sorti du poulailler de maman Vauquer, vous à qui le cœur a failli pour saisir les millions du papa Taillefer quand le plus fort de l'ouvrage était fait, sachez [. . .] que si vous ne vous comportez pas avec Lucien comme avec un frère que vous aimeriez, vous êtes dans nos mains sans que nous soyons dans les vôtres. [. . .] Choisissez entre la vie et la mort. Votre réponse?"
>
> Rastignac eut le vertige comme un homme endormi dans une forêt, et qui se réveille à côté d'une lionne affamée. (55)

> "Young cock who has left the henhouse of mommy Vauquer, you who lacked the heart to seize the millions of papa Taillefer when the most

> formidable part of the work had been done, know [. . .] that if you do not behave with Lucien as you would with a brother you love, you will be in our hands without our being in yours. [. . .] Choose between life and death. Your response?"
>
> Rastignac felt dizzy like a man fallen asleep in the forest who wakes beside a famished lioness. (my trans.)

Rastignac, returned to life and to Paris, has effectively evaded the choice "between life and death," put to him bluntly by the one character whose devotion to life—to its drama—has made cheating death his profession. If by fooling death in the guise of others Vautrin lives "his" life in a perpetual present, we may say of Rastignac what is said of Goriot on Goriot's dying breath: he lived by fooling himself, by cheating life:

> Trompé sans doute par les larmes, Goriot usa ses dernières forces pour étendre les mains, rencontra de chaque côté de son lit les têtes des étudiants, les saisit violemment par les cheveux, et l'on entendit faiblement: "Ah! mes anges!" Deux mots, deux murmures accentués par l'âme qui s'envola sur cette parole.
>
> "Pauvre cher homme," dit Sylvie attendrie de cette exclamation où se peignit un sentiment suprême que le plus horrible, le plus involontaire des mensonges exaltait une dernière fois.
>
> Le dernier soupir de ce père devait être un soupir de joie. Ce soupir fut l'expression de toute sa vie, il se trompait encore. (358–59)

> Deluded no doubt by the tears he had felt, Goriot gathered all his remaining strength to stretch out his hands, which on either side of the bed encountered the students' heads. He clutched at their hair convulsively, and they heard a faint whisper,
>
> "Ah! my angels!"
>
> Two words, two murmurs given meaning by the soul which fled as they were spoken.
>
> "Poor dead man," said Sylvie, touched by that exclamation, the expression of a supreme tenderness, aroused for the last time by a most ghastly, most involuntary lie.
>
> The last sigh of this father was to be a sigh of joy. This sigh was the expression of his whole life: he continued to fool himself.
>
> (297, with modification)

Finally one must ask, What is this life that Vautrin repeatedly "dies" for and must live through others, that Goriot lives as self-deception, that Rastignac will conquer by becoming it? *Le Père Goriot* is not the narrative of the discovery of Goriot *père*; nor is it—at least for the reader—the story of the education of Rastignac, who, if he has lost illusions, has also decided to make himself an illusion, to cheat life for the sake of cheating it. What is this life of striving to which, each in his own way, Vautrin, Rastignac, and Goriot all sacrifice their lives?

The illusion no education can dispel is that something is worth this sacrifice; the illusion this novel of education cannot dispel is that of education in, or disillusionment with, life itself. For the very force of life, this novel suggests, resides in sustaining illusion. "Ma vie à moi est dans mes filles"—"My life is lived through my two girls"—is more literally if self-contradictorily rendered: "The life that belongs to me is in my daughters." The stunning energy of Goriot, his incalculable physical and mental (as opposed to monetary) resources, is devoted to the acquisition of what can never be acquired, the happiness of his daughters and, thereby, his own. In the place of that already displaced happiness he acquires the furnishings of happiness, the things required to acquire titled husbands, who inevitably show themselves only to be expensive, part of the decor, and then goes on to acquire the additional furnishings required to acquire lovers, who inevitably show themselves no less capable than husbands of reconverting decor from illusory aspirations back into decor. While referring immediately to the context of the Maison Vauquer, Mme Vauquer's enigmatic pronouncement—"La vie est dans les meubles"—coincides with Eugène's return from the richly appointed apartment in the rue d'Artois in which Delphine has just proclaimed: "Eh bien! Eugène, les choses que je vous offre sont les armes de l'époque, des outils nécessaires à qui veut être quelque chose" 'Well, Eugène, the things I offer you are the weapons of the times, tools needed by a man who wants to make himself someone of consequence' (280; 233). "Things" acquired toward the goal of becoming "something" ("quelque chose") are Delphine's (and Goriot's) offering to her lover: life, if the future of illusion, is in the furnishings indeed.

Yet the "things" Goriot offers Eugène are as far removed from the furniture Mme Vauquer's statement concerns as is the feast given Telemachus, a picture of which lines her dining-room walls. And this is where the force of Balzac's descriptions and the plot of his narrative of education most clearly conflict. For the Maison Vauquer and the inhabitants that resemble it are dressed in illusions past: "shoes like those left abandoned in the gutters in smart districts, frayed linen, clothes which were only the shadow of their former selves. The women had old-fashioned dresses, dyed and faded and redyed again [. . .]" (36). The narrative of *Le Père Goriot* is driven by the kind of self-deception that keeps a fatally weakened Goriot alive and talking, animated by the delusion that his daughters will still come, as if his dying could ever change what he has known "depuis dix ans" 'for the last ten years': "Non, elles ne viendront pas!" 'No, they will not come!' (343; 284). The narrative of *Le Père Goriot* has Eugène join forces with a world whose venality he "now" knows intimately, ending the novel not by learning from Goriot but by taking up where the dead man left off. The narrative of *Le Père Goriot,* in short, sustains Delphine's view—also the view of Vautrin, Rastignac, and Goriot—that "things" are the "necessary tools" ("outils nécessaires") for making someone "something," while description in the novel represents people and objects in such immediate, borderless proximity that "something" and "things," present aspiration and past disillusionment, barely appear distinguishable.

Thus it is realist description in this novel that educates us as the novel's narrative cannot, indicating where "life" remains when illusion and furnishings no longer serve the future: when people and things are neither reconvertible to blank ingots nor stamped with narrative exchange value, but "démonétisés." Realist description in this novel images the out-of-date, the hopelessly outmoded (see Moretti, *Way* 144). The paths of Delphine and Anastasie cross the threshold of the Maison Vauquer, touch their father and their past punctually, when their narratives of acquisition require it; the Maison Vauquer, a place in which the past lives as context, presents to us concretely the ends of such narratives. The *maison*'s description offers the reader images of "things" that remain while past experiences have proved to be illusory, that is, composed of the desire to make "things" amount to "something." That ongoing description and its component images remain with us because, like the pensioners' "effaced," "solidly built bodies," it is the iron hand of such desire they "have resisted" ("avaient résisté"). Description in *Le Père Goriot* attests to the life we ascribe to life's "furnishings," to the context we wish to transform into action, to the action from which we imagine we will fashion future happiness without incurring loss or death; and description in *Le Père Goriot* ascribes a certain life to all those things our actions leave behind: "ces meubles indestructibles, proscrits partout, mais placés là comme le sont les débris de la civilisation aux Incurables" 'indestructible furniture which every other household throws out [but which] finds its way to the lodging-house, for the same reason that the human wreckage of civilization drifts to hospitals for the incurable' (27; 32).

The furnishings of the "incurable" are not the props of credited illusion or disillusion, "fiction" or "romance." They are the "indestructible" things of a "drama" of a different kind, a specifically untheatrical or unmelodramatic drama, whose "life" "continues" after the plot of education and social assimilation ends (32; 36). At odds with dramatic narrative, with such narrative's inherently forced and false denouements, these "mute" (32; 36) dramas of things removed from circulation continue within Balzacian description as the contextual relation of things recalling images of things we "may" or may not "have seen" (Auerbach 471) in the context of delusions past: things, in other words, that remind us that, in reality, no narrative buries the past.

So it is that only now, looking back on this narrative, we can see that "[r]ien n'est plus triste à voir que ce salon meublé [. . .]," '[n]othing could be more depressing than the sight of this sitting room,' the unending drama of things denuded of social value, and that the drama of education and illusion, with its many colorful characters, ends in "the human wreckage of civilization," persons and things deprived of any but a temporary face value. That the plot appears to lead us away from this recognition does not make the novel a false representation but rather implies that there is little education to be had from within a narrative realm of relentless circulation. Persons who mistake life for its furnishings (in the larger sense), the novel suggests, will be outlived by those furnishings if not directly meet their death. And this is not only because, whatever subsequent actions they may take as subjects, they have already transferred the life accorded them to objects, to things, but because, unlike them, when the course of narrative action—transformation and exchange—is exhausted, those things that cannot be changed live on in the images of memory and description.

"La vie est dans les meubles" is both the delusion of this novel's protagonists and the reality the novel's descriptions represent. In *Le Colonel Chabert* an indestructible man, risen from the surrounding dead only to be contextually effaced by the living, ends as a human embodiment of historical debris because he could not be cured of life; if there is to be a "human comedy" there can be only one Chabert, one person who suffers in both body and story the contradiction *within* being between being at once a thing *and* a person, and Chabert, who ends "aux Incurables," came early to Balzac. In *Le Père Goriot* Balzac begins the separation of the contradiction contained in Chabert, a contradiction that Balzac will sustain and elaborate throughout the *Comédie humaine,* in which the "things" that becoming "something" depends on, the exchanges that compose narrative advancement, and the objects that are the necessary context of plot also threaten, sooner or later, to efface the very subjects of such plots. For it is not only murderous Trompe-la-Mort who must engender action incognito—although the very character of Vautrin serves as further camouflage for that fact—but it is also the devoured Goriot, and it will be Rastignac. And like Rastignac, the future will not resolve this contradiction; rather, like Rastignac, this contradiction represents the future, the currency of illusory, dramatic narratives and the "drames continus" 'continuing dramas' (32; 36) of their "muet" 'mute' (32; 36) objectification. In Balzac's bildungsroman contradiction remains edifying: "Rien n'est plus triste à voir [. . .]," and "[*a*]*ll is true.*"

NOTES

[1]It should be noted that all available modern translations of the novel paraphrase—and in so doing change considerably—Mme Vauquer's extraordinary declaration "La vie est dans les meubles," which states directly: "Life is in the furniture." The clearest attempt I have found to include in a translation a periphrastic explanation of Mme Vauquer's brief and startling observation is the following sequence of sentences from the Signet Classics edition of *Père Goriot:* "My house, stripped of its men! *They were like furniture to me. You can't live without furniture, can you?*" (210; my emphasis). In every case, an explicit analogy or parallelism meant to parse Mme Vauquer's meaning is constructed and added by the translator, with the result that both the unsettling equation of men with furniture effected by "démeublée de ses hommes" and the subsequent shifting of life to furniture alone—"La vie est dans les meubles"—are virtually imperceptible to the English reader. Yet it can be argued that the paired definitions of life offered by Goriot, speaking for himself ("Ma vie à moi, est dans mes deux filles"), and Mme Vauquer, speaking for everyone ("La vie est dans les meubles")—categorical statements whose nearly identical wording by Balzac is infelicitously lost in translation—are what

the novel attempts to represent, and what any analysis of its contents and reception as an education in life, or bildungsroman, must ponder.

[2]Here the translation of the novel inevitably detracts from the novel's direct, verbal effect: although the French nickname *père* is indeed almost synonymous with the English term of familiarity, *old,* the appearance of *père* in the original text literally designates Goriot as "father" nearly from the start of the narrative.

[3]"Depuis ce jour, il n'a plus été question de la princesse de Cadignan, ni de d'Arthez. La princesse [. . .] passe tous les étés à Genève dans un villa avec le grand écrivain. [. . .] D'Arthez ne se montre qu'à la Chambre. Enfin, ses publications sont devenues excessivement rares. Est-ce un dénouement? Oui, pour les gens d'esprit; non, pour ceux qui veulent tout savoir" 'From this day on there was nothing more to be said about either the Princess of Cadignan or d'Arthez. The princess spends every summer in Geneva in a villa with the great writer. [. . .] D'Arthez only makes an appearance at the Chamber of Deputies. Finally, his publications have become terribly rare. Is this a denoument? Yes, for people of spirit (or intelligence); no, for those who want to know everything' (309; my trans.).

Fathers and Sons in *Old Goriot*: The Symbolic Dimension of Balzac's Realism

Ruth Amossy

To seek out the essential reality beneath the surface in order to expose the internal mechanism of society: such, according to Georg Lukács, is the principal goal of realistic art. Thus Balzac, in *Old Goriot,* does not simply mimic a preexistent world already endowed with meaning, nor is he content to show things as they appear. If, as some writers and critics would have it, the novel is a mirror, it is a mirror that reveals the hidden logic of human and social formation. While creating an illusion of reality through detailed description and true-to-life characters, *Old Goriot* in effect provides us with an in-depth analysis of French society in the first half of the nineteenth century.

Balzac constructs a fictional world that might usefully be decoded on at least two levels. On the first level, the novel constitutes a true-to-life representation, replete with vivid detail. On the second level, all the elements that advance the representation are woven into a web of complex relations through which they acquire symbolic meaning. The composition of *Old Goriot* thus allows for a significant distribution of its material: the Vauquer boardinghouse is one of three Parisian spheres staged by the novel; Goriot is related to a series of father figures, among whom are Taillefer and Vautrin; Rastignac and Bianchon embody two of the options open to youthful ambition. This combination of verisimilitude and symbolic organization, of mimesis and carefully crafted structure, is at the very core of Balzac's realism. It offers a comprehensive scheme for both describing and interpreting the social formation. Formal patterns yield social meanings; more or less explicit configurations of elements such as characters, places, and scenes uncover the logic of postrevolutionary France. These principles are illustrated by a close reading of the father-son relationships in *Old Goriot.*

Although Goriot's drama of paternity derives from his neglect by his two daughters, who are his sole and absolute passion, clearly his paternal function is not confined to these painful relationships. It has often been observed that Eugène de Rastignac nourishes filial sentiments toward Goriot, who in turn looks on Rastignac as a son and is delighted when the young man has a love affair with Delphine de Nucingen, Goriot's daughter. "So you wish to be my dear child too?" says Goriot to Rastignac (171). On another occasion, the two men express their feelings in a significant exchange: "[D]ear Father Goriot, you know very well that I am fond of you," says the student to the old man, who answers: "Yes, indeed, I can see that you are; you are not ashamed of me! Let me embrace you" (197). Admiring Father Goriot's qualities and appreciative of his immense generosity and self-sacrifice, Rastignac willingly accepts the old man, uneducated as Goriot is, while his own daughters, in shame, hide him from the world. "He says nothing about what he has endured, but anyone can guess it.

Well, I will look after him as though I were his son; I will fill his life with happiness," thinks the young student to himself (216). The adoptive son even takes on himself the duties Delphine and Anastasie fail to perform. When the old man is on his deathbed, Rastignac is constantly at his side, trying to comfort him in his anguish while Goriot's daughters claim to be delayed by personal concerns. Deeply moved by Goriot's despair, Rastignac spares no effort to induce Anastasie and Delphine to pay one last visit to their dying father: "Well, then, promise me," he says to M. de Restaud, Anastasie's husband, "you will tell her that her father has not a day to live; that he looked for her at his bedside, and cursed her when she did not come." M. de Restaud, "impressed by the fierce indignation expressed in Eugène's voice," answers, "You may tell her that yourself" (292–93). It is Rastignac who takes charge of the funeral arrangements, and he and the Vauquer servant are the only mourners present at a burial ceremony that the daughters decline to attend. This painful ordeal is a significant factor in the hero's apprenticeship and constitutes the final stage in the process of his disillusionment: "He looked at the grave, and in that place the last tear of his youth was shed" (304).

What, then, is the meaning of a symbolic paternity bestowed on a man unable to play the role of a spiritual father? Goriot is deprived of all paternal attributes, since he has no knowledge and no power. Rastignac rapidly acquires in Paris experience of the world and a capacity to behave according to the rules of society—a capacity the old man will never have. Rastignac begins to grasp the hidden mechanisms that move people in familial and social situations, while Goriot remains forever unable to analyze, and thus to master, the world around him. Moreover, in the Vauquer boardinghouse, Rastignac protects the old man, who has become the laughingstock of his fellow boarders: "'Anyone who annoys old Goriot shall answer for it to me from now on,' said Eugène, looking at the old vermicelli-maker's neighbour. 'He's worth more than all of us put together [. . .]' (107). Balzac's novel thus presents a striking reversal of the traditional roles. The man endowed with understanding and savoir faire, the benevolent protector, the parental caretaker is not old Goriot, but young Rastignac. The novel stages the fall of the father and the rise of the son.

A glance at another work, *Colonel Chabert* (1832), in which the same reversal of hierarchy occurs, may help us to understand the meaning of a recurrent pattern in Balzac's fictional world. One should recall that in the final order chosen by Balzac for his *Human Comedy, Old Goriot* is placed together with *Colonel Chabert* in the *Scenes of Private Life*. The two books, both set in Paris, raise issues of paternity, family, and law in modern society.

Colonel Chabert tells of the tragic return of a Napoleonic hero who is reported dead but who reappears during the Restoration to reclaim his wife and family fortune. Chabert's wife, who meanwhile has married an aristocrat and borne two children, takes advantage of the fact that, having been severely wounded, Chabert's outward appearance has changed beyond recognition: she stubbornly refuses to acknowledge Chabert. The unfortunate colonel, unable to grasp the complexities of the law, seeks help and succeeds in enlisting the support of a well-known lawyer, Derville. The young lawyer, familiar with jurisprudence as well as with the mechanisms of the new French society, has to guide and teach the old man, who eventually becomes completely dependent on Derville. Fallen from glory, immured in useless military knowledge, the powerless father now obeys the son. This reversal of roles has to be understood against the background of radical change that French society underwent following the abrupt transition from Napoleon to Louis XVIII. Emerging out of a past that the new regime wishes to efface, Chabert is like an unwelcome ghost. The new society refuses to recognize the elevated status attained by a child of the Revolution with the support of the emperor. Moreover, whatever knowledge the brave combatant may have acquired in the Napoleonic army no longer has any currency. Chabert's norms and values are now dead and buried, and Chabert feels he should have stayed dead and buried himself instead of returning to a society that seeks to discard everything he represents. Rejected by everyone, the former hero is eventually driven to the margins of society, to an asylum where he completely loses his identity.

The parallel between, on the one hand, Colonel Chabert and Derville the man of law and, on the other, Old Goriot and Rastignac the law student, is evident. The symbolic son, rather than the father, is now the representative of the law. The two paternal figures, who at one time enjoyed success and power in a world where ordinary citizens had ample opportunity to scale the social ladder, are no more than unwanted ghosts in a country looking to erase the memories of the Revolution. Goriot and Chabert embody a past that has to be buried in order to allow for the restoration of the Old Regime. Thus the reversal of the father and son roles and of the power structure is not the sign of a natural progression whereby sons take over paternal responsibilities and the past is replaced by new achievements. Rather, this reversal is symptomatic of a profound political and social crisis. Let us, then, explore in *Old Goriot* the particular meaning of the symbolic father-son relationship in the context of France's historical situation after the Revolution.

Balzac chose to set his novel in the Restoration years of 1818 and 1819, when Louix XVIII had ascended the throne following Napoleon's ultimate exile to Saint Helena. The text was published in the years 1834 and 1835, that is to say, after the revolution of 1830, under the July Monarchy. By 1834, the writer had sufficient critical distance to analyze the last desperate attempt of the foundering aristocracy of the faubourg Saint-Germain to restore past glory—the aristocracy all the while behaving as if the French Revolution had never taken place. Balzac shows the ascendant force of another milieu, the bourgeoisie of the Chaussée d'Antin, who embody the new source of power, namely, wealth. There is a third sphere, the faubourg Saint-Marceau, the neighborhood in which the Vauquer boardinghouse is located. Rastignac is the only one to move between these three spheres—the old aristocracy, the wealthy bourgeoisie, and the simple poor. But he is not the only connection between them: each milieu constitutes a social space in which one member of the Goriot family evolves. Anastasie has married a representative of the old noblesse, the count of Restaud; Delphine is absorbed into the world of finance when she becomes the wife of the banker Nucingen. The tensions between these two segments of French society battling for power during the Restoration account for the difficult relationship between the two Goriot sisters, endowing them with a symbolic meaning that goes beyond the mere psychological grounding. As for Father Goriot, he is an "old '93 man" (101): he represents the simple people who became prosperous during the Revolution and gave their children an opportunity to ascend the social ladder.

Balzac calls up Goriot's biography by enabling his hero to pick up information on the father of Anastasie and Delphine. The original version of Goriot's story is told to Rastignac by a member of the aristocracy, the duchess of Langeais, and this version is followed by an account provided by the man who bought Goriot's business after Goriot retired. The most salient elements of the biography are these: Goriot was at first "an ordinary workman employed by a vermicelli-maker"; thanks to the Revolution, he managed to make his fortune. He bought his business when his employer "fell a victim to the first upheaval in 1789" (111). Goriot was then "President of his Section during the Revolution; he was in the know about the notorious famine, and laid the foundation of his fortune at that time by selling flour for ten times as much as it cost him" (101). He thus acquired power that was derived from money. As for his knowledge, it went no further than his business enterprise:

> His dealings in grain seemed to have absorbed all his intelligence. [. . .] Take him from his specialty, from his humble obscure counting-house [. . .] and he became once more the uncouth, slow-witted workman, incapable of following an argument, insensible to all the pleasures of the mind. (112)

His situation during the Restoration, after he had achieved an advantageous marriage for each of his two daughters, is cannily described by the duchess of Langeais:

> You can quite understand that so long as Buonaparte was Emperor the two sons-in-law did not much mind having the old '93 man in their houses: but when the Bourbons were restored it was a different story; the old fellow was in Monsieur de Restaud's way, and even more tiresomely in the banker's. (101)

It is thus evident that Goriot embodies times that are no more: their founding principles have been dismissed by the Restoration, and their memory is to be erased. Just as the Napoleonic colonel's military wisdom is of no consequence in the new civil society, Goriot's business acumen serves him not at all in the powerful circles of postrevolutionary France. The uneducated workman cannot cut a figure in society. Goriot is aware of his ignorance and of the embarrassment his presence causes his family. He evokes thus the "agony that Anastasie inflicted upon [him] with the first look that made it clear to [him] that [he] had just said something stupid which made her feel humiliated" (285). The "old '93," as the duchess of Langeais rather derisively calls him, no longer fits in the world in which his beloved daughters triumph. The old man is at a loss in a society that has rejected him and whose complexity he is unable to grasp. He fails where Rastignac, the young man come from a distant province, easily succeeds.

What, then, is the knowledge acquired by the son that completely escapes the father? One of the main things Rastignac learns during his Parisian apprenticeship is never to confuse the principles of law with their practical application in real-life situations. To conquer a position in the world, the young man has not only to study law but also to become proficient in the ways of the world. He has to understand how laws are adapted to the needs of influential people and thus enabled to serve money and power. The distinction between legality and legitimacy remains beyond Goriot's understanding. A close and solid connection between law and justice is at the base of the reforms pursued by the Revolution and intended to put an end to the arbitrary power of an absolute monarch and to ensure the equality of all citizens. The "old '93" believes in the efficiency of law to protect defenseless citizens against illegitimate measures. When Delphine reveals that her husband, the banker Nucingen, has invested all his money in a questionable business concern and has offered her personal freedom in return for placing her fortune at his disposal, Goriot naively protests: "But there are such things as laws! [. . .]. There's a Place de Grève for that sort of son-in-law! I would guillotine him myself if there were no public executioner to do it for me!" Delphine responds, "No, no, Father, the law can't touch him" (249).

It is the daughter who teaches the father that morality and family respectability cannot be protected by laws. She reveals to him the crooked ways in which Nucingen has built a fortune, "swindling poor people out of their money" behind a lawful facade (249). She tells Goriot that the banker has straw men who build houses on his land, pay the contractors with postdated bills, sell the properties to him for small sums, and then "slide out of their debt to the duped contractors by going bankrupt" (249). The wisdom of the son-in-law, as explained by the daughter, is something that the father can neither understand nor admit. To fight it, he sees no other recourse than turning to the tribunal and applying the letter of the law.

This appeal to a law designed to protect natural rights, that is to say, moral principles enshrined in nature, reappears in hyperbolic form when the old man lies on his deathbed. Seeing that his two ungrateful daughters do not care enough to sustain him in his final moments, Goriot cries out in a terrible instant of despair, "My daughters! My daughters! Anastasie! Delphine! I must see them. Send the police to fetch them, compel them to come! Justice is on my side, [. . .] natural affection, and the law as well. I protest!" (286). Later he cries out, "Pass a law for dying fathers. It is shocking! It cries for vengeance!" (290). Rastignac has no answer for the unfortunate man. Did he himself not abandon his studies in law when he understood that law and morals do not apply to the wealthy, since money is the world's ultima ratio?

In short, the father, who symbolically stands for the law, no longer represents its power, does not know its real use, and calls in vain for its support. The breakdown of paternal authority and the increasing gap between law and natural rights threaten the very existence of the new society. The raving Goriot expresses it dramatically in his final protest: "The country will go to ruin if the fathers are trampled underfoot. The thing is clear as day. Society, the whole world, turns on fatherly love, everything falls to pieces if children do not love their fathers. [. . .] Go and tell them that not to come is parricide!" (286, 289). On both personal and emotional levels, Goriot's words echo the obsession of postrevolutionary France, which was still reeling from the killing of King Louis XVI, the almighty representative of human and divine law on earth, and the fall of the emperor Napoleon I, who was called the Père du Peuple. It has been observed that the dates marking Goriot's progressive degradation parallel those charting Napoleon's downfall: Goriot leaves his business in 1813, the year of Napoleon's first important defeat, at Leipzig; moves from the first to the second floor of the Vauquer boardinghouse in 1815, the fatal date of Waterloo; and dies in 1821, the year of Napoleon's death. These events were present in everyone's memory when Balzac published his novel. Even the plain Mme Vauquer evokes the fatal passing of Louis XVI and the emperor's reversals of fortune. Beyond Goriot's personal demise, the theme of the father's death or, rather, murder, thus has a political echo that considerably broadens the scope of the story.

The new French society is characterized not only by the disintegration of paternal authority but also by the breakdown of the family cell. Family as an institution on which society is built, an institution that lends order and stability to society, tends to disappear. The two daughters who neglect their father are also torn apart by savage rivalry. They are driven by personal interests and social ambition, which leave little room for family affection. "[T]he desertion of the father by the two daughters who wish he were dead is hideous enough," says Mme de Beauséant, "but there is something still more hideous, the rivalry of the two sisters among themselves" (103). Moreover, relationships in Delphine's and Anastasie's respective families are also subverted. The marital ties between Delphine and her husband are nothing but a cold business relationship devoid of love and even respect. A terrible war takes place between Anastasie and the count of Restaud, who wants to compel his wife to waive the inheritance of the children she has from her lover, Maxime de Trailles, in favor of the Restaud's elder son, who is the only legitimate heir. The rich banker Taillefer, the father of the young Victorine who lives in the Vauquer boardinghouse, deprives his daughter of her fortune on the grounds that she is illegitimate and intends to leave everything to Victorine's brother, who pays scant attention to Victorine. The disintegration of the family in Parisian circles is thus displayed with all its dire consequences.

Family seems to survive only as an archaic memory in the distant provinces. Thus Rastignac takes pleasure in a warm family where relationships between parents and children, brother and sisters, are based on true love and devotion. Whereas the Parisian families are consumed by envy and conflict of interests, the provincial family is still united by a feeling of deep solidarity. Rastignac's mother and sisters are habitually generous and self-sacrificing. Faced with the Parisian world of opportunism and sheer self-interest, the young man sadly recalls his home: "He remembered the pure happiness of his uneventful life there: he recalled the days spent among beings who loved him dearly. Those creatures conformed to the natural laws of the domestic hearth, and in so doing found a full and constant happiness [. . .]" (271). However, the young student, who is bent on social advancement, does not hesitate to exploit the situation. He himself compares his deeds to those of Goriot's daughters when he asks his mother and sisters to deprive themselves of the little they possess in order to send him money:

> He thought of old Goriot breaking up his silver plate and selling it to pay his daughter's bill of exchange. [. . .] "Your mother has broken up her jewels!" he said to himself. [. . .] "What right have you to condemn Anastasie? You have just done selfishly for your own future what she did for her lover!" (116)

The sad lucidity arrived at in Paris allows Rastignac not only to denounce his own acts but also to gain a new insight into the family idyll. He now understands the real nature of a life based on meager resources and a daily series of petty deprivations:

> His increased knowledge, his kindled ambition, had opened his eyes, so that once he was back in the manor-house in the family circle he saw things clearly as they were. [. . .] Eugène noted the constant worry about money [. . .]. He watched the parismony with which every crumb was hoarded [. . .]. (56)

As Vautrin cynically puts it: "The family eats more chestnut soup than white bread" (126). Eugène thus realizes "that the uncertain future of this large family [depends] upon him" (56). The provincial family is indeed like an island of feeling and true love. But it can no longer be autonomous. Its whole existence is threatened by insufficient material conditions and thus subordinated to a success governed by Parisian rules.

The young hero's relationship with his family expresses a nostalgia for a lost harmony, a nostalgia shared by other characters. Old Goriot often recalls his former life with his two daughters when they were still young and lived with him in a loving home. He tries to revive it by setting up a love nest for Delphine and Rastignac. The old man dreams of sharing the happiness of the young couple and restoring a lost family cell dominated by true feeling. Taking Rastignac to the apartment he has furnished, he is thrilled at the idea that they are going to have dinner with Delphine: "The three of us are dining together, together! do you understand? [. . .] Ah! it's a long, long time since I've had such a peaceful happy time with her as we shall have now" (229). Goriot's desperate efforts thus produce a parody of the original family unit. Other parodic substitutes of the lost paradise are provided in the narrative. One substitute is, of course, the boardinghouse, where the "breakfast had the air of a family meal": "Everyone came down in slippers, and tongues were loosed in the atmosphere of intimacy [. . .]" (35). In an even more ironic mode, Vautrin dreams of living a "patriarchal life on a great estate, say a hundred thousand acres, in the United States of America, in the deep South," where he intends "to be a planter, to have slaves" (131). "Negroes, you see," he explains to Rastignac, "are children ready-made that you can do what you like with [. . .]" (131). These questionable substitutes lay further stress on the loss of an idealized patriarchal life.

Beyond the psychological dimension, the novel denounces a society where all familial and personal ties are mediated by money. The blessed transparency of human relationships based neither on power nor on wealth is nothing but a nostalgic dream. "Money buys everything, even daughters," says the dying father to Rastignac in a moment of horrible lucidity (284). From beginning to end, the text implicates the personal and the socioeconomic levels. Emotional or spiritual planes have no self-sufficiency in Balzac's novels: love, lust, parental affection are all subordinated to material components. The hero's love for Delphine cannot be separated from his social ambitions. Delphine's beauty and the desire Delphine arouses in the young man greatly derive from the luxury surrounding her and the splendor of her dress. Rastignac does not fall in love with Victorine Taillefer, although she is naturally pretty, because she does not have the seductive qualities of a sophisticated Parisian socialite. Rastignac himself, in order to seduce Delphine, has to spend his money on fashionable clothes, since "[o]ne glance at Monsieur de Trailles had made Rastignac realize the influence that tailors exercise in young men's lives" (118). Moreover, he has to be introduced as Mme de Beauséant's relative to attract the attention of the ladies. The intimate relationship between Delphine and Rastignac starts with the young woman's confession of her financial problems. It develops thanks to the apartment that old Goriot brings as a present to his protégé, laying out his last franc. Money runs the world; it gives life and love, as Goriot aptly puts it in his misery.

Viewed from this perspective, the lesson of the novel is no less cynical than that offered by Vautrin. The hero's apprenticeship begins with the initial steps taken by an impoverished law student anxious to make his way in the world through university studies. He soon discovers that hard work is by no means the only way to succeed and that knowledge of the world is of far greater value than knowledge itself. At first he is "resolved to open two parallel lines of attack on Fortune, to lean on Knowledge and on Love, to be a learned doctor of law and a man of the world" (106). Eventually, however, he is obliged to concede, together with the narrator, that the two lines are "asymptotes" that can "never meet" (106). Abandoning the classroom, Rastignac serves his entire apprenticeship in the world, learning more between the blue boudoir of Mme de Restaud and the pink boudoir of Mme de Beauséant than he could ever have done at university. What he aims to study is Parisian law—without which no fortune can ever be made.

Thus in *Old Goriot,* parallels and oppositions between symbolic sons and fathers and their relation to the law are designed to reveal the hidden meanings of the new French society's sociopolitical and economic dimensions. The novel raises problems without trying to provide solutions or even unequivocal answers. It exposes the various and often contradictory attitudes adopted by its fictional characters in accordance with their individual perceptions of society at large. Readers, then, are invited not to pass judgment based on moral precepts already in place but rather to analyze, to configure the elements in meaningful patterns, to compare viewpoints, and to reflect on a fictional world intended to equip them with a better understanding of their own.

Balzacorama: Mass Culture in *Old Goriot*

Dean de la Motte

Strictly speaking, it may be anachronistic to discuss mass culture in *Old Goriot*, but there can be no doubt that Balzac's novel stands at a crossroads in literary history: it starkly reveals a new, bourgeois society heaving into view in the wake of the French Revolution. The purpose of this essay is neither to claim Balzac's novel for the burgeoning field of culture studies nor to suggest that its undergraduate readers be led into the labyrinths of cultural theory. Instead I would like to suggest how, through Balzac's own analysis of a society in transition, we might help our students begin constructing a historical, political, and even theoretical backdrop not only for *Old Goriot* specifically but also for canonical nineteenth-century French literature in general. To this end, I suggest three interrelated microapproaches to Balzac's text, which consider (1) the book as an object of art or a consumer good; (2) the narrator's use of details to establish an aesthetic hierarchy of class or authenticity analogous to the social; and (3) the introduction of the larger aesthetic, political, and social events and discourses that frame the writing of *Old Goriot*.

In the novel's opening passage, its narrator moves outside the narrative frame to address the privileged, and most likely female, reader in terms that underscore the production of novels as commodities, mass-produced entertainment:

> Ainsi ferez-vous, vous qui tenez ce livre d'une main blanche, vous qui vous enfoncez dans un moelleux fauteuil en vous disant: Peut-être ceci va-t-il m'amuser. Après avoir lu les secrètes infortunes du père Goriot, vous dînerez avec appétit en mettant votre insensibilité sur le compte de l'auteur, en le taxant d'exagération, en l'accusant de poésie. Ah! sachez-le: ce drame n'est ni une fiction, ni un roman. *All is true,* il est si véritable, que chacun peut en reconnaître les éléments chez soi, dans son cœur peut-être. (22)

> And you will show the same insensibility, as you hold this book in your white hand, lying back in a softly cushioned armchair, and saying to yourself, "Perhaps this one is amusing." When you have read of the secret sorrows of old Goriot you will dine with unimpaired appetite, blaming the author for your callousness, taxing him with exaggeration, accusing him of having given wings to his imagination. But you may be certain that this drama is neither fiction nor romance. *All is true,* so true that everyone can recognize the elements of the tragedy in his own household, in his own heart perhaps. (28)

This celebrated passage, usually quoted in the context of discussions of Balzac's realism, is rich with possibilities for classroom discussion. Clearly in 1834 the novel, like the dinner that follows it, is to be digested without an afterthought. It is, after all, a fiction. Why else would Balzac need to insist to the contrary? The mimetic claims are used, among other things, to differentiate *Old Goriot* from the sensationalist, gothic, and melodramatic potboilers that were the rage in the 1820s and to which Balzac himself made a prolific—if pseudonymous—contribution. Balzac's new tragedy, his rewriting of William Shakespeare's *King Lear,* offers itself as a work of serious fiction, not—or not simply—a commodity.

Most accepted definitions of mass culture in France place its development in the final quarter of the nineteenth century or, at the earliest, during the Second Empire (Schwartz 7–8). And yet this fiction—or "drame," as Balzac calls it—reveals a society where, if mass culture has not yet fully become the dominant cultural model of production and consumption, the material and intellectual conditions that enable it are nevertheless developing with astonishing rapidity. Mass culture, based as it is on mass production, has inscribed in its logic both an absent original, provoking nostalgia for authenticity, for the "aura" that "withers in the age of mechanical reproduction" (Benjamin, "Work" 221), and the mediated or "mimetic desire" that René Girard elaborates in his *Deceit, Desire, and the Novel* (see esp. 1–52) and that Mme de Beauséant describes in the following manner: "Il y a des femmes qui aiment l'homme déjà choisi par une autre, comme il y a de pauvres bourgeoises qui, en prenant nos chapeaux, espèrent avoir nos manières" 'There are women who love a man because he has been chosen by another, just as there are poor middle-class women who copy our hats and think by doing so to acquire our manners too' (116–17; 104). It is hardly a coincidence that Balzac, through Mme de Beauséant, has succeeded in fusing his novelistic interest in mimetic desire on two levels, sex and class, in a single detail. The hat represents the mimetic logic that will inspire the bourgeois consumption of mass-produced goods, and this specific brand of mimetic desire adds considerable momentum to the industrial revolution, which will reach its apex later in the century.

At this point instructors may wish to remind students that the miming or aping of one's "betters"—and by extension one's betters might include anyone who possesses what one does not—is not only a stock device of the French comic tradition, from Molière to Marcel Proust, but also a constant in explanations of the psychological dynamics of consumer desire, from Marx to Roland Barthes's *Mythologies.* The parroting that for Gustave Flaubert is almost always a sign of bourgeois *bêtise* makes its appearance in Balzac's novel in the mindless repetitions that emanate from the former *fonctionnaire* Poiret, who is early on described as "une espèce de mécanique" 'a kind of automaton,' who "semblait avoir été l'un des ânes de notre grand moulin social" 'appeared to have been one of the drudges of our great social treadmill' (33, 34; 37). Balzac, who would go on to write *Physiologie de l'employé* ("Physiology of the Bureaucrat" [1841]), itself to be incorporated into a later version of *La Femme supérieure* entitled *Les Employés* (*The Bureaucrats*), is one of the earliest and most penetrating critics of the bureaucracy created under Napoleon and usually associated with the mechanized, scientific approach to administration synonymous with modern life. Like Delphine (Goriot) de Nucingen—not only the daughter of a vermicelli merchant who cleverly used his position during the Revolution to make a fortune but also the wife of a newly ennobled Jewish Alsatian banker—Poiret does not have an original idea in his head: his entire existence is mediated.

Another site of mediated repetition in the novel is, of course, the "plaisanterie de parler en *rama*" 'pleasantry of "talking 'rama"' (80; 74)—the series of playful neologisms forged on the popular panorama. As Vanessa Schwartz has demonstrated, although the panorama did not become an attraction affordable to the masses until much later, it is clearly a precursor to wax museums, the cinema, and other Parisian mass entertainments that would evolve throughout the century (149–76). In *Old Goriot,* however, the precocious pensioners of the Maison Vauquer are in fact already possessed by ramamania—the suffix enters and playfully but parasitically clings to their speech throughout the novel. While one would be well advised not to read too much into Balzac's use of the device (Marion Crawford, in the introduction to her Penguin Classics translation of the text, points out that such conversation is a universal of student speech [22], and similar examples could certainly be cited from texts at least as early as Rabelais's *Gargantua* and *Pantagruel*), the device reinforces not only the quality of repetition personified by Poiret but also the shabbily derivative existence—at least from the narrator's elitist, we might even say essentialist, point of view—led by all but a privileged few. This existence is, in fact, best embodied by the Maison Vauquer itself.

Before moving through the opening passages with students, I suggest returning to the two passages quoted above and to the question of the status of the text of *Old Goriot* itself. Once students understand the series of parallel dichotomies, real or imagined, set up by the narrator between authenticity and sham, art and entertainment, true nobility and the likes of the Nucingens, they might better appreciate the swarming detail of Balzac's overture to the novel. The famous description of the Maison Vauquer is, in this context, less remarkable for its rendering of the dilapidated state of the boardinghouse or the corollaries to be drawn between character and environment than for the split it invokes between original and copy that in turn implies all the other dichotomies and that so clearly and insistently hints at a nascent mass culture.

Outside the boardinghouse a statue of "l'Amour" 'the God of Love' is placed in a "renfoncement que simule cette peinture" '[painted] imitation shrine' (24; 29); inside, in the gloomy sitting room, stands 'ce cabaret en porcelaine blanche ornée de filets d'or effacés à demi, que l'on rencontre partout aujourd'hui" 'a white china tea-service with its gilt decoration half worn away, the kind of tea-service that is inevitably found everywhere today' (26; 30), and on the wall is hung "un papier verni représentant les principales scènes de *Télémaque,* et dont les classiques personnages sont coloriés" 'a varnished paper on which the principal scenes from *Télémaque* are depicted, with the classical characters in colour' (26; 31). Over the hearth are "deux vases pleins de fleurs artificielles, vieillies et encagées, qui accompagnent une pendule en marbre bleuâtre du plus mauvais goût" 'two vases full of faded artificial flowers imprisoned under glass shades, set on either side of a bluish marble clock in the worst possible taste' (26; 31). The emphasis, beyond the obvious misery of the place, is on the ersatz—what will later come to be known as *industriel* or mass-produced—quality of the furnishings of this "respectable" establishment. But the narrator only truly hits his stride as he leads the reader into the dining room:

> Vous y verriez un baromètre à capucin qui sort quand il pleut, des gravures exécrables qui ôtent l'appétit, toutes encadrées en bois verni à filets dorés; un cartel en écaille incrustée de cuivre; un poêle vert, des quinquets d'Argand où la poussière se combine avec l'huile, une longue table couverte en toile cirée assez grasse pour qu'un facétieux externe y écrive son nom en se servant de son doigt comme de style, des chaises estropiées, de petits paillassons piteux en sparterie qui se déroule toujours sans se perdre jamais, puis des chaufferettes misérables à trous cassés, à charnières défaites, dont le bois se carbonise. (27–28)

> In this room you would find a barometer with a monk who appears when it is wet, execrable engravings bad enough to spoil your appetite and all framed in varnished black wood with gilt beading, a clock with tortoise-shell case inlaid with copper, a green stove, Argand lamps coated with dust and oil, a long table covered with oil-cloth so greasy that a facetious boarder can write his name on it with his finger-nail, broken-backed chairs, wretched little esparto grass mats unravelling endlessly without ever coming completely to pieces, and finally miserable foot-warmers, their orifices enlarged by decay, their hinges broken and their wood charred. (32)

While such images are particularly concentrated in the novel's opening pages, they recur a number of times, from Mme de Beauséant's allusion to the counterfeit hats of the bourgeoises to the carefully distinguished carriages, homes, and furnishings of, respectively, the princely de Beauséants, the noble de Restauds, and, finally, the nouveaux riches Nucingens, whose home, Eugène discovers, is

> une véritable maison de banquier, pleine de recherches coûteuses, de stucs, de paliers d'escalier en mosaïque de marbre. Il trouva madame de Nucingen dans un petit salon à peintures italiennes, dont le décor ressemblait à celui des cafés. (192)

> a true banker's house, full of costly showiness, with stucco-work on the walls, and landings of marble mosaic. He found Madame de Nucingen in a little drawing-room hung with paintings in the Italian style and decorated like a restaurant. (161)

Of course Balzac's novel, like the entire *Comédie humaine*, is the portrait of a society in flux, with old standards of class, taste, and beauty under siege, and it certainly will not harm students to be reminded of the aesthetic revolution announced by Stendhal in *Racine et Shakespeare* (1823) and Victor Hugo in the preface to *Cromwell* (1827), familiar though this revolution may be to all teachers of French literature. Moreover, as Peter Brooks (*Melodramatic Imagination*), Julia Przybos, and Marie-Pierre Le Hir have shown, the enormously popular and influential melodrama competed first with classical, then with romantic theater (Le Hir 1); we recall that Vautrin invites Mme Vauquer to *Le Mont sauvage*, a melodrama by Guilbert de Pixérécourt, and that the good woman then proceeds to attribute the play, in a comic triple error, to "Atala de Chateaubriand" (240; 202). François Chateaubriand, the wrong author, is given the first name of one of his own protagonists and, by far the worst insult, is a serious poet confused with a popular playwright. Ma Vauquer, Balzac's own Mme Malaprop, should know better, "*née* de Conflans" as she is (21; 27). One notes here that Balzac's acute analysis of postrevolutionary society shows the possibility of not only upward but also downward mobility—through the "malheurs" '*peck of troubles*' (29; 33) of Mme Vauquer and the privations of the noble de Rastignacs. Despite the attempts of the Bourbon Restoration to turn back the clock, democracy and its attendant institutions—capitalism, industry, and mass culture—are beginning to make themselves felt, to disturb the rigid hierarchies of the ancien régime in a more profound, lasting way than did even the Revolution itself.

One need not be a Marxist critic to see in Balzac's opening description of the pension and its inhabitants a direct link between politics and aesthetics and, specifically, a startling view of the birth of a modern society where financial success, as Rastignac soon comes to understand, is the "*ultima ratio mundi*" (117; 105). It is all too easy for students and instructors alike to forget, however, that Balzac, although "one of the first novelists to understand the dominating importance of money in the dawning world of capitalism, when the old values of the landed aristocracy were being challenged by the rising commercial and industrial classes" (Brooks, Introduction vii), is writing as a reactionary royalist rather than as a progressive or a revolutionary. It is thus crucial that we help our students situate the Restoration in relation to the ancien régime, the Revolution, the Empire, and the July Monarchy (during which the novel was published) and, more generally, in relation to the political, economic, and cultural forces at play in the France of 1834. Despite the novel's ostensible dates of 1819 to 1820, *Old Goriot* was originally to be set in 1825 (which explains the existence of a number of anachronisms) and, I would suggest, may be read as a text not only of but also about the early years of the July Monarchy. Those years saw a number of momentous changes, many of which would only become wholly realized under the Second Empire and Third Republic, but all of which were certainly in the air of intellectual Paris—one need only peruse the newspapers of the period—and lurk just beneath the surface of *Old Goriot*. The July Revolution of 1830, largely provoked by repression of the press, brought with it a loosening of censorship. In 1833 the Guizot Law offered elementary education to all French males, and in 1836 Emile de Girardin—with whom Balzac had earlier collaborated and in whose new journal *La Presse* he would publish the first roman-feuilleton, *La Vieille Fille* (1837)—introduced the first information-based, inexpensive daily newspaper, whose drastically reduced subscription price was to be made up through advertising. Instructors might point to Mme Vauquer's use of advertising to attract boarders (44; 45) and Vautrin's parody of a sales pitch to mock Rastignac as examples of Balzac's sensitivity to this incipient mass culture:

> —Monsieur a une épouse? Demanda Poiret.
> —Une épouse à compartiments, qui va sur l'eau, garantie bon teint, dans les prix de vingt-cinq à quarante, dessins à carreaux du dernier goût, susceptible de se laver, d'un joli porter, moitié fil, moitié coton, moitié laine, guérissant le mal de dents, et autres maladies approuvées par l'Académie royale de Médecine! excellente d'ailleurs pour les enfants! meilleure encore contre les maux de tête, les plénitudes et autres maladies de l'œsophage, des yeux et des oreilles, cria Vautrin avec la volubilité comique et l'accentuation d'un opérateur. (191)

> "Have you a spouse?" asked Poiret.
> "Yes, a spouse with compartments, watertight and buoyant, fast colour guaranteed, prices from twenty-five to forty, checked patterns in the latest fashion, washes well, looks pretty, half-linen, half-cotton, half-woollen, cures toothache and other complaints approved by the Royal College of Physicians! Excellent for children as well! Better still as a remedy for headaches, feelings of fullness and other maladies of the oesophagus, eyes and ears!" cried Vautrin, with the comic volubility and patter of a quack at a fair. (160–61)

The patter of a quack, yes, but also very much the language of the *annonce* that will soon come to dominate not only the mass press but also the visual spaces of Paris as the century progresses.

The 1830s also saw pioneering experimentation in both photography and railways, perhaps the two inventions that would most transform perceptions of time and space. Finally, the decade of *Old Goriot* was one of enormous ideological ferment, and beneath or alongside the visionary mysticism of the utopian socialism of the Saint-Simonians and Fourierists lay the movement's most basic tenet: that increased economic production and consumption would alone be the key to future social equality. Despite the disillusionment of 1848 and the ridicule heaped on the utopian thinkers, progress became, thanks in large part to its popularization in the early mass press, what Pierre Larousse, in his article "Progrès" in the *Grand Dictionnaire*, would call "la foi de notre siècle" 'our century's religion.' The *Saint-Simoniens* and *Fouriéristes* would go on to become some of the most influential architects of the French industrial revolution: bankers, engineers, publicists, and railway magnates.

As Albert Béguin long ago pointed out in his seminal *Balzac visionnaire* (1946), Balzac had the paradoxical capacity to be at once "the apologist of the established order and of the strictest social hierarchies" and yet fully "attached only to the characters, from among those he created, who broke through boundaries" (qtd. in Balzac, *Père Goriot* [Norton] 268–69). One way this contradiction plays itself out in *Old Goriot* lies in the claims of artistic integrity and seriousness of purpose made by a hopelessly indebted former hack and practicing journalist known for his ability to produce enormous quantities of what Sainte-Beuve would condemn as early as 1839 as "littérature industrielle" 'mass-produced literature.' The parvenu here refashions himself, not only by becoming Honoré de Balzac but also by rewriting the tragedy as novel in an attempt to join the aristocracy of letters.

Balzac's alter ego, Eugène de Rastignac, learns from Vautrin that "il faut se salir les mains si l'on veut fricoter; sachez seulement vous bien débarbouiller: là est toute la morale de notre époque" 'you have to dirty your hands if you want to live well. The only thing that matters is to know how to get them clean again; in that art lies the whole morality of our times' (153; 130). *Old Goriot,* produced at great speed to satisfy both the author's creditors and the "main blanche" 'white hand' of the literary consumer, represents the former scribbler and failed printer's attempt to cleanse his own soiled hands. Visionary and penetrating critic though he was, Balzac, in creating the novel, enacted and yet perhaps did not clearly see what the likes of Théophile Gautier, Charles Baudelaire, Gustave Flaubert, and Joris-Karl Huysmans would come to experience so painfully throughout the century: the widening gulf between, on the one hand, artistic integrity and originality and, on the other, the increasingly commodified, mediated mass culture born in the 1830s and inescapably present ever since. Happily, the distinction between serious and popular literature is one our students, assigned to read *Old Goriot* instead of the latest best-seller, understand perfectly. Balzac has, of course, long ago "made it."

Chronologically and thematically positioned at the moment of mass culture's emergence in nineteenth-century France, *Old Goriot* thus provides a privileged point of departure for classroom discussions of the new literature, culture, history, and politics—not to mention the psychology and sociology—of mediated desire. Such an approach not only brings Balzac's text into sharper focus but can also illuminate much of nineteenth-century literature, helping students to establish connections between apparently disparate works. After all, Flaubert's *Madame Bovary* may be read as the story of Mme de Beauséant's hat retold from the perspective of the desiring bourgeoise, and later in the century Emile Zola's *Nana* and Guy de Maupassant's "Le Collier" are subsequent rewritings, this time from the point of view of the *ouvrière* and petite bourgeoise, respectively. As Balzac does in so many other ways (his interest in society from top to bottom, his realism, his creation of a distinctly French brand of bildungsroman), in *Old Goriot* he lays down a template for a penetrating analysis of mass culture that will serve novelists from Flaubert to Proust and beyond. Indeed, as I hope I have demonstrated, Balzac's model of interpretation—of both society and literature—is one from which students and teachers of the novel can learn a great deal.

Reading Social and Historical Space in *Le Père Goriot*'s Descriptions

James H. Reid

One of the great challenges to teaching *Le Père Goriot* is the first twenty pages, which describe in painstaking detail the poor *quartier* and pension in which much of the story takes place as well as the characters who inhabit the pension. It is tempting to skip over these descriptions to the dramatic accounts of Goriot's fall into poverty and Rastignac's rise to power. The temptation is increased by the many vocabulary words that the student—and even the teacher—may not recognize.

But to skip Balzac's descriptions is to neglect a central role of his realist narrator's discourse. French realist narrators use descriptions to reconstruct society at a particular historical moment by giving society the form of a perceivable and coherently structured space. This space is constituted by fixed relations between people, between places, and between people and places, all of which, according to the fiction, can be observed by narrator or character. Realist narrators reconstruct this social space by describing the habitual actions of a novel's characters and the physical environment. Balzac's narrator interprets the characters' habitual actions and the place as means by which society reproduces its fixed hierarchical relations between rich and poor, strong and weak, at a particular historical moment.

Balzac's descriptions do more than reconstruct a static place or set of characters; they reconstruct the dynamic, ongoing processes by which the spatial structure of society reproduces itself. Thus they provide a counterweight to his narrative passages, in which the narrator often constructs the historical moment quite differently: as a struggle between powerful, deceitful, and manipulative individuals who compete for the authority to guide society's reproduction of its social space in the increasingly capitalist world of early-nineteenth-century France.

By learning to recognize how Balzac's descriptive and narrative passages construct the historical moment students can also discover, as I argue here, the ways in which Balzac felt that his narrator's words actually acted in history. They can appreciate the richness and complexity of Balzac's realist discourse.

Before my students read *Le Père Goriot,* I tell them that each set of descriptions in a particular text often repeats a recognizable pattern. To understand a description, they must look up the minimum of words necessary to reconstruct this pattern. They must then interpret how the description functions by honing in on short passages in the description.

I begin discussion by asking students how they reacted to the initial descriptions of the Parisian *quartier* where the pension is located. Many note the apparent excess of perceptible, especially visible, details, such as falling plaster, the silence of the *quartier,* or the smell in Mme Vauquer's dining room. I then ask what the purpose of such detail could be. Some say that the copious details of place and character provide a background for the action. Others mention that place names, like Montmartre, refer to real places. Most conclude that the background is "real," and they point to the sentences: "Ah! sachez-le: ce drame n'est ni une fiction, ni un roman. *All is true,* il est si véritable, que chacun peut en reconnaître les éléments chez soi, dans son cœur peut-être" 'But you may be certain that this drama is neither fiction nor romance. *All is true,* so true that everyone can recognize the elements of the tragedy in his own household, in his own heart perhaps' (22; 28).

Having established the students' general presupposition that realist descriptions provide a real background, I ask students how readers can know that Balzac describes Paris as it was. How many readers in the class know Paris or have knowledge of early-nineteenth-century Paris? Does Balzac's narrator reconstruct every detail or even a majority of the details that make up a *quartier*? The narrator himself says that he does not: "Pour expliquer combien ce mobilier est vieux, crevassé, [. . .] il faudrait en faire une description qui retarderait trop l'intérêt de cette historie [. . .]" 'This furniture is all old, cracked [. . .]; but its state could not be described fully without breaking the thread of the story and putting too great a strain on the tolerance of impatient people who read it' (28; 32).

Once students sufficiently doubt the completeness of Balzac's descriptions and of their own knowledge of nineteenth-century Paris, they generally realize that the narrator is providing them only with some typical details of a conventional city and a few Parisian proper names to identify Paris. They conclude that Balzac provides a "real" background only when they mentally complement these details with other details of a conventional city, organize them according to the narrator's directions into a spatial representation of a city, then convince themselves that they are seeing, in their mind's eye, a real *quartier* of Paris. Rather than describe a real Paris, Balzac's descriptions guide, or prescribe, the reader's act of building an imaginary place and create the illusion that this imaginary place is real.

If one reminds students that Balzac's descriptive details are only words, not perceptions, then they can see that these details are stereotypical less of a poor area of early-nineteenth-century Paris than of how Parisians at that time talked about such an area. Balzac's narrator encourages readers to transform this conventional descriptive discourse into mental images and to confuse these images with reality. Instructors can guide students in discovering how Balzac structures the reader's act of mentally constructing a place by (1) qualifying the entire place with a noun, such as *quartier;* (2) listing common names, such as *houses, walls, streets, gutters, pension, students,* that are typically associated with a *quartier* and that help readers construct an image of one in their minds;

(3) adding adjectives, adverbs, and so on, such as "plâtras incessamment près de tomber et [. . .] ruisseaux noirs de boue" 'crumbling stucco and gutters black with mud' (22; 27), that individualize the mental image of a *quartier* as a stereotypically poor place with poor inhabitants; and (4) adding (mostly non-aristocratic) proper names, such as Montmartre, Mme Vauquer, and Mlle Michonneau, that give identities to the individualized places and characters in the *quartier* (Hamon 92–139).

Some students may note (or the teacher can point to passages that suggest) that Balzac's narrator encourages readers to confuse a constructed image with an accurate representation by acting as if he is giving readers a tour of the area and making them physically see the parts he is pointing out. As one descends the street toward the pension Vauquer, "de marche en marche, le jour diminue" 'a traveller [. . .] sees the light of day grow dim' (23; 28); "on entre dans cette allée par une porte [. . .]" '[t]he path is reached by a side gate [. . .]' (24; 29). The narrator speaks as if he were a sociology teacher taking his students down the street, through the gate into the yard, around the yard, into the house, upstairs, and so on (Terdiman 86). He also encourages readers to confuse a mentally constructed image with a physical perception by (1) using the historical present tense to heighten the illusion that readers are in the process of touring and seeing the pension; (2) adding numerous sensory details of things that can be seen ("le plâtras [. . .] près de tomber" 'crumbling stucco' [22; 27]), smelled ("l'air chaudement fétide" 'stuffy air' [28; 33]), heard ("le chant du conducteur" 'the sing-song of his guide' [23; 28]), or touched; and (3) comparing his descriptions to paintings: "on ne saurait trop préparer l'intelligence par des couleurs brune, par des idées graves" 'the mind must be prepared by gloomy colours and heavy thoughts' (23; 28).

After the teacher has established the artificial, and thus partially deceptive, nature of Balzac's realist descriptions, it is essential to remind students that these descriptions are not totally fictional. For example, the French edition states that Balzac modeled Mme Vauquer's pension on the real house (not pension) of a relative named Mme Vauquer (21n1). Historical studies thus confirm that many details accurately describe, rather than prescribe, real parts of Balzac's Paris. Balzac saw himself as, in part, an objective scientist. He dedicated *Goriot* to the zoologist Geoffroi St.-Hillaire and claimed, in the preface to the *Human Comedy*, to be presenting a scientific typology of the over 2,000 characters typical of the era.

No matter how accurate Balzac's descriptions may be, however, their artificially constructed nature redefines the questions we can ask about the text. Rather than ask whether or not a background is "real," we must ask, as we have just done, how his descriptions construct the illusion of a real background and which details are historically verifiable. We can also ask how this descriptive illusion functions in the narrative. The narrator provides a possible answer to this last question at the beginning of the novel:

> [L]'œuvre accomplie, peut-être aura-t-on versé quelques larmes *intra muros et extra.* Sera-t-elle comprise au-delà de Paris? le doute est permis. Les particularités de cette scène pleine d'observations et de couleurs locales ne peuvent être appréciées qu'entre les buttes de Montmartre et les hauteurs de Montrouge. (21–22)

> [P]erhaps some tears may be shed over it in the reading—*intra muros et extra.* Will it be understood outside Paris? One may doubt it. Only between the heights of Montmartre and Montrouge are there people who can appreciate how exactly, with what close observation, it is drawn from life. (27)

One must see the *quartier* in order to understand the narrative of the events that will take place in it. But if that is true, why did Balzac follow this comment with ten pages of descriptions of the place? Clearly, the descriptions' role is to enable readers, who cannot see the *quartier* physically, to see it in their mind's eye in order to comprehend the story.

What do the narrator's descriptions add to the narrative and how do they make the narrative comprehensible? One might turn students' attention to the sentence where the narrator describes the *quartier* as a "vallée remplie de souffrances réelles, de joies souvent fausses, et si terriblement agitée" 'valley full of real suffering and often deceptive joys' (22; 27). The area he will describe is so full of real suffering and false joy that few from the outside would care to look at it. Sometimes, however, great suffering, such as Goriot's, is so noble that outsiders momentarily stop and pay attention: "Cependant, il s'y recontre çà et là des douleurs que l'agglomération des vices et des vertus rend grandes et solennelles: à leur aspect, les égoïsmes, les intérêts, s'arrêtent et s'apitoient" 'Yet now and then in some overwhelming tragedy evil and good are so strangely mixed that [. . .] selfish and self-centred people are forced to pause in their restless pursuit of their own affairs, and their hearts are momentarily touched' (22; 27 [translation incorrectly puts "these" before "selfish"]). Soon, however, "le char de la civilisation, semblable à celui de l'idole de Jaggernat, à peine retardé par un cœur moins facile à broyer que les autres et qui enraie sa roue, l'a brisé bientôt et continue sa marche glorieuse" 'The chariot of civilization, like the chariot of Juggernaut, is scarcely halted by a heart less easily crushed than the others in its path' (22; 28).

What Balzac's narrator invites us to see in his descriptions is evidence of the historical processes by which society's powerful, who ride on civilization's chariot, inevitably destroy the weak, who live in areas like the *quartier* he describes. Balzac's descriptions are thus not static, like a painting; they contain signs of dynamic, historical processes of transformation. One process is destroying poor areas and their socially weak inhabitants: "L'homme le plus insouciant s'y attriste comme tous les passants [. . .]" 'The most carefree passer-by feels depressed [. . .]' (23; 28). The other process is raising up wealthy areas and their socially strong inhabitants.

Balzac's descriptions appear static because the parallel but reverse historical transformations that are structuring the city of Paris and its social space cancel each other out. These transformations repeatedly reproduce the same hierarchical, spatial relation between the people and areas rising up and those falling down. Balzac attributes this equilibrium to universal human nature: "Peut-être est-il dans la nature humaine de tout faire supporter à qui souffre tout par humilité vraie, par faiblesse, ou par indifférence. N'aimons-nous pas tous à prouver notre force aux dépens de quelqu'un ou de quelque chose?" 'Perhaps it is a part of human nature to pile burdens on those who make no protest because of their true humility, their weakness, or their indifference. Do we not all like to prove our strength at the expense of another person or a thing?' (40; 42). For each Rastignac who takes advantage of the weak in order to succeed in society, there is a Goriot who asks to be taken advantage of and beaten down. Zoologists of the human species, like Balzac, may identify different types of characters and areas in different historical eras; but these differences will always add up to the same atemporal equilibrium between the psychologically strong and the psychologically weak. Every historical era will thus reproduce the universal and fixed structure of society.

Signs of society's historical self-reproduction can be found in a number of the narrator's descriptions, as when he describes the *quartier* as "cette illustre vallée de plâtras incessamment près de tomber et de ruisseaux noirs de boue" '[an illustrious] valley of crumbling stucco and gutters black with mud' (22; 27). The present historical tense, like the present participle in the translation, constructs this space as an ongoing moment of transformation, of physical destruction. Plaster is constantly crumbling.

Balzac's narrator presents this historical crumbling as a visual reality that ironically undercuts the romantic symbols with which some of the *quartier*'s occupants, especially students, or some of Balzac's readers might idealize the area. Balzac published *Goriot* in 1834, fourteen years after the publication of Alphonse de Lamartine's *Méditations*. He repeats Romanticism's nature vocabulary—"vallée" ("valley") and "ruisseau" (the latter meaning both "stream" and, as in the translation, "gutter")—both metaphors for the eternal memory of self, ideal other, and love. But he undercuts these metaphors by adding empirically observable details—"crumbling plaster" and "black with mud"—that ironically negate the invisible, literal meanings of "valley" and "stream." The *quartier* hardly looks like a natural valley, its gutters do not recall natural streams, and neither this valley nor this stream suggests romantic love.

Balzac's descriptions, containing as they do not only romantic metaphors but also realist visual details that ironically undercut these metaphors, demystify the illusion that these metaphors create. His descriptions teach readers to momentarily face up to the stark, historical reality that we ("vous qui vous enfoncez dans un moelleux fauteuil" 'you [. . .] lying back in a softly cushioned armchair' [22; 28]) would prefer to ignore: society's continual reproduction of its hierarchies through the subordination and destruction of the weak. Some may rise out of poverty and others may fall out of wealth, but the overall structure of society, the gap between rich and poor areas, rich and poor people, remains.

The historical mechanism of social reproduction that Balzac's descriptions reconstruct demystifies the romantic illusion—held by Goriot and the inexperienced Rastignac—that society is motivated by love rather than by power and self-interest. This historical mechanism also produces the reverse process of remystification, a repetition of the social hypocrisy by which the rich and powerful repress any knowledge of the violence of civilization's chariot. The rich choose not to see the area and its demystifying message: "Nul quartier de Paris n'est plus horrible, ni, disons-le, plus inconnu" 'It is the grimmest quarter of Paris and, it may be said, the least known' (23; 28). And Balzac's readers, in their cushioned armchairs, blind themselves to the realist mirror he holds up to the readers' greed for power and pursuit of self-interest by transforming his realist narrator into a purveyor of fictions, "en le taxant d'exagération, en l'accusant de poésie" 'taxing him with exaggeration, accusing him of having given wings to his imagination' (22; 28).

Students can thus come to see that the narrator constitutes his realist description both as a means of reconstructing Paris as an empirically observable, historically self-reproducing social space and as a means of demystifying the readers' romantic illusions about this space. Students can comprehend the demystifying function by interpreting a description of a painting on Mme Vauquer's garden wall. The painting represents a statue of Love protected within an imaginary recess in the wall: "A voir le vernis écaillé qui la couvre, les amateurs de symboles y découvriraient peut-être un mythe de l'amour parisien qu'on guérit à quelques pas de là" 'and its chipped scaling surface makes it look like a patient for one of the nearby hospitals, and provides an allegory [of love] for those who are fond of symbols' (24; 29). If one tells students from the outset that the nearby hospital treated patients for venereal disease (Balzac, *Père Goriot* [Gallimard] 412), then students can interpret the ironic relation that the narrator establishes between the invisible, immaterial romantic illusion of love and the visible, material consequences of physical love. The representation of romantic love is made possible, in this urban reality, by material paint. But this material means of producing romantic signs is—unlike the romantic meaning of these signs, eternal love—destroyed by time. The visible evidence of time's erasure of this image thus ironically negates and demystifies the illusion that love is anything more than a physical act, an illusion also cured by the nearby hospital.

One can help students visualize the urban reality that Balzac evokes by mentioning that, during the Restoration, there were few paved streets or sewers. Sewage streamed continually down the unpaved, often muddy streets, adding to the sights and smells of the garbage in this illustrious valley. This is why the wealthy rode in carriages, especially when passing through poor areas, and descended within the courtyard of another wealthy person's *hôtel*.

Students might better understand the self-reproducing nature of this urban space if they discuss how modern capitalism may reproduce the gap between rich suburbs and poor cities. One might ask students whether children in the poorest areas of our largest cities are dragged down and children in the middle- and upper-middle-class suburbs buoyed up by the areas into which they have been born. One might also ask whether the media and superhighways discourage the American middle and upper-middle classes from confronting evidence of America's urban and rural poor. The entire structure of Balzac's social space, by the way, comes to the fore only later in the novel, when Vautrin reveals that in addition to society's visible separation between rich and poor, there is an invisible criminal underworld.

Although we can explain how Balzac artificially constitutes Paris as a historically self-reproducing social space, it is not evident that Balzac understood that he was not representing a preexisting real space. Balzac's descriptions give the impression that the author was a naive realist. His narrator reassures readers that the descriptions of high society are objective, since they are based on the empirical observations of the protagonist, Rastignac:

> Sans ses observations curieuses et l'adresse avec laquelle il sut se produire dans les salons de Paris, ce récit n'eût pas été coloré des tons vrais qu'il devra sans doute à son esprit sagace et à son désir de pénétrer les mystères d'une situation épouvantable, aussi soigneusement cachée par ceux qui l'avaient créée que par celui qui la subissait. (31)

> But for his observant curiosity, and the adroitness with which he contrived to introduce himself into the salons of Paris, this story would not possess the colour of reality. It undoubtedly owes its truth to his alert mind and to his desire to fathom the mysteries of an appalling state of affairs, which was being as carefully concealed by the victim as by those responsible for it. (35)

But when we look at how Balzac's characters interpret the events narrated, we find that Balzac is much more aware of how words operate than his descriptions might lead readers to suppose. We also discover the complexity of his realist discourse. In narrative passages, we find a different notion of history, one according to which unique individuals construct social space, instead of being determined by the self-reproduction of social space. Below, I briefly sketch this reading and mention some useful passages to discuss in class.

In many narrative passages, Balzac dramatizes a struggle between the narrator's assertion that words represent reality and characters' assertions that words construct reality. Balzac's narrator associates Goriot with the belief that words accurately reproduce reality. Goriot sincerely confesses his emotions and wealth to characters like Mme Vauquer, as if his words will be interpreted by others as mere representations of his real state. But Mme Vauquer, who recognizes only what words do, interprets his confession of wealth as a promise of marriage and punishes him when he does not keep that promise. Goriot's illusion that words function to represent reality repeatedly makes Goriot a pawn of those who, like his daughters, use words unscrupulously, only to further their self-interest. Goriot's representational illusion thus subordinates him to society's self-reproduction of its fixed, hierarchical relation between the rise of the powerful and the fall of the weak.

At first, Rastignac believes in sincerity, in Goriot, and in the descriptive illusion of realist representation. But he learns from high society (Mme de Beauséant) and the criminal underworld (Vautrin) that, in order to succeed, he must never use words as if their primary function were to represent. He learns this lesson because he is one of those Balzacian individuals who construct their own future, who "se préparent une belle destinée en calculant déjà la portée de leurs études et, les adaptant par avance au mouvement futur de la société, pour être les premiers à la pressurer" 'carefully lay the foundations of a great career. From the beginning they plan their studies as means to an end, adapting them in advance to the probable turn of events in the future, so that they may be the first to squeeze a profit from social changes' (31; 34–35). Not only is Rastignac an acute observer, he also learns that the honest description of one's observations, of society's realities, like the narrator's initial description, is socially self-destructive. As Vautrin tells him: "L'honnêteté ne sert à rien" 'Honesty is of no avail' (152; 129); "Aussi, l'honnête homme est-il l'ennemi commun" 'So the honest man is the common enemy' (152; 130). For Vautrin, Rastignac is one of the few who can "se mett[re] au-dessus de tout, même des lois" 'climb above everything, even above laws' (153; 130).

What Rastignac learns is the social reality of words. They are a means of acting on others. In the social act of persuasion, misrepresentation may be just as useful as representation. Mme de Beauséant tells him: "si vous avez un sentiment vrai, cachez-le comme un trésor" 'if you have any real feeling, hide it like a treasure [. . .]' (115; 103). He must use words to increase his power to satisfy his desires while not allowing others, through his honesty, to use him: "N'acceptez les hommes et les femmes que comme les chevaux de poste que vous laisserez crever à chaque relais, vous arriverez ainsi au faîte de vos désirs" 'Regard men and women only as you do post-horses that you will leave worn out at every stage, and so you shall arrive at the goal of your desires' (115; 103).

The arch criminal Vautrin tells Rastignac that words in society do not signify a right or a wrong, a truth or a falsity. Such ideals do not exist: "Si j'ai encore un conseil à vous donner, mon ange, c'est de ne pas plus tenir à vos opinions qu'à vos paroles" 'If I have one more piece of advice to give you, my sweet lad, it is this—don't stick any more firmly to your opinions than to your [words]' (158; 134; "words" incorrectly translated as "work"). Words are a pure means of exercising individual power: "Il n'y a pas de principes, il n'y a que des événements;

il n'y a pas de lois, il n'y a que des circonstances: l'homme supérieur épouse les événements et les circonstances pour les conduire" 'There are no such things as principles, there are only events; there are no laws, there are only circumstances; the man who is wiser than his fellows accepts events and circumstances in order to turn them to his own ends' (158; 134). The mature Rastignac concludes that Vautrin is "plus grand" 'greater' than all the others he has known, since the criminal is willing to act according to his knowledge of society's infamy (326–27; 271). And in the novel's last words, Rastignac chooses to follow the advice of his noble and criminal mentors. After Goriot's funeral, he goes to dinner with the daughter who virtually killed the old man. Because he loves her? Or because she is the best means to his end of achieving social success?

Rastignac's education, in this novel of education, raises serious questions about whether Balzac can be identified with his narrator, who at the beginning of the novel claims to describe society as it is. If Balzac truly believed that his narrator's words objectively represented a historically self-reproducing society, he would run the risk of being a loser, like Goriot, rather than a winner, like Rastignac. But if Balzac accepted Mme de Beauséant's and Vautrin's lessons on individual power, then he would use words in the way that Rastignac learns to do, as a means of subordinating society to the destiny one is preparing and calculating for oneself.

Are we the passive receivers of Balzac's observations of a self-reproducing Parisian society? Or are we apprentices to the narrator, who as one of a few strong individuals seduces us, persuades us to accept Vautrin's cynical view of language and of a society dominated by power? Is it not possible that it was in the conservative Balzac's interest for readers to believe that society's gap between rich and poor, powerful and weak, was inevitable? But if Balzac's describing narrator, like the wigged Vautrin, is the mask for a seducing narrator, then why should we believe him any more than we believe Vautrin?

Le Père Goriot does not decide between the representational function of its describing narrator and the seductions of its seducing narrator. The novel opts for neither a historically self-reproducing social space nor a space constructed by the historical acts of elite individuals. On the one hand, Rastignac ultimately chooses to emulate the seducing, rather than the descriptive, narrator. On the other hand, the supposedly all-powerful individual Vautrin is rendered impotent, at least temporarily, by the petty Mlle Michonneau and her boyfriend, who disclose his disguise and get him thrown in prison.

The different ways in which the narrator of *Le Père Goriot* constructs contemporary reality—both by describing a self-reproducing social space that determines individual lives and by narrating acts of individual power that construct social space—suggest the complexity and richness of Balzac's realist discourse. The narrator is, in part, a naive realist who thinks that his words accurately represent contemporary social space. But he is also a cynical pragmatist who uses descriptive and narrative representations as mere means of exercising power. Our students might ask questions similar to those suggested here about the present-day Balzacs who describe the world market as a space determining an inevitable gap between rich and poor yet narrate individual life as the universal freedom to become a free-market Rastignac.

NOTE

The interpretation set forth in this essay draws in part from James Reid's *Narration and Description in the French Realist Novel.*

Moral Complexity in *Le Père Goriot*: Balzac between Kant and Nietzsche

David R. Ellison

Families, Parisian and Provincial

Balzac's novel *Le Père Goriot* is a story about families and family relationships, in which the simplicity and solidly grounded moral foundations of the provinces contrast sharply with the fragmented social bonds and decadence of the capital. Although most of the plot centers on Paris and its multifaceted, kaleidoscopic cast of characters, the narrator alludes to the families of both Eugène de Rastignac and Bianchon, Eugène's friend and companion at Mme Vauquer's *pension bourgeoise,* in order to emphasize the difference between the stable and centered quality of provincial life and what, in today's vocabulary, we would call the dysfunctional nature of the family unit in its city context. Among other things, *Le Père Goriot* provides lucid and sometimes scathing social commentary on the excesses and vices that inhabit the nineteenth-century city and post-Napoleonic society as the bourgeois middle class begins its ascent and as money begins to speak louder than the privileges of inherited nobility. The hero, Eugène *de* Rastignac, is an aristocrat; but, as the reader is continually reminded, he is always low on funds, and it is only through the sacrifice of his long-suffering family members that he can hope to arrive, to succeed, *parvenir,* in the labyrinth of Paris. The novel's central moral problem, which emerges quite early in the narrative development, can be summarized as follows: Will it be possible for Rastignac, while making use of his family's scant financial resources, to retain the simple virtues of his home as he navigates his way through the disorienting maze of Parisian corruption, greed, and power worship? Put another way: What is the moral status of ambition, the driving force that propels the hero along his way? Is it possible to be ambitious and also a good person, or do ambition per se and goodness constitute an insuperable contradiction in terms? In nineteenth-century Paris, is it possible to disentangle the desire for success from the snares of money (of value in the material sense of that word)? Or are values in the moral sense of the term antithetical to the constant compromises one has to make along the road to an influential position and social inclusion? These are some of the questions raised by Balzac's complex and polyvalent text, questions for which, I contend, no unilinear or unequivocal answer can be provided.

It might be objected that, at least at first glance, the moral universe of *Le Père Goriot* is clearly structured according to a traditional Christian model of interpersonal relationships—not only that goodness is contrasted unambiguously with evil but also that the narrator himself makes obvious his condemnation of vice in its various appearances. Victorine de Taillefer's innocence and virtue are presented to the reader in sentimental tones but without irony, whereas the desire for money that inhabits both Mlle Michonneau and Mme Vauquer is depicted in its unadmirable, even detestable, colors. When Goriot dies, Mme Vauquer's decision to furnish (for a price) already used sheets for his shroud, saying, "Goodness knows, they're quite good enough for a corpse" (357; 296), is a decision whose moral reprehensiveness cannot be doubted by the reader. In the same way, one might be tempted to say that Eugène's two father figures, Goriot and Vautrin, are depicted, respectively, as "le Christ de la paternité" 'the Christ-like father' (282; 235) and as Satan—the seductive criminal's face, in the moment of his arrest, is illuminated by "the flames of Hell" (263; 219)—precisely in order to establish beyond all doubt that the psychodrama of *Le Père Goriot* is staged on firm moral, even theological, ground. Like Christ, who sacrificed himself for the future salvation of sinful humankind, Goriot sacrifices himself for undeserving daughters: his death resonates with pathos and is represented with a melodramatic theatrical intensity. The criminal Vautrin is discovered, unmasked, and finally shackled, his dangerous satanic influence neutralized as he is brought under the control of the law. Certainly the temptation exists for the reader to see Goriot-Christ as the good father and Vautrin-Satan as the bad father, with Rastignac finally adopted by the former and providentially removed from the latter's harmful and insidious charm.

There are several problems with this interpretation, however, a notable one being that the highly sentimental love father Goriot professes for his daughters is obsessive and disquieting in its boundless scope. Not only is Goriot profligate in meeting his children's every desire but the narrator goes so far as to assert that "il aimait jusqu'au mal qu'elles lui faisaient" '[h]e even loved them for the pain they caused him' (129; 114).[1] Here, paternal love is dangerously close to masochism. Love of this kind knows no limits: it is what the French would call *un amour démesuré.*

Goriot is a man of exorbitance and extravagance who made his fortune thanks to the false famine of the revolutionary period and drove to financial ruin a competitor who had the bad sense to upset the "Christ-like father" about the health of one of Goriot's daughters (127–28; 113–14). The father figure Eugène admires is not so much a paragon of virtue in the classical sense (Goriot is, for example, completely devoid of altruistic impulse) as he is what Vautrin calls "un homme à passions" '[a man] with a passion': a man who will sacrifice everything for his one obsession—in this case, his daughters (75; 71). Goriot's personality, like that of Molière's Harpagon, is stitched from one cloth: the reader is fascinated by his monomaniacal focus and obliviousness to any aspect of his environment that does not have a direct bearing on his daughters' welfare.

When viewed in this light, Goriot/Christ is uncannily similar to Vautrin/Satan. Like Goriot, Vautrin is a man of passion and is capable of sacrifice: after all, he served a prison term for "un très beau jeune homme qu'il aimait beaucoup, un jeune Italien" 'a very fine young man whom he had taken a fancy to, a young Italian' (223; 186).[2] Although popular wisdom has it that there is no honor among thieves, Vautrin acts as banker for the other members of his criminal society: he is, at least within the criminal netherworld, a trustworthy man. Balzac further complicates his depiction of Jacques Collin–Vautrin by staging the celebratory dinner preceding Vautrin's arrest as what one might call an inverted Last Supper. The devil who tempts Rastignac with an unholy pact (involving the death by duel of Victorine Taillefer's brother, which would presumably make of Victorine a wealthy prize for the ambitious young provincial) is represented as Jesus Christ surrounded not only by his faithful disciples but also by Judas—that is, Mlle Michonneau, who is soon to betray Vautrin to the Paris police (235–51; 196–209). At the moment of his arrest, Vautrin, speaking for the members of his criminal society and alluding to the prison identification letters on his shoulder, TF (meaning *travaux forcés* [forced labor]), addresses his fellow boarders at the *pension bourgeoise* thus: "We bear the mark of shame on our shoulders, but there's a deeper mark in your hearts, you flabby members of a rotting society [. . .]" (265; 220–21). Later, he contrasts himself to Mlle Michonneau: " 'There's some good in there,' he said, tapping his heart; 'no one has ever been betrayed by me!' " (267; 222).

The reader of Dante's *Inferno* will remember that the perpetrators of betrayal and treachery are lodged in the ninth circle of hell, the lowest point of the infernal regions. Is Mlle Michonneau, the betrayer of "Vautrin," to be situated lower on the scale of vice than Jacques Collin himself? Certainly, unlike Judas Iscariot, she betrayed not a holy man but a known criminal, and yet the scene in which Mlle Michonneau, along with her faithful Poiret, is expelled as "Judas" from the pension Vauquer is an unforgettable moment, one in which it is impossible not to wonder whether the narrator is appealing to the reader's sense of indignation at the unhappy woman's insidious collusion with the police (268–72; 224–27). Is it possible that the narrator admires Vautrin and expects the reader to do so as well? In what way is the character of Vautrin containable within a traditional ethical framework based on Christian doctrine and the classical tradition of Western philosophy? What kind of moral doctrine does Vautrin espouse? These questions need some attention, I think, if the reader of *Le Père Goriot* is not to become disoriented by the disconcerting, shifting relations Balzac establishes between Christ and Satan, good and evil, the admirable and the distasteful.

Values and Their Transvaluation

> Duty! Sublime and mighty name embracing nothing charming or insinuating but requiring submission [. . .] what origin is there worthy of you, and where is to be found the root of your noble descent which proudly rejects all kinship with the inclinations and from which to be descended

> is the indispensable condition of the only worth which men can give themselves?
>
> —Immanuel Kant, *Critique of Practical Reason*

> The judgment *good* does not originate with those to whom the good has been done. Rather it was the "good" themselves, that is to say the noble, mighty, highly placed, and high-minded who decreed themselves and their actions to be good, i.e., belonging to the highest rank, in contradistinction to all that was base, low-minded and plebeian. It was only this *pathos of distance* that authorized them to create values and name them. [. . .] There is no *a priori* necessity for associating the word *good* with altruistic deeds [. . .]. In fact, it is only after aristocratic values have begun to decline that the egotism-altruism dichotomy takes possession of the human conscience; to use my own terms, it is the herd instinct that now asserts itself.
>
> —Friedrich Nietzsche, *The Genealogy of Morals*

Written almost exactly one century apart, Immanuel Kant's *Critique of Practical Reason* (1788) and Friedrich Nietzsche's *The Genealogy of Morals* (1887) delineate two radically opposed moral universes, between which Balzac's *Le Père Goriot* (1834) situates itself, borrowing from Kant's dutiful rigorism in places and anticipating Nietzsche's transvaluation of values in others. If we look briefly at the epigraphs above (Kant 89; Nietzsche 160), we find that Kant structures his apostrophe to duty on an apparent paradox, namely that the "sublime," "mighty," and "noble" qualities of duty are based on one's submission to duty's commands. We must humble ourselves in order to act according to the moral law, and only in this lowly posture can we be worthy of the "noble" descent of duty itself. Our worth as individuals lies in submission: to gain in the area of moral value, we must sacrifice in the domain of self-assertion and self-affirmation.

The passage from Nietzsche overturns this logic by asserting that nobility, and the noble class itself before the advent of Christianity, is based on power and domination. The Kantian paradox, founded on the New Testament idea of "the last shall be first, and the first last" (Matt. 20.16), is, for Nietzsche, empty rhetoric that conceals (badly) the resentment (*ressentiment*) of the ruling caste, the aristocrats, by the lower and weaker classes, who call themselves good. Christianity, for Nietzsche, is an insidious lie perpetuated by the weak, who, being in reality powerless, compensate for their subservience by creating and eventually imposing on multitudes of gullible people the myths of self-sacrifice and altruism. For Nietzsche, values are not universally valid and timeless—as they are for Kant. Rather, values emerged in a pre-Christian era, when those of highest rank, whose lives were completely consumed in action and who themselves had no need of fine ethical distinctions, created the values good and evil by equating the good with their own will to power and by designating as evil whatever lay in the lowlands of "plebeian" passivity and rancor. Nietzsche's historical scheme supposes that the dichotomy of egotism versus altruism, to which classical ethical systems, including Kant's, assign an immutable valuation (egotism is always bad, altruism is always good), is in fact a derivative conceptual pair, born after the decline of the aristocrats, and truly at home only in the world of the "herd"—of the unthinking masses.

My contention, which I sketch briefly below, is that the moral complexity of *Le Père Goriot* derives from the novel's alternation between moments in which a Kantian ethics is affirmed and moments in which the text prefigures, with uncanny fidelity, the ethos of the superman, or overman (*Übermensch*)—one who has uncovered the origins of moral values and has undertaken to transvalue them according to how they enhance or prove detrimental to one's goals, to one's flourishing as an affirmer of human vitality. I look at two of the novel's characters, Bianchon and Vautrin, both of whom present Rastignac with moral problems to solve and lessons to be learned.

Bianchon and the Riddle of the Absent Chinaman

At the midpoint of the novel, when Rastignac has begun to hesitate between his incipient passion for Delphine de Nucingen and the lure of Victorine de Taillefer's potential fortune, he has a significant conversation with Bianchon—a conversation that adds nothing to the development of the plot but that constitutes a crucial moral crossroads for the protagonist. Eugène asks his friend:

> Do you remember the passage where he [Rousseau] asks the reader what he would do if he could make a fortune by killing an old mandarin in China by simply exerting his will, without stirring from Paris? (186; 157)

Rastignac asks the question because he, like "Rousseau's" imaginary reader,[3] could become rich without himself committing a crime in the active sense: it would be Vautrin's accomplice who would kill Victorine's brother; and if Eugène were to marry Victorine later on, he would not, in the strict sense, be guilty of her brother's unfortunate demise. Yet the protagonist is bothered by his conscience because he senses that his involvement, however passive, however indirect, is still involvement; and he wonders if he could live with the knowledge of the crime, which his guilty conscience would store within him. Bianchon, who does not have Rastignac's ambition for social success, answers the riddle with elegant simplicity:

> I'm quite content, myself, with my humble fortune, to live the quiet country life I mean to fashion for myself, and step into my father's shoes in due course like any stick-in-the-mud. A man's affections are just as fully satisfied within the smallest circle as in a vast circumference. [. . .] I come to the conclusion that the Chinaman should be allowed to live. (187; 158)

Explicitly, the young medical student explains that he would spare the Chinaman's life because he has modest needs and an assured professional future. Implicitly, he is following Kant's lead in refusing to use another human being, however distant and unknown to him, as a means toward the end of his own personal advancement. In Kant's resonant formula:

> The moral law is holy (inviolable). Man is certainly unholy enough, but humanity in his person must be holy to him.[4] Everything in creation which he wishes and over which he has power can be used merely as a means; only man, and, with him, every rational creature, is an end in itself. (90)

Bianchon understands and subscribes to this ideal. But Rastignac, at this stage of the novel, is unsure of which way to orient his moral compass, for he has heard, from the mouth of Vautrin, a very different philosophy.

Vautrin and the Philosophy of "Superior Man"

Shortly after the end of the novel's expository section, Vautrin has a conversation with Rastignac in which Vautrin elaborates, at some length, his philosophy of life. The tone of the discourse could be called cynical, in that Vautrin has, on the one hand, nothing but disdain for the classical moral values of abnegation and self-sacrifice and, on the other, a hearty contempt for the festering corruption of society. He looks beneath the appearance of virtue and finds vice. It would be a mistake, however, to see in Vautrin an avatar of Goethe's Mephistopheles, whose formulaic self-description, "Ich bin der Geist, der stets verneint!" 'I am the spirit that always denies (or negates)!' (47; my trans.), could be the cogent motto for the cynic's mode of being. Rather, Vautrin's tirade is in the mode of affirmation and is, in this sense, a remarkable anticipation of Nietzschean thought. The *Übermensch* in Nietzsche is a powerful person belonging to the ruling caste whose action is spontaneous and who most resembles an artistic genius. It is significant that Vautrin describes himself in these very terms. Compare what Nietzsche, in his criticism of Rousseau's *Social Contract,* says about "born rulers" with what Vautrin says about himself:

> What do men who can command, who are born rulers, who evince power in act and deportment, have to do with contracts? Such beings are unaccountable; they come like destiny, without rhyme or reason, ruthlessly, bare of pretext. [. . .] Their work is an instinctive imposing of forms. They are the most spontaneous, most unconscious artists that exist.
> (Nietzsche 219–20)

> Je suis ce que vous appelez un artiste. J'ai lu les Mémoires de Benvenuto Cellini, tel que vous me voyez, et en italien encore! J'ai appris de cet homme-là, qui était un fier luron, à imiter la Providence qui nous tue à

> tort et à travers, et à aimer le beau partout où il se trouve. [. . .] Il n'y a pas de principes, il n'y a que des événements; il n'y a pas de lois, il n'y a que des circonstances: l'homme supérieur épouse les événements et les circonstances pour les conduire. (146, 158)

> I am what you might call an artist. Such as you see me. I have read the *Memoirs* of Benvenuto Cellini, and in Italian too! He was a rare sportsman [*un fier luron*], and he taught me to follow the example set by Providence who kills us right and left haphazard, and also to love beauty wherever it is to be found. [. . .] There are no such things as principles, there are only events; there are no laws, there are only circumstances: the man who is wiser than his fellows accepts events and circumstances in order to turn them to his own ends. (125, 134)

For Nietzsche and for Balzac's Vautrin, the "born ruler," or "superior man" ("homme supérieur"), needs no preestablished code of conduct in the form of "contracts" or "principles." In Nietzsche's terms, the *Übermensch* acts "ruthlessly." Vautrin proposes to imitate Providence and to conduct events and circumstances according to his own urges for power and self-realization. Like Nietzsche, Vautrin has nothing but disdain for those citizens who object to the powerful using their power and who, wallowing in rancorous abjection, opt for "stupid obedience" rather than glorious revolt (147; 125). What both Nietzsche and Vautrin are proposing is an elitist philosophy in which the superior being, in a very un-Kantian manner, dominates those who are inferior, makes use of them as a means to an end, in the very act of affirming life. The idea is: it is natural to affirm life, to "espouse events" ("épouse[r] les événements") with one's own vital purposiveness. Moral precepts and social contracts are unnatural superimpositions that stifle human striving.

What of Rastignac in all this? Balzac has structured his novel so that the young protagonist is caught between the Kantian and Nietzschean philosophies. One might say that he remembers Kant as a vestige of his provincial mode of upbringing but is tempted by the proto-Nietzschean thought of Vautrin, which seems to better explain and correspond to the actual events and practices of the Parisian world. The reader arriving at the end of the novel must wonder, despite the narrator's constant efforts to show Rastignac's good heart and pure sentiments, whether the young man is not poised to follow in Vautrin's footsteps. When Rastignac cries out, on the last page, "A nous deux, maintenant!" 'It's war between us now!' (367; 304), he is echoing the phrase "A nous deux!" (147; 126) that Vautrin used with Rastignac at the very beginning of his presentation of himself as "artist" and "superior man." Is Rastignac's verbal gesture of defiance toward the city of Paris an imitation of Vautrin's challenge to the impressionable hero? But what does Balzac mean when he adds, as a coda, "Et pour premier acte du défi qu'il portait à la Société, Rastignac alla dîner chez madame de Nucingen" 'And by way of throwing down the gauntlet to Society, Rastignac went to dine with Madame de Nucingen' (367; 304)? In the discrepancy between the exalted philosophical ideas of Vautrin-Nietzsche and the rather mundane act of going to dinner, does the reader not glimpse a protagonist mocked? It may be that the moral victor in this novel is neither Kant nor Nietzsche, but the rhetorical figure of irony. It is irony that, speaking through the voice of France's sixteenth-century philosopher of moderation, Michel de Montaigne, reminds the reader that even the loftiest successes to which ambition can lead us, and to which our affirmation of life pushes us, cannot veil our essential humanity, which is far from lofty in its common constitution:

> Si, avons nous beau monter sur des eschasses, car sur des eschasses encores faut-il marcher de nos jambes. Et au plus eslevé throne du monde, si ne sommes assis que sus nostre cul. ("De l'expérience" 1096)

> A fine thing to get up on stilts: for even on stilts we must ever walk with our legs! And upon the highest throne in the world, we are seated, still, upon our arse. ("On Experience" 1269)

Pedagogical Issues

The reading I have offered here, which stresses a rhythmic alternation in *Le Père Goriot* between a classical Kantian ethics and a Nietzschean emphasis on the "genealogy of morals" and the transvaluation of values, has encountered some resistance in the classroom setting.

The vast majority of students I have taught are the purest of Kantians (often without having read a line of Kant). Moral laws, for them, are those of which Kant speaks in his ethical writings and are filtered through the precepts of Christianity, especially the New Testament. Students are so familiar with the terms *good* and *evil* that the terms go unquestioned—hence the students' usual discomfort with the morally deconstructive aspects of Nietzschean thought. When Nietzsche states that "good" is an invention of a resentful slave mentality and has a specific historical origin, this statement leads to the subversive idea that morality, in its historicity, is also relative to this or that given culture and therefore not timeless or eternally valid in its prescriptions. Translated into Balzac's novel, this idea would mean that Vautrin's proto-Nietzschean philosophy of passion and vitality calls into question the apparent bedrock solidity of the traditional values expounded by Rastignac's family and his friend Bianchon. The question for the student then becomes: Is it possible to choose between Vautrin and Bianchon? Does Balzac give the reader the interpretive means to make that choice?

I have never tried to impose my own interpretation on my students, but I have used Vautrin's philosophical pronouncements as a way to incite them to an examination of the presuppositions that underlie moral thought in general. I always emphasize the importance of the narrative choices made by Balzac in his novel and am careful to indicate that *Père Goriot* is not a philosophical treatise but rather a carefully structured work of literature in which context is all-important. Thus, although the discussion between Bianchon and Rastignac on Rousseau's absent Chinaman takes place during a pause in the novel's action and is presented as a kind of puzzle possessing a timeless quality, the killing of Victorine's brother takes place, most conveniently, while Rastignac is sleeping; the departure of the now rich young woman and her guardian very conveniently eliminates the "Victorine problem" from the novel. Rastignac's early hesitation between Delphine and Victorine constituted a full-fledged moral dilemma, but what does it mean when Balzac simply removes Victorine from the equation? Is there not some form of complicity between the narrator and his protagonist in the narrative act whereby one pole of the moral dilemma is simply made to disappear? In a remarkably similar way, Vautrin's arrest makes the dangerous seducer vanish and causes the incipient Faustian bargain between the professor of desire and his putative pupil to evaporate into thin air. At the end of the work, Rastignac is alone. Is he still virtuous? Or is his virtue the result of some rather outrageous narrative manipulating?

The points I am making can best be resumed in the following way. The Kant-versus-Nietzsche underpinning allows class discussion to crystallize around well-defined philosophical positions; but the very resistance of students to the Nietzschean paradigm opens up discussion and allows both students and teacher to attend to Balzac's impressive art of the novel, which doubtless consists of asking more questions than it answers.

NOTES

[1]Balzac's statement, which would be translated literally as "he loved even the suffering they inflicted on him," is stronger than Crawford's rendition, which turns Goriot's love back to his daughters as cause rather than toward suffering per se as object of a strange and excessive love.

[2]There are two problems with this translation: (1) in the French "un très beau jeune homme" there is no hint of moral rectitude or of moral content at all, so that the word *fine* is a pure invention of the translator; (2) the French phrase "qu'il aimait beaucoup" suggests a homosexual relationship but does not denote it with the finality of "whom he had taken a fancy to." Vautrin's homosexuality, like that of Charlus in Proust's novel, is a mystery to be deciphered gradually, as the text unfolds, not a given, not a bland *factum*. Part of the humor of the passage in the original lies in the possibility that the rather dense Michonneau and Poiret do not understand what is implied in the expression "qu'il aimait beaucoup."

[3]A helpful footnote in the French edition of the novel (426) informs us that the moral problem of the old Chinese mandarin is to be found not in Rousseau's works but in Chateaubriand's *Le Génie du christianisme*.

[4]This phrase finds an ironic echo at the end of *Le Père Goriot*, when the attending doctor, while concluding that Goriot's death is imminent (and that any further material aid or expense for his needs is now superfluous), nevertheless recommends that Goriot be treated with decency: "Il faudrait cependant le changer de linge [. . .]. Quoiqu'il n'y ait aucun espoir, *il faut respecter en lui la nature humaine*" (355; my emphasis). The Kantian resonance of the passage is lost on Crawford, who translates the final phrase as "some respect is due to suffering humanity" (295).

Balzac and the Modern City: Mapping Paris in *Old Goriot*

David F. Bell

A student who opened and scanned—even in the most cursory manner—a standard social history describing the nineteenth and twentieth centuries in the West would inevitably encounter numerous passages devoted to the development of the modern city. Industrialization and the concentration of production in Europe and the United States led to an increasingly rapid growth of urban areas as the nineteenth century progressed and thus ultimately to a social and political situation in which cities became a major economic and ideological phenomenon of our modern world. Balzac was an acute observer of the social, economic, and cultural trends of his time, and it is therefore not surprising that he quickly began to thematize the opposition between the city and the country, to describe the urban concentration that was already well under way in the society in which he lived. In Balzac's France (I mean, of course, both the France Balzac observed around him and the France Balzac created in his fiction—it is impossible to separate the two!),[1] the opposition between the urban and the rural took the characteristic form of a dichotomy between Paris and the provinces. The modern city, the ultimate product of the trend toward urban concentration, is inevitably symbolized in his novels by Paris, the great developing metropolitan center that has had and continues to have an enormous impact on France as a social, economic, and cultural entity. As a result of a novelistic perspective that clearly privileges Paris, when Balzac speaks of provincial cities and towns (take Angoulême in *Illusions perdues* as one of many possible examples), they are invariably linked to the backwaters of French culture in his period. In stark contrast, Paris occupies a position at the center of all that is complex and dynamic in modern French culture and society.

Le Père Goriot, written in 1834 and published in 1835, is a key founding text in Balzac's developing portrait of the city and of how individuals must deal with this important social and cultural phenomenon. In fact, one may describe the social and cultural education of Eugène de Rastignac as a veritable mapping of the city space of Paris, which allows him to understand social relations in a way that is impossible for him at the beginning of the novel. The topography of urban space is an essential source of information that Rastignac must explore and understand in some coherent way in order to progress socially and fulfill his ambitious designs. One need only reflect for a moment on the contrast between the opening and closing sequences of *Le Père Goriot* to grasp the fundamental importance of urban topography in the novel.[2] The first sentence of the novel brings Mme Vauquer's boardinghouse into fictional existence, situating it in a very particular way: "For the last forty years the elderly Madame Vauquer, *née* de Conflans, has kept a family boarding-house in the Rue Neuve-Sainte-Geneviève between the Latin Quarter and the Faubourg Saint-Marcel" (21;

27). Much has been said about the realist device at work here—the address that solicits readers, even dares them, to go look on their own in the streets of the city to verify that the boardinghouse is really there. What interests me more, however, is the geographical placement of Mme Vauquer's establishment in relation to the rest of the city. The rue Neuve-Sainte-Geneviève is between the Latin Quarter, a well-known neighborhood of Paris and one of the centers of Parisian cultural life (the hub of student life in the city), and the faubourg Saint-Marceau, which is only marginally a part of the city.[3] In fact, the rue Neuve-Sainte-Geneviève is a sort of border space between the city and its outside. Although the area within which the rue Neuve-Sainte-Geneviève is located can technically be called a neighborhood of the city, the street is nonetheless simultaneously located on a border, removed from the normal traffic and circulation of Parisian thoroughfares. For, as we soon discover, the streets found in this part of Paris are narrow and steep, and they are therefore impracticable for normal urban circulation: "The lodging-house [. . .] stands at the lower end of the Rue Neuve-Sainte-Geneviève where it slopes so abruptly towards the Rue de l'Arbalète that carriages rarely use it" (22–23; 28). The neighborhood of the rue Neuve-Sainte-Geneviève thus strangely resembles what in French would be termed a *banlieue,* a neighborhhood that is at a certain distance from the city (*lieue*) but that is linked to it in specific legal ways (*ban*), in other words, a tributary of the city that is not actually a part of the city. From the outset, the story establishes that the rue Neuve-Sainte-Geneviève is situated in an ill-defined peripheral region that, even if not technically a *banlieue,* certainly functions symbolically as one.

All the more so in the sense that a *banlieue* is a space inhabited by *bannis,* by those who are banished from the inner city for one reason or another—*au ban de la société,* as the French expression would have it. The list of boarders in the pension Vauquer soon confirms this rule, since all of them are at a certain remove from the social and cultural heart of the city. The first boarder mentioned is Victorine Taillefer, who, as the reader eventually discovers, has been disinherited by her father and lives in poverty as a result of her social disgrace. Rastignac, the son of a poor provincial nobleman, also lives in the boardinghouse. He knows nothing about how life in Paris functions and is poised to discover the city's secrets as the novel begins. The peripheral space of the rue Neuve-Sainte-Geneviève is also inhabited by the mysterious Vautrin who, the reader will ultimately discover, is an archetypal outsider, a criminal at total war with society and therefore pitted expressly against the sociocultural heart of the city. Finally, old Goriot himself is a characteristic member of the population inhabiting Mme Vauquer's boardinghouse. He has slipped into poverty and become increasingly confined to the marginal domain represented by Mme Vauquer's neighborhood. One could easily lengthen this list, but by now it is evident that every character in the boardinghouse corresponds surprisingly closely to the topographical city space in which Mme Vauquer's building is located.

One way of describing the problem that confronts Rastignac as the novel opens would thus be to say that he must learn how to penetrate the heart of the city, learn to understand Parisian topography from the vantage point of the ill-defined space of the socioeconomic *banlieue* to which he is initially confined. The rue Neuve-Sainte-Geneviève is only tenuously related to the city proper, as I have suggested, and the passage from one domain to the other is thus difficult—it will require a sustained effort to grasp a complex set of relations. Rastignac's inevitable blindness as outsider and newcomer is compounded by his spatial marginalization. Rastignac must develop a sense of the subtle distinctions that lie at the heart of the city and thus obtain the proper vision for making lucid mappings. The symbolic distance his education covers in the novel is strongly foregrounded by the story's final sequence, which, like the opening sequence, is intersected by a thematics of topography. The novel's concluding passage reworks the initial sequence and takes place in a very different space. Rastignac attends the pauper's burial of old Goriot in the Père Lachaise cemetery accompanied only by Mme Vauquer's domestic servant Christophe and eventually by servants from the Restaud and the Nucingen households—both households have sent empty carriages but no representatives to the funeral. At the end of the service, Rastignac goes to one of the highest points in the cemetery, from which he has a full view of the city's center:

> Thus left alone, Rastignac walked a few steps to the highest part of the cemetery, and saw Paris spread out below on both banks of the winding Seine. Lights were beginning to twinkle here and there. His gaze fixed almost avidly upon the space that lay between the column of the Place Vendôme and the dome of the Invalides; there lay the splendid world that he had wished to gain. He eyed that humming hive with a look that foretold its despoliation, as if he already felt on his lips the sweetness of its honey, and said with superb defiance,
>
> "It's war between us now!" (367; 304)

The scene signifies openly that Rastignac has accomplished his journey of initiation: having set out from the indistinction that characterizes the space of rue Neuve-Sainte-Geneviève, into which he was plunged with little perspective to help him grasp subtle connections, he has now obtained a vantage point with a bird's-eye view of the city. He encompasses the panorama in a single glance and identifies not only its borders (Place Vendôme, dome of the Invalides) but also its essence (the honey that his understanding and accomplished gaze now draw out of the scene). To plunge into the city from the banishment of the rue Neuve-Sainte-Geneviève was a gesture of blind faith. To plunge into the city now from the vantage point of the Père Lachaise cemetery is a risk that can be at least partially calculated. Rastignac has learned enough to begin to manipulate people and events himself—instead of simply remaining prey to those events and to the maneuvers that characterize Parisian life.

The problem for the reader is to understand how Rastignac gets from one place to the other—both figuratively (from ignorance to understanding) and literally (from one region of the city to another). What strongly characterizes the structure of the novel is that the two kinds of journeys (figurative and literal) are constantly superimposed on each other. For Rastignac, to learn the city space means, at least in part, to walk in the city; a fundamental activity of his apprenticeship is to navigate the city on foot. At first glance, this seems to be a rather simple, straightforward statement. One must not, however, neglect its theoretical significance. One must not underestimate the differences between the act of circulating about a given space in a conveyance and the act of circulating on foot. The insight into the detail of a terrain that one obtains by exploring the terrain's irregularities on foot has little common measure with the knowledge that one gathers when enclosed in a carriage. Transportation by vehicle depends directly on the fact that the space in question has been rearranged into a costly infrastructure. A network of streets, for example, has the effect of carefully directing and limiting the way one can move about the city. Imagine that a passenger in a carriage in Paris at the historical moment described by Balzac (the early 1820s) wanted to descend suddenly into the street to explore something perceived from within the carriage. Such a gesture would be frankly dangerous—the passenger would run the risk of being immediately struck by another vehicle. It would also be extremely disruptive of the traffic flow and doubtless would elicit reprimands from other travelers.[4] In other words, the passenger is ultimately a prisoner of the vehicle and, as such, is confined to the infrastructural network already laid out by urban authorities. The chance to make aleatóry connections, to work toward a deeper understanding of the complexity of the landscape, is precluded. Jean-Marc Lévy-Leblond sums up these points succinctly. While his perspective is modern, the lesson remains the same:

> No doubt planes, trains, and automobiles go faster than the walker. But have we really understood the extreme limitations they impose on the trips we take? Their effectiveness comes at a price, namely, a heavy and restrictive infrastructure. A few airports or railroad tracks, a network of highways will never cover more than an infinitesimal portion of the planet. Wherever you go, you will finish your trip on foot. In bed, at the table, on the beach, in the middle of the forest, only your body will reach its goal. (39)

What Lévy-Leblond is driving at here and what I have been suggesting is the importance of the body's kinetic displacement in space as a device for understanding the detail of the terrain in which one is moving. The teeming subtleties of the links, passages, and possibilities of the Parisian cityscape cannot be understood in quite the same way by a passenger in a vehicle. The fact, then, that Rastignac is poor as the novel begins, which means that he must move about without the help of a vehicle, should not be taken as a mere socioeconomic descriptive detail. Quite the contrary, this necessity is an important characteristic of the educational initiation he undergoes.

An emblematic sequence that develops this problematic is the first and only visit Rastignac makes to Anastasie de Restaud's house. After dressing in his finest clothes, he sets out toward her neighborhood on foot—with the anticipated results:

> Eugène walked with a thousand precautions against splashing himself with mud, but with his mind wholly fixed on what he would say to Madame de Restaud. He laid in a stock of wit; he invented scintillating retorts to imaginary remarks; he prepared his polished lines, his phrases in the style of Talleyrand, for imaginary situations favourable to the declaration on which he was to found his future. And so he became spattered with mud after all, poor student, and was forced to have his shoes polished and his breeches brushed at the Palais-Royal.
>
> "If I were rich," he said to himself as he changed a five-franc piece that he had brought *in case of need,* "I should have gone by cab, then I could have thought at my leisure." (85; 78–79)

Perhaps Rastignac would have been able to think more clearly about the anticipated conversation had he taken a cab, but the trip is more than an occasion for inventing witty repartee; it is also the experience of a route, a necessary prospecting of the itinerary between his living quarters and the aristocratic neighborhood in which the Hôtel de Restaud is to be found. The practicalities that Rastignac encounters—mud and the necessity of cleaning it off his clothing—are not extraneous, but central. A carriage might have spared his shoes and pants, but it would not have allowed him to fill in essential details to the indispensable map of the city he is formulating by experience. The scene demonstrates, moreover, that the topographical problem of transition between the Vauquer pension and the Restaud residence hides other complexities—the first problem is doubled by a second, namely, the transition between the street and the Restaud household itself. Obliged to cross the courtyard on foot, Rastignac becomes the butt of the servants' jokes, because the domestics in the household are used to visitors who arrive only in the most stylish conveyances. The awkwardness of Rastignac's entry is a prelude to his failure within the house—where he immediately betrays his ignorance of the layout of the rooms, that is, of the interior topography, and ends up crossing through the service back rooms of the house while attempting to enter the parlor. Decidedly, Rastignac has a lot to learn about spatial relations! The first part of the scene in the Restaud household ends, moreover, with Rastignac looking out the window and beholding the courtyard through which he just walked and in which, to his surprise, he espies another visitor on foot—Goriot. Rastignac, who does not yet know of the familial connection between Goriot and Anastasie de Restaud, catches sight of Goriot just as the old man is leaving after having visited his daughter. Goriot's apparition in this context is both surprising and mysterious to Rastignac. How is it that the space between the Vauquer household, where Goriot lives, and the Restaud household can be connected, that is, how can an obscure inhabitant from one of the spaces be displaced into the other? The question applies to Rastignac himself as well as to Goriot, and Rastignac's inability to grasp how this transport is possible is precisely what leads to the social faux pas that will permanently close the door of the Restaud household to him—Rastignac mentions Goriot to the count Restaud. One might add, moreover, that the reversal of perspective that occurs in the scene prefigures the reversal that characterizes the novel's final scene. Rastignac is plunged into the space of the Restaud courtyard without any perspective possible—everyone, including the servants of the household, has the advantage and is thus able to adopt an ironic stance toward his behavior. Once within the house and able to look back at the courtyard, Rastignac sees someone like himself (old Goriot) and immediately assumes a position of perspectivist mastery with respect to this other person. Unhappily for Rastignac, the reversal of perspective in this case is quite premature. He is unable to use the reversal to understand it, and is therefore unable to transform it into a strategy—in fact, his attempt to mobilize his momentary superiority over Goriot by mentioning their acquaintance is precisely what leads to Rastignac's ultimate downfall in the Restaud household.

If this sequence can be considered archetypal in the context of Rastignac's development of mapping skills relevant to itineraries created by walking, experiences obtained through other means of transportation quickly make their appearance as well. Rastignac, bitter over his defeat in the Restaud household, impulsively hails a cab that takes him to see his cousin, Mme de Beauséant. In other words, the scene as a whole contains both a trip on foot and one in a carriage. The carriage portion contains yet another lesson and a considerable dose of irony. On asking to be taken to the hôtel de Beauséant, Rastignac is informed that his request is ambiguous:

> "Where to, sir?" asked the driver, who had already taken off his white gloves.
>
> "The devil take it," said Eugène to himself, "since I'm going the pace I must at least get value for my money! Drive to the Hôtel de Beauséant," he added aloud.
>
> "Which?" said the driver.
>
> This lofty question shook Eugène's composure. The unfledged dandy was not aware that there were two Hôtels de Beauséant; he did not know how rich he was in relations who did not care two straws about him.
>
> "The Vicomte de Beauséant, Rue—"
>
> "De Grenelle," interrupted the driver, nodding his head. "You see," he added as he pulled up the step, "there's the Count's house and the Marquis's in the Rue Saint-Dominique."

> "Yes, of course," replied Eugène drily. "Must everybody jeer at me today?" (97; 88)

Even to circulate about Paris in a cab requires some knowledge of how the city is laid out, and in the absence of such knowledge one risks looking like a fool—Rastignac's ignorance is immediately exposed. At this point, Rastignac simply decides to throw himself on the mercy of the only one who can begin to show him where the bridges between the parts of the city can be found, namely, Mme de Beauséant herself. It is interesting to note that his transition into her domestic space at the end of his cab ride is every bit as clumsy as his entry into the Restaud household only minutes earlier:

> As Eugène was getting out of the cab he heard smothered laughter from the peristyle. Three or four lackeys had been cracking jokes at the expense of this plebeian bride's turn-out. A moment later the student knew in a flash what they were making merry over, as he compared his carriage with one of the most elegant broughams in Paris. (98; 89)

Little has been changed by Rastignac's extravagant, impulsive decision to take a cab. The comparison between the cab and the elegant carriage parked in the courtyard of the Hôtel de Beauséant is enough to elicit the mirth of the servants once again, because to arrive in a cab is hardly better than to arrive on foot. At Mme de Beauséant's, suffice it to say, Rastignac makes exactly the same mistakes he made previously and is saved only by the fact that he is her cousin. For this reason alone Mme de Beauséant does not throw him out on his ear. Rastignac receives a detailed geography lesson from her and discovers the relation between old Goriot's space and that of his daughters. A map begins to be established.

If Rastignac moves throughout the city on foot and by public conveyance, others do as well, and the shortcuts and short circuits suggested by such displacements add further complexity to his topographical knowledge. A striking example occurs early in the novel, on the morning after Rastignac has attended his first ball at Mme de Beauséant's *hôtel* (this sequence occurs before the one analyzed above). He espies Anastasie de Restaud—whom he met for the first time at the ball—in the neighborhood of Mme Vauquer's boardinghouse. This apparition of the elegant countess in surroundings that are utterly foreign to her normal social regions is extremely surprising to Rastignac. Immediately he tries to discover what bridge leads from the faubourg Saint-Germain to the area around the rue Neuve-Sainte-Geneviève:

> "Well, this morning I met this divine countess, about nine o'clock, on foot, in the Rue des Grès. My heart started thumping." [. . .]
>
> "She didn't see me," said Eugène; "but was it not strange to meet one

> of the prettiest women in Paris in the Rue des Grès at nine o'clock, when she could not have come from the ball before two in the morning? It's only in Paris you meet with such adventures." (73, 75; 69, 70)

Not only did Anastasie venture into a sector of the city far removed from her normal domain but, when Rastignac sees her, she is on foot—surely not to be expected of a wealthy and apparently powerful woman. Anastasie's passage from one part of the city to another appears to be an inexplicable short circuit that collapses distinct topographical regions onto one another. Not surprisingly, the key to the enigma belongs to Vautrin, who, although he does not provide a full explanation, hints that he knows where the bridge is located:

> "Yesterday dancing at a Duchess's ball," said Vautrin, "this morning visiting a money-lender; from the highest arc of fortune's wheel to the bottom of the social ladder: behold the progress of Parisian women! If their husbands can't support their unbridled extravagance they sell themselves." (74; 70)

The second geographer in the story is obviously Vautrin himself. His knowledge and expertise are emblematically represented by the fact that only he possesses a passkey to the Vauquer boardinghouse. His ability to come and go as he pleases at any hour of the day or night demonstrates the extent to which he has free run not only of the Vauquer household but also, by extension, of the city with which this domestic space communicates. Open doors lead to other doors, to bridges, to connections that Vautrin has thoroughly explored, as the reader learns progressively when the story begins to unfold.

A topographical analysis structured around the idea of mapping in *Le Père Goriot* would have to deal with other spaces as well—the public garden where Vautrin is betrayed, for example—but the brief remarks I have made allow the reader to grasp the extent to which Rastignac's education is tied to learning how to navigate within a city space that is the result of nineteenth-century urban growth. That growth brought prominence to a new kind of perception of the city. The unfamiliar had to be made familiar in new ways, and one of the most important of the senses that had to be developed was that of the connections between and among apparently separate regions of the city. The city had dispensed with the familiarity of well-organized, semipermanent spaces resulting from spatial habits formed across generations. Such permanence over long periods of time was characteristic of rural culture. The new situation encountered in cities confronted citizens with the need to decipher mysterious and rapidly changing connections in a conglomeration that had to accommodate very diverse groups amassed on a relatively small territory. As Balzac shows in his construction of Rastignac's character, topographical intelligence therefore became an indispensable element of every young man's cultural knowledge.

NOTES

[1]One need only think about how historians habitually use Balzac's novels as documents for reconstructing the history of the Restoration period in France to begin to grasp the difficulty of separating fiction from historical observation in his work. The ambiguous nature of Balzac's novels, simultaneously fiction and document, merits reflection, because the ambiguity is related both to Balzac's ambition (he saw himself as a historian) and to the nature of the realist novel of which he was a founding father.

[2]It is often pedagogically worthwhile to compare the opening and closing sequences of a Balzac novel—of any novel, in fact—once students have finished reading the whole work. The relations between the two sequences frequently recap the fundamental themes of the novel and provide a convenient means for pointing out something like the symbolic trajectory of the novel as a whole. The last sentence of Flaubert's *L'Education sentimentale,* for instance, provokes the utter collapse of the whole lived experience of Frédéric Moreau and, I would claim, is a conscious rewriting of the end of *Le Père Goriot.*

[3]A quick reminder of the etymology of the term *faubourg*: *foris* ("outside"), the *bourg* ("the city"). Although Paris has obviously grown by absorbing various faubourgs, which have often retained their designations as faubourgs despite their incorporation into the city, the term nevertheless refers to the original status of such neighborhoods—not quite yet a part of the city—and has a clear significance here.

[4]It is dangerous to exit from a vehicle in the middle of an urban street, and thus the act of exiting must be accomplished carefully, after the vehicle has moved out of the mainstream of the traffic flow. Such caution is not needed for a conveyance in a rural setting. One of the major differences between railroad travel and carriage travel between cities and towns turned out to be the fact that when traveling in a carriage, the voyager often descended to walk periodically (for example, when the carriage was going up a steep hill), while the train passenger was and is very much a prisoner of the train—for all sorts of reasons, one of which is, of course, the speed of the vehicle.

A Narratological Approach: The Narrator in *Le Père Goriot*

Gerald Prince

There are many characteristics of Balzac's narrative fiction and, specifically, of *Le Père Goriot,* that "archetypal Balzacian novel" (Kanes 10). For example, there is the writer's recourse to an essentially dramatic form, to crisis and conflict, exclamatory presentation and coups de théâtre, the cramming of a large number of events into a small amount of time. In fact, *Le Père Goriot* is self-described as a drama or tragedy (21, 22, 128; 27, 28, 115) and divided into three well-delineated acts, each taking up about a third of the text (Gaudon 154). There is also the device of reappearing characters, which opens up the novel onto other works in *La Comédie humaine,* extends its duration, and increases its naturalness (Lotte 234–35; Pugh 235–37); Balzac first exploited this device systematically with *Le Père Goriot* (Delphine appears in seventeen of his texts, Rastignac in twenty-five, Bianchon in twenty-nine, Nucingen in thirty-one). There is the author's propensity for patient and minute description; his tireless linking of the concrete and the abstract, of physical features and mental or emotional ones; his emphasis on the intimate connection between characters and their environment. Mme Vauquer's entire person, for example, "explique la pension, comme la pension implique sa personne" 'provides a clue to the boarding-house, just as the boarding-house implies the existence of such a person as she is' (29; 33). Above all, perhaps, there is the Balzacian narrator.

Like the narrators of most of Balzac's novels, the narrator in *Le Père Goriot* is heterodiegetic and extradiegetic: neither a participant in the events recounted nor situated in any diegesis. Moreover, he is trustworthy (no feature of the text undermines the veracity of his account) as well as reliable in the Boothian sense of the term (behaving in accordance with the implied author's norms, values, and tastes).[1] He is, furthermore, omniscient or quasiomniscient, aware of the characters' past and of their future (136–37, 166, 203, 328; 119, 142, 172, 274), capable of viewing events from the periphery or the center, capable too of reporting not only physical actions but also thoughts and feelings, and subject to no perceptual or conceptual restrictions. If he sometimes seems to hesitate (34, 40, 41, 187; 37, 42, 43, 159), his uncertainty is less a symptom of his possible limitations than a sign of the very murkiness—the very hesitancy—of the world depicted. It allows him to underline his good faith, his conscientiousness, the importance of a questioning state of mind and of a regard for evidence, the difficulty of his explorations and decipherments. It allows him, moreover, to emphasize his difference from a character like Vautrin, who is himself an eloquent narrator but who is betrayed by excessive confidence in his own powers of understanding, prediction, and control: had Vautrin paid more attention to Mlle Michonneau's "bosses de Judas" 'bumps of Judas' (81; 75), for instance, he might have been more careful (Mozet, "Description" 113). Finally, the narrator is intrusive. So much so that, according to Gérard Genette, the multiplicity, variety, and complexity of the narrator's intrusions underscore the very arbitrariness of fictional narrative that they attempt to conceal. The invasion of story by discourse, of the narration of situations and events by narratorial commentary, constitutes for Genette one of the "modern" aspects of a reputedly "traditional" novel ("Vraisemblance" 11–13). In *Le Père Goriot,* the narrator fulfills not only a narrative function (the recounting of what took place) but also the other possible narratorial functions described in Genette's *Narrative Discourse* (255–57): the "testimonial function," or "function of attestation," whereby the text indicates, maintains, or characterizes the links between the narrator and the narratee; the "directing function," whereby the text concentrates on its own nature, its functioning, its organization, and the meaning or import of its constituents; and, lastly, the "ideological function," whereby the text comments on, explains, or justifies the action and serves as an instrument of plausibility and realistic motivation.

Many of the narrator's interventions foreground his self-consciousness, his awareness of telling a story. From the very beginning of the novel, in fact, he points to the difficulty of his task:

> Sera-t-elle [cette histoire] comprise au-delà de Paris? le doute est permis. [. . .] Après avoir lu les secrètes infortunes du père Goriot, vous dînerez avec appétit en mettant votre insensibilité sur le compte de l'auteur, en le taxant d'exagération, en l'accusant de poésie. (21, 22)

> Will it [this story] be understood outside Paris? One may doubt it. [. . .] When you have read of the secret sorrows of old Goriot you will dine with unimpaired appetite, blaming the author for your callousness, taxing him with exaggeration, accusing him of having given wings to his imagination. (27, 28)

At several other points in the text, he explicitly comments on the narrative moves he performs, the reasons for performing them, and the accuracy of his representation (28, 57, 97, 175; 32, 56, 89, 150). He is never reluctant to express his thoughts and emotions about the events he relates or the participants they involve. Paris, human nature, modern civilization, Rastignac's ambitions, Victorine's emotions, Gondureau's machinations—nothing is mentioned without the narrator making his stance manifest (34, 40, 166–67; 37–38, 42, 143). Nor is he reluctant to indicate the sources on which his material and its representation depend. The very look of the French version of the text, which is sprinkled with mimetic and citational italics, reflects the diversity of languages making up the narrator's language (21, 91, 229; 27, 84, 193), and, early in the novel, he suggests that the latter owes much of its authentic quality to Rastignac and that the narrator himself often functions simply as a transcriber:

> Sans ses observations curieuses et l'adresse avec laquelle il sut se produire dans les salons de Paris, ce récit n'eût pas été coloré des tons vrais qu'il devra sans doute à son esprit sagace et à son désir de pénétrer les mystères d'une situation épouvantable, aussi soigneusement cachée par ceux qui l'avaient créée que par celui qui les subissait. (31; see also 182)

> But for his observant curiosity, and the adroitness with which he contrived to introduce himself into the salons of Paris, this story would not possess the colour of reality. It undoubtedly owes its truth to his alert mind and to his desire to fathom the mysteries of an appalling state of affairs, which was being as carefully concealed by the victim as by those responsible for it. (35; see also 155)

If Rastignac is identified as one of the important sources of the story, he is also portrayed more directly as a teller and thus constitutes a possible foil for the narrator. Rastignac may possess "la chaleureuse éloquence du jeune âge" 'the vehement eloquence of youth' (329; 272), but he lacks knowledge (96, 98, 100, 187; 88, 90, 92, 159)—a major weakness (etymologically speaking, a narrator is one who knows); he lacks patience (120; 108); and he lacks the capacity or will to report the facts: "L'étudiant répéta les paroles de la baronne en les embellissant" 'The student repeated the Baroness's words, with some embellishments of his own' (180; 152). Thus, even when Rastignac proves narratively effective, he is not entirely compelling: Delphine weeps when she hears him tell of Goriot's self-devotion and Anastasie's cruelty, but she does not forget that tears will spoil her looks (329; 272–73).

Rastignac is not the only teller that the Balzacian narrator refers to or portrays in order to specify his own qualities. Walter Scott as well as Lord Byron are mentioned, for example (176, 281; 150, 237), and many of the novel's characters—from Mme Couture and the servant Thérèse to Mme Vauquer, Vautrin, and Goriot himself—appear as narrators (see Bellos 27–29). Sometimes, their accounts help justify the heterodiegetic narrator's attitudes and claims. The duchesse de Langeais, for instance, who tells Mme de Beauséant and Rastignac how Goriot gave his daughters everything and yet was cast off by them, insists on the tragic dimension of the story as well as on the dramatic nature of life and the mire of the modern world (110–13; 100–02). More often, the defectiveness of the characters' accounts helps delineate the narrator's manner and foreground his superiority. The narrow-minded Mme Vauquer is incapable not only of properly designating people and things (25, 240, 255; 29–30, 202, 214) but also of considering why events happen (47; 48), and she provides platitudes in lieu of analysis and explanation (251; 212). Similarly, Poiret proves unable to tell anything other than pointless, incoherent, and interminable narratives:

> Après avoir entamé un premier sujet, il était conduit par ses parenthèses à en traiter de tout opposés, sans avoir rien conclu. En arrivant à la Maison-Vauquer, il s'était faufilé dans une suite de passages et de citations transitoires qui l'avaient amené à raconter sa déposition dans l'affaire du sieur Ragoulleau et de la dame Morin, où il avait comparu en qualité de témoin à décharge. (229)
>
> The first subject he broached led him by way of one parenthesis after another to others entirely different, and he went on and on without putting a period to any topic on the way. By the time they reached the Maison Vauquer a chain of examples, quotations and incidental allusions had brought him to an account of the evidence he had given in the case of the Sieur Ragoulleau *versus* Dame Morin, when he had appeared as a witness for the defence. (191)

Vautrin, however, is of an entirely different caliber. He seems to know everything and see everything (140; 122), can enter the mind of others (228; 192), and can handle the language of gallantry as easily as the language of criminals (245, 262–63; 122, 140). Capable of exemplary terseness when recounting his life (143; 124), he is also capable of torrential eloquence when describing society, its mechanisms, and its movers. He has read Benvenuto Cellini's *Memoirs* in the original (144; 125), makes judicious reference to Bernardin de Saint-Pierre and *Paul et Virginie* (244; 205), and comments ironically on the conventions of sentimental stories: "'Enfin,' dit-il à haute voix, '*ils furent considérés dans tout le pays, vécurent heureux, et eurent beaucoup d'enfants*. Voilà comment finissent tous les romans d'amour'" '"In short," he added aloud, "they were esteemed throughout the land, lived happily ever after and had lots of children. That's how all the romances end"' (243; 203). Besides, he himself is, of course, a masterful plotter. Contrary to the narrator, however, and as mentioned above, he is not always sufficiently modest, cautious, and attentive to the world around him. Whereas the narrator believes in fixed principles and general laws, Vautrin believes only in circumstances and events (156; 134). Whereas the narrator equates poetry with exaggeration and fabulation rather than with truth (22; 28) and would call himself a historian rather than a fiction writer, a describer and explicator rather than a creator (see, e.g., van Rossum-Guyon, "Texte" b7), Vautrin defines himself as a poet (152; 130) and compares himself to God (155; 134). But, like the devil, Vautrin can only create evil and illusion (see Milner, "Poésie" 329–30). Goriot also compares himself to God (178, 339; 152, 285), and he too proves to be a fabulator, for instance when he paints deluded pictures of life with Rastignac and Delphine (231–32; 195). As his passion for his daughters becomes overwhelming, he produces increasingly rambling, disjointed, delirious quasi narratives (340–45; 284–89).

Just as the narrator of *Le Père Goriot* amply fulfills the testimonial function, he pays a lot of attention to the function of communication. Indeed, he evokes his narratee on the very first page of the novel. Subsequently, he spares no effort to establish multiple links with him, and—through numerous direct and indirect addresses, explicit and implicit instructions—he attempts to orient the narratee's perceptions; guide his reflections; make him see, think, understand. As indicated above, this is no simple task. In the first place, perhaps "[l]es particularités de cette scène pleine d'observations et de couleurs locales ne peuvent être appréciées qu'entre les buttes de Montmartre et les hauteurs de Montrouge" '[o]nly between the heights of Montmartre and Montrouge are there people who can appreciate how exactly, with what close observation, it [this story] is drawn from life' (22; 27). Moreover, the narratee is probably callous (22; 28) and impatient (28; 32). Besides, he must be used to another kind of story (amusing, superficial, fictional) and must expect mere entertainment rather than more substantial fare (22; 28). Still, the narrator is not easily discouraged. For one thing, some stories are "si véritabl[es] que chacun peut en reconnaître les éléments chez soi, dans son cœur peut-être" 'so true that everyone can recognize the elements of the tragedy in his own household, in his own heart perhaps' (22; 28). For another, like a good mentor—*Télémaque* is mentioned early on (26; 31)—the narrator may show his narratee the way. Questions, some rhetorical, and plain directives abound, especially in the French version of the text, challenging the narratee, calling on his experience, addressing his concerns, silencing his objections (see, e.g., 40, 100, 126, 209; 42, 91, 113, 177). Plentiful as well are passages that include demonstrative terms that, instead of pointing to an anterior or posterior element in the novel, point to another text, to another world that the narratee presumably knows and can profitably use as a reference. My favorite such passage? Perhaps it is this one: "[une] de ces balourdises dont on dit pittoresquement en Pologne: *Attelez cinq bœufs à votre char!*" 'one of [those] blunders in regard to which they stay picturesquely in Poland, "Yoke five oxen to your cart!" ' (101; 92). Finally, there are numerous general explanations clarifying circumstances, actions, and motivations as well as metanarrative commentary recognizing the reasons for the narratee's resistance, prevailing over his prejudices, allaying his apprehensions:

> A qui ne paraîtra-t-il pas invraisemblable que Poiret, ancien employé, sans doute homme de vertus bourgeoises, quoique dénué d'idées, continuât d'écouter le prétendu rentier de la rue de Buffon [. . .]? Cependant, rien n'était plus naturel. (220)

> It is not easy for anyone to believe that Poiret, a retired clerk, and no doubt a man of middle-class virtues although lacking in intelligence, continued to listen to the so-called gentleman of means from the Rue Buffon [. . .]. Nothing, however, was more natural. (184)

Unlike Goriot, who gives up all control over his daughters, or Vautrin, who wants total mastery over his newfound child Rastignac, or Taillefer, who refuses to recognize Victorine's existence, or the elder Rastignac, who never even appears on the scene, the narrator proves to be a proper father. He chides the narratee but also cajoles him, dispenses criticism as well as praise, shows disapproval as well as tolerance, uses an exclusionist "you" but also a unifying "we" (40, 139, 161, 200; 42, 121, 138, 170). Warning the narratee against pettiness and coldheartedness (39, 49; 41, 50); requiring him to be patient and judicious, observant, and vigilant (63, 164, 166; 62, 140–41, 143); providing him with the tools necessary for understanding; and recognizing his potential for enlightenment, the narrator is a good teacher—which probably explains in part why his instructions and appeals gradually decrease as the story develops. *Le Père Goriot* is the story of a double education: that of Rastignac but also that of the narratee (Mozet, "Description" 109).

I have already mentioned the narrator's self-consciousness, and I have referred to his definition of *Le Père Goriot* as something other than ordinary fiction. Not once does he characterize the text as a novel or himself as a novelist (van Rossum-Guyon, "Texte" b7). He is rather an explorer, a philosopher, a dramatist, a painter, or a historian (see, e.g., 34, 40, 161; 38, 42, 138). He likes to use terms like *peindre* (paint) or *expliquer* (explain); *peinture* (painting), *scène* (scene), or *drame* (drama); *comprendre* (understand) or *voir* (see) to designate his production, its constituent parts, and its reception (see, e.g., 218, 243, 266; 184, 204, 224). And, by offering numerous negative and positive descriptions of the story he tells and its components, he repeatedly makes it clear that story and components are painterly, dramatic, and philosophical rather than novelistic. With three protagonists, several "endings" (Vautrin's fall, Mme de Beauséant's farewell to the world, Goriot's death, Rastignac's challenge to society); and elements evocative of a mystery story, a melodrama, a bildungsroman, a history of Parisian manners and society, and a tragic tale about the human heart (see Kanes 10), *Le Père Goriot*—which Balzac included first among his *Scenes of Parisian Life,* then later among his *Scenes of Private Life*—can, of course, be characterized in a number of ways. According to the narrator, the novel can be said to relate "les secrètes infortunes" 'the secret sorrows' of Goriot (22; 28), the terrible self-destruction and agony of "[un] Christ de la

Paternité" '[a] Christ-like father' (282; 235). But the novel can also be said to depict a poor student "dans sa lutte avec Paris" 'in his struggle with Paris' (169; 143) or "des sinuosités dans lesquelles un homme du monde, un ambitieux fait rouler sa conscience, en essayant de côtoyer le mal, afin d'arriver à son but en gardant les apparences" 'the devious paths into which a man of the world, a man of ambition, forces his conscience, as he tries to sail close to the wind to reach his end while keeping up appearances' (178; 150) or, more generally, "[une] obscure mais effroyable tragédie parisienne" '[an] obscure but terrible Parisian tragedy' (130; 115) or, indeed, human life itself (140; 120). *Le Père Goriot* is not "dramatique dans le sens vrai du mot" 'dramatic in the real sense of the word,' though the term "drame" 'drama' is undoubtedly suitable (21; 27). It is certainly "ni une fiction ni un roman" 'neither fiction nor romance' (22; 28). No, it is made up of frequently overlooked or unpublished truths (34, 219; 38, 184) and it is truth itself: "*All is true,* il est si véritable, que chacun peut en reconnaître les éléments chez soi, dans son cœur peut-être" '*All is true,* so true that everyone can recognize the elements of the tragedy in his own household, in his own heart perhaps' (22; 28). Now, the narrator clearly has the qualities required for transmitting this truth, and the narratee can be taught to receive it. As for the medium of transmission—language (oral but also written [161; 135])—it proves unproblematic. No doubt, some words can become discredited through inconsiderate use (21; 27), some things do not have a name in French (91, 100–01; 84, 92), and other things are difficult to express (27, 63; 31, 61). But the topos of the inexpressible is seldom relied on; there is always German or Polish or a myriad of other languages if French seems inadequate; and even an overworked term sometimes turns out to be appropriate. The narrator exhibits little linguistic anxiety, and, through allusion and citation, comparison, explanation, and invention—"Cette première pièce exhale une odeur sans nom dans la langue, et qu'il faudrait appeler l'*odeur de pension*" 'This first room exhales an odour without a name in the language; it ought to be called *boarding-house smell*' (26–27; 31)—he consistently shows himself capable of saying what has to be said. Though the map is not the territory, the word not the thing, the language not the idea (182; 154), the distance between sign and referent is bridgeable, in part because the latter itself signifies. Everything in the diegesis—a bearing, a glance, the inflection of a voice—functions as a text (22, 164; 39, 140–41). Affections are "les poésies de la volonté" 'the poetry created by the mind' (180; 154), different temperaments are linked to different genres (188; 160), and the theme of the world as book is explicitly mentioned (114; 103). Indeed, as Françoise van Rossum-Guyon argues, the use of terms like *picture* or *scene* to designate various aspects of the world and the encroachment of discourse on story, of metalinguistic commentary on the narration of events, points to an equivalence between reality and its representation ("Texte" b7–b9). Besides, the narrator makes it clear that he does not aim simply to provide a copy of the real. He summarizes the many thoughts that float through Rastignac's mind (97, 175; 93, 150), for instance, just as he summarizes the information gathered by the young man about Goriot's history (124; 111). His point is not merely to represent things in their silent materiality and to reproduce what took place. Rather, it is to represent things in their telling concreteness and to convey the meaning of reality.

In *S/Z* Roland Barthes writes that (Balzacian) realism "consists not in copying the real but in copying a (depicted) copy of the real" (55). This is perhaps another way of saying that, contrary to what happens in much of Gustave Flaubert, for example, or in much of Alain Robbe-Grillet, the Balzacian narrator endeavors to present the real as an interpreted and interpretable complex of signs. *Le Père Goriot* constitutes, among many other things, an exercise in language teaching, and Balzac (or his narrator) is perhaps, above all, a language teacher.

NOTE

[1] The narrator's gender is not explicitly identified in the novel, though much of the narrator's stance may be considered masculine. The same is true of the gender of the narratee, though the early reference to the "main blanche" 'white hand' (22; 28) connotes femininity. For the sake of brevity, I use masculine pronouns when referring to both figures.

A Feminist Approach: Realism and Its Others: Reading Bodies in Balzac's *Le Père Goriot* and Girardin's *La Canne de M. de Balzac*

Margaret Waller

Early in my teaching career, I made a serious miscalculation. After the vague ennui and slow-moving narratives of the Romantics in my survey of nineteenth-century French literature, I imagined that the students would be grateful for a novel like *Le Père Goriot* with its far more exciting plot. I assumed that they would readily identify with Rastignac, the poor but ambitious young provincial coming of age in a corrupt, materialist world, and relate easily to the ethos of social advancement as well as to the discourse about its pitfalls. Even the seemingly interminable description of the Maison Vauquer and its inhabitants, I reasoned, was so classically realist that it was perfect for the classroom. On all accounts, then, it looked as though Balzac's *Père Goriot* was not just a classic must-read for my undergraduates at Pomona, a selective liberal arts college; the novel would also be pleasurable reading.

In a word, I was wrong. *Le Père Goriot* may be a paradigmatic readerly text, but teaching it successfully to American undergraduates takes forethought and, in the best of all possible worlds, a course that places the novel in historical context. What follows are four teaching strategies I have devised that work particularly well. The first two are especially appropriate for less-advanced students, and the second two, which may or may not be used in tandem, for an upper-level seminar in French literature and cultural studies.

The first strategy is simple and is one I use in all my literature classes. Rather than discourage students from talking about how bored or unmoved they may have been by their reading, I make all their reactions—including negative ones—key heuristic devices. Indeed, students' various forms of emotional resistance to the text are an excellent starting point for class discussion of *Le Père Goriot*. Saying exactly where they were irritated, for example, helps students identify important features of the novel: the narrator's loquacious intrusiveness; the lengthy descriptions; the highly charged, melodramatic moments. Close examination of some of these passages in the light of students' resistance usually leads to a productive discussion: What is it about these moments in the text that makes the novel seem dated? How do our notions of plausibility differ from those underlying the text? What makes a character sympathetic for us as modern, American readers, and what do these changing notions tell us about what seems normal and natural?

Ironically, many passages that students identify as being the most difficult and unsatisfying are precisely those that most resemble movie scripts. Thus a second teaching strategy I have used builds on this similarity in order to head off students' resistance to the text. Before they begin reading Balzac on their own, I ask the students to imagine that they are going to turn *Le Père Goriot* into a film.[1] Reading the first paragraphs together, we identify which parts read like factual description and which seem more speculative. Would students start out with a long-distance shot of nineteenth-century Paris that then closes in on the Latin Quarter? If they used a voice-over, what kind of actor would they choose—male or female, young or old—and why?

Using preliminary discussions of this kind as a model, the students read the first thirty pages or so of the text at home and, in teams of two, create a screen treatment of an assigned paragraph or section, noting what well-known actors they would cast for the main characters, justifying their choices, and identifying drawbacks as well. Class discussion then revolves, for example, around whether or not a film adaptation should convey the heaviness of the text's description and commentary. If we eliminated the voice-over, what kind of information could be communicated through other means, and what would be lost?

The students soon discover that the visual details and contextual background that at first seemed heavy-handed in Balzac are no more redundant—and are usually far more revealing and interesting—than the information they pick up more passively and often unwittingly in traditional films through the "neutral" eye of the camera. Similarly, analysis in class of a brief clip from a well-known movie or TV program demonstrates that a dramatic yet fundamentally predictable plot is exactly what most students find appealing about contemporary romance, horror, Western, spy, and action shows. As a result, the unreadable and hopelessly dated Balzac becomes strangely familiar—almost modern—while contemporary film and TV come to seem more and more strange. These first two teaching strategies thus work by highlighting similarities and differences between Balzac's text and modern readers' expectations.

I have the greatest pedagogical success with the novel when I teach *Le Père Goriot* at a more advanced level and, in particular, in the context of a cultural studies seminar I designed on the prestige of the visible in the literary, cultural, and artistic representation of bodies in nineteenth-century France. This highly contextualized approach gives the students firsthand knowledge of the many discourses competing with realism for dominance during this period. Whenever possible, I pair Balzac's novel with *La Canne de M. de Balzac,* the witty, parodic novella by Delphine Gay de Girardin published in 1836, just a year after the publication of *Le Père Goriot.* Taken together, the two works foreground the questions of vision, knowledge, power, and gender that were so instrumental in establishing realism not only as a canonical literary genre but also as a dominant form of knowledge and power.

Devised as a seminar in nineteenth-century French cultural studies for undergraduates, Reading Bodies situates Balzac in the larger historical context to ask questions about the privileging of vision in postrevolutionary France. In the course, we ask how and since when vision has been considered a crucial sign of truth or a means to it; why and whose bodies have been the focus of efforts to establish truth; and at what cost. Did the privileging of vision work as a progressive, democratic force, or did it give rise to increasing anxieties about the instability of social and sexual identities and the disjunction between appearance and reality, and thus to an insistence that different bodies mattered differently?

In the syllabus, Balzac's novel comes about midway, well after the students have read pornographic pamphlets against Marie Antoinette from the 1780s and 1790s, François-René de Chateaubriand's versions of otherness in *Atala* (or *René*), photocopies of fashion magazines and beauty manuals from the Empire, and the story of racial alienation in Claire de Duras's *Ourika* and after they have studied representations of the male nude in paintings from Jacques-Louis David to Théodore Géricault.[2] By the time we get to Balzac, therefore, the students have been seeing what reading bodies has to do with the constitution of a new body politic after the Revolution, with the place of exoticism and race in French national identity, with the construction of class and gender in the rise of consumer culture, with the development of a new reading public, and with changing notions about masculinity and new representations of the male body. The shift to *Le Père Goriot* marks a key literary turning point as we move from Romantic texts, which gain their moral authority in large part from the personal narrative of exceptional, isolated individuals recounting their emotional suffering, toward realist works, in which a supposedly disinterested narrator exposes a highly material and materialist world of false appearances that baffles and bedevils a young outsider who longs to succeed in it. On all narrative levels—the characters, the narrator, the reader, and the author—Balzac's text lends itself to the overarching questions of the course about vision and bodies: Where does knowledge come from? What are its limits? Who claims to possess it? How is this knowledge secured? And at what costs?

Advanced, motivated students, I find, raise many of the pertinent points on their own and can readily identify key passages for discussion. However, study questions can help students who are new to literary analysis focus their reading, especially in the beginning of the semester. In my own preparation for the discussion I find it useful to prepare notes on the text in the form of questions—some leading, to be sure the students have understood the basics, others open-ended, to elicit genuine debate.

For the first session on *Le Père Goriot*, we focus, in particular, on the narrator. Questions to be given in advance or to be used to guide class discussion might include the following:

> What does the narrator reveal about himself directly? indirectly?
> When and where does he say "I" or "we"?
> Can or should we call the narrator male?
> If the narrator is disembodied, does this make us more or less likely to trust what he says?
> From what source does his cultural authority derive?

Does he put his own knowledge into question or set up a vantage point without blind spots? Could such a perspective exist?

Do you find what he says trustworthy, unbiased? Give specific examples.

Focusing on the narrator, discussions naturally turn toward key questions about objectivity and omniscience and about what the famous phrase "*All is true*" might mean in the context of a work of fiction (22).[3]

I ask the students to note the various enigmas in the text as they occur and how, when, and by whom they are explained, for example, the speculations and eventual revelations about Goriot and the fashionably dressed young woman who visits him (50–52, 73–77, 87). Why would a *fille* (daughter) be mistaken for a mistress or even a *fille* (prostitute)? Who is fooled by appearances and who is not? Vautrin, is, of course, a centerpiece for such discussions. From his ability to see *through* the hero, Eugène de Rastignac (160), to his knowledge about what goes on behind the scenes at all levels of society, Vautrin seems to share with the narrator a kind of omniscience. We discuss whether the ability to see through appearances to what is "real" gives Vautrin and the narrator similar moral attitudes toward the world of corruption and illusions, and we consider what difference it makes that Vautrin, unlike the narrator, is frank about his interests in "playing God" (146, 157, 218). The most dramatic scene in the novel is Vautrin's unmasking (262–69), which comes as a surprise to most of the characters but not to the narrator or to us as readers since we have been let in on the secret. How does this knowledge affect our attitudes about the characters?

Tracing the metaphors of vision in the novel, particularly in the relationship between Vautrin and Rastignac, reveals the novel's association of vision with masculinity. To get to this subject and to help the students understand its significance, I ask questions such as the following:

What do the images of uncovering, unmasking, piercing, and penetration in the text imply about the observer and about the object being observed?

What are the gender and sexual connotations of Vautrin's gaze and of Rastignac's status as transparent object (160)?

How does Rastignac react to his implicit feminization?

How are these questions tied up with presumptions about heterosexuality and masculinity?

Discussion of the final pages of the novel draws together these points at several levels to show how knowledge is figured as vision and vision, as power. Questions might include the following:

If, by the end, Rastignac learns Vautrin's lessons about using keen observation for one's own self-interest (166), does this mean that he has adopted Vautrin's moral code?

What, finally, do students make of the last scene of the novel, in which Rastignac, from a vantage point above Paris, gazes from afar at the fashionable world he wanted to penetrate?

When Rastignac grandly announces that he will take on the city as if in a duel, is this insistence on besting a phallic world at its own game the final proof of his accession to "manhood"?

And if so, to what extent is the narrator's penetrating vision, which works to keep ignorance at bay and the characters at an emotionally safe remove, gendered masculine as well?

For showing what a stance of disembodied omniscience may have to do with notions of masculinity in the France of the 1830s, I have found no other reading assignment as pedagogically effective or just plain enjoyable as Girardin's parodic spoof *La Canne de M. de Balzac.* In Girardin's novella, irony and reversals call into question gender, social, and literary hierarchies by making Balzac an explicit focus of attention rather than an omniscient figure invisible behind the scenes or a famous author lit with the halo of genius. In the novella, Balzac, far from all-knowing, learns from Tancrède Dorimont, Girardin's hero, what he does not know from personal experience: "the misfortune of being handsome" (140).[4] More important still, Tancrède's eagle-eyed gaze, indiscreet curiosity, and tenacious ambition help the hero penetrate Balzac's dirty little secret: carried in the left hand, Balzac's cane makes its bearer invisible. Thus the famous author's vaunted ability to know so much about so many different kinds of people—not only their public views or physical appearance but also what they think at home in their bathrobes (190)—is explained as a result not of his genius but of his shameless use of a magic cane. By situating Balzac and his works in a historically specific place and time but viewing them from an ironic distance, Girardin's novella foregrounds with witty panache the questions about objectivity and universality that are at the heart of discussions about realism and the canon.

The text is a perfect fit for the course Reading Bodies but could easily be incorporated into other courses in nineteenth-century French literature and culture. Reasonably short (about 140 pages) and written in a bantering tone and colloquial style, Girardin's text, unlike its canonical counterpart, is eminently readable. Though the novella features flat characters, it avoids the melodrama typical of Balzac's novels by employing its characters for comic, satiric, and even farcical effect. After heavy-handed texts like Balzac's, students are amazed and relieved to find a nineteenth-century work that uses a deft, light, "modern" touch.

One obvious focus for an initial discussion of Girardin's work is her short preface. There the author puts gender front and center by foregrounding the tight constraints on form and substance within which women writers are held. So as to forestall any mistaken assumptions, however, it is important to let students know right away what readers of the novella in the 1830s would have known about the author.[5] Instead of experiencing hardship and prejudice because of her sex, Delphine Gay de Girardin, the self-styled "Muse de la Patrie" (Sainte-Beuve, "Madame Emile" 388), not only was Balzac's equal in literary fame in the 1830s, she also enjoyed far greater social clout than did Balzac. Though both authors were of relatively modest origins, Delphine enjoyed advantages Balzac did not: her mother was Sophie Gay, the popular novelist and *salonnière*; Delphine's beauty and success in poetry brought her considerable fame early on; and her marriage in 1831 to the up-and-coming journalist and editor, Emile de Girardin, helped ensure her continuing literary and social prominence. If any woman might have been given some leeway to bend the rules of gender conformity, it would have been Delphine. Girardin's preface insists, however, that women writers are given far less latitude than men are. In other words, for Girardin, her own status as exception merely proves a larger rule.

Study questions such as the following can help students new to literary analysis identify key elements in the preface:

> The text is staged as "an interrupted preface" in which the voices in dialogue are unnamed. What are the probable identities of the voices?
> What are the names of famous contemporary male writers doing here?
> Characterize the author's tone in the preface.
> What does Balzac's simple dedication of *Le Père Goriot* seem to imply now by contrast?

In *La Canne,* one man's privilege is another's opportunity. Having found out Balzac's compromising secret, Tancrède blackmails Balzac into lending him the magic cane and quickly learns to use it for his own less than upstanding purposes. In one farcical sequence, for example, the invisible hero finds himself trying to control a sudden coughing fit as he slips into a meeting between the king and the king's advisers; later he uses the confidential information he has overheard to his financial advantage. He also employs the cane to gain access to a married lover, and then, as a chaste but assiduous voyeur, he spies on Clarisse Blandais, a young provincial poet who, his observations reveal, is as good at heart—and as in love with him—as his ego could desire.

Like *Le Père Goriot,* the novella features an ambitious young outsider who learns to make his way in a cold, cruel Paris. The following questions could guide an initial comparison of the two works:

> Are Tancrède's actions and his compromising of honesty any less or more objectionable than Rastignac's?
> What is the narrator's attitude toward the hero's moral development in each work?

> In *Le Père Goriot* Paris is described as a battlefield (111, 167), and the plot details an "elegant parricide" (326). Characterize the world Tancrède enters.

In both works, appearances are crucial. Discussion focuses on passages in *Le Père Goriot* where opportunities open up to Rastignac in part because he considers himself handsome (36–37, 61) and where he takes care, with good reason, of his appearance (208). In *La Canne,* by contrast, time and again Tancrède's good looks deny him employment, despite his marketable talents and proven skills. Although the temporary use of Balzac's magic cane gives Tancrède an entry into the political and cultural elite, he is neither privileged enough nor ambitious enough to join the ranks of those like Rastignac who, if they play the game right with a woman of fortune, can afford to be ornamental. Does a difference in social class account for Tancrède's more prosaic fate and the different treatments of the handsome heroes in the two works?

Although appearance is capital in Girardin's novella, physical description plays a minimal role. What might account for this apparent contradiction? I have the students note when, where, and for what purposes the narrator describes the physical appearance of persons or things and have students compare the lengthy description of M. Poirceau's house in disarray (149–50) with the description of the ground floor of the Maison Vauquer in Balzac (26–28).[6] I pose questions such as the following:

> Which description is more "realistic"? According to what definition of realism?
>
> What kind of reader does each work assume or construct?

We also ask whether the fantastic elements in Girardin reinforce or subvert the text's realist premises. We consider, for example, the scene in which the badly dressed Tancrède feels embarrassed—even though he is invisible—in the exclusive literary salon of Mme de D*** (231). The following questions help focus the discussion:

> Do the cane's magic properties serve or undercut a realist exposition of social mores?
>
> Similarly, does the hero's on-again, off-again invisibility offer a critique of "objective" vision?

We discuss Clarisse's mother, who remains blind to Tancrède's momentary appearances in the house, despite Clarisse's insistence that a young man keeps appearing there. We note how characters account for magical appearances and disappearances (see, e.g., 216) and ask whether the fantastic ironically undercuts traditional realism's faith in causality and claims to truth.

Another key question is whether the fantastic reinforces or calls into question the various reversals of gender commonplaces in the text. Students see right away that in Girardin's novella, the hero is a sex object, feared as though he were a Fatal Man and likened to a male Medusa (160). It may be less obvious that Girardin's text shows heterosexuality as triangulated by male homosocial desire and rivalries between men. If women are Tancrède's downfall (170), it is not because they seduce and then abandon him but rather because other men, fearing that their wives and daughters will be unable to resist Tancrède, seek to exclude him even from the world of work. Similarly, while a pretty woman at the opera simpers coquettishly, assuming that Tancrède is intently watching *her,* the reader knows that the hero has eyes only for Balzac's cane (171). "Cherchez la femme," the traditional motto of narrative causality, becomes "Cherchez la canne."

Comparing Girardin's and Balzac's works, we find that the role of the narrator is crucial. Discussion often focuses on the following questions:

What kinds of judgments or generalizations do the narrators permit themselves?
Do they adopt a superior tone toward the characters?
If so, on the basis of what knowledge or experience?
Is the long paragraph on Madame Malvina Thélissier, "une bonne petite femme" (Girardin 204), sympathetic or hostile, feminist or misogynist?
How do the two works represent the relation between vanity and gender?

To answer this last question, we look at the passage in *Le Père Goriot* where the narrator details Rastignac's new vanity (162) along with the passage in *La Canne* where vanity is defined as a wholly human and even animal trait rather than as a uniquely feminine foible (240) and those on the unfortunately named M. Legrand, which explicitly skewer male vanity (157).

Questions like the following help focus a comparison of the narrators in the two novels:

Does the irony of Girardin's narrator distinguish her from Balzac's or does it unite the two narrators?
What are the narrators' class assumptions and identifications—or lack thereof?
Is Girardin's narrator more or less disembodied than Balzac's? Does the narrator claim a more or less universal point of view?
What should we think when Girardin's narrator includes herself in a description of what women are like when they are in love (223)?
Does Girardin's preface tend to make us identify the narrative voice with the author? What, if anything, identifies the narrator in Balzac as male?

No discussion of the two works would be complete without considering their very different conclusions. Rastignac, his eyes open to the corruption around him, has learned by the end of the novel how to justify his own ambitious collusion in it: "And in his first act of defiance to Society, Rastignac went to dine with Madame de Nucingen" (367). In *La Canne de M. de Balzac,* by contrast, the hero and heroine choose—though for far less desperate reasons—the dramatic option taken by Mme de Beauséant in Balzac's novel: a decisive escape from Paris and all that is illusory and disillusioning about the city. We discuss whether this is supposed to be a happy ending.

Given the milieu described in the novella, the heroine's characterization as a talented young poet, the part played by extraordinary beauty, and the prominent place given to the friends and literary men and women in Girardin's circle, the author is clearly flirting with the possibility of being identified with the heroine. However, whereas Girardin seems to have had the best of both worlds in her own life, her youthful and less-talented provincial heroine chooses the happiness promised by marriage over the promise of literary glory in the big city. A final discussion of the novel explicitly examines the text in the light of its author's gender. I ask questions like the following:

What is the moral of the novella? What are its views on poetry, status, success, and celebrity, especially for women?

Given Girardin's own fame as a poet, how can we understand the prominent place accorded in the novella to her friend, Lamartine, and to her female contemporaries and rivals: Amable Tastu, Marceline Desbordes-Valmore, and Elise Mercoeur?

Is Girardin attempting to make a place for women like herself in a more egalitarian canon? If so, why choose as a heroine a woman poet who decides against pursuing her literary ambitions?

Reading Girardin's *La Canne de M. de Balzac* after Balzac's *Le Père Goriot,* students usually understand immediately how Girardin's work reverses gender truisms and, by making visible the invisible gaze as well as the faith in a penetrating vision that founds Balzac's novel, how the novella questions the social privileges and male identity such a vision implies. However, a key question we debate in class is whether featuring Balzac in the novella works as a tribute and further enhancement of his considerable reputation in 1836, as a barbed put-down, as a form of friendly teasing, or as a biting critique. When the source of Balzac's secret power—his famous cane—is described as ridiculous, oversized, monstrous, ugly, and cumbersome (174), what are the implications? Students are quick to get the phallic reference, especially in the light of Girardin's ironic preface to the novel, which identifies disembodiment, invisibility, and the power to go anywhere and to write about anything and everything as privileges—like brandishing a cane—given only to men of a certain social standing, not to women of whatever class.[7] However, it is important to remind students that, in the novel, the magic cane is easily mistaken for other, everyday canes. It is lost, stolen, misplaced, and exchanged almost as often as it is used as a tool for illegal or immoral entry. In other words, the power the cane represents can go wildly out of its bearer's control. Asking questions like the following can help forestall simplistic understandings of the cane and generate discussions about its larger significance:

> What should we make of the cane's farcical transferability and its use by a child, a gentleman, a servant, and the police?
>
> Why does the narrator liken the magic cane to one of those newfangled marvels, like trains and binoculars, that will soon be within everyone's reach (189)?
>
> Does this idea denaturalize even further men's "natural" association with privileged knowledge and show technological progress as a democratizing force? Or would this marvel in fact be available only to the male elite who could afford it?
>
> Finally, does the obvious focus on gender in the novel tend to obscure or lay bare inequities of wealth and social class?

By the end of Reading Bodies, students have seen that Balzac's text helped fashion discourses on society, family, and morality that are still familiar today and that have largely overshadowed some of the alternative literary, political, and social values and discourses from the nineteenth century, like those of Girardin. Revealing literary studies as dynamic, not inert, this kind of contextualized pedagogical approach actively involves the students in current debates about the texts that can and should figure in their education. Reading *Le Père Goriot* with *La Canne de M. de Balzac,* they learn not only what a canon is but also what is missing when we fail to read its others.

NOTES

[1]Similar results could be achieved by comparing a Balzac story or novel, such as *Le Colonel Chabert,* with its film adaptations. In any case, when teaching the novel in French, I recommend providing students right away with a sheet on film vocabulary for use in this assignment.

[2]The rest of the syllabus has included Grandville's caricatural "Les Animaux," Charles Baudelaire's "Peintre de la vie moderne," selections from *Le Spleen de Paris,* Barbey d'Aurevilly's writings on the dandy, a history of the scandal caused by Edouard Manet's *Olympia*, Gustave Flaubert's correspondence from Egypt, Emile Zola's *Germinal,* Rachilde's *Monsieur Vénus,* and documents related to the Dreyfus Affair.

[3]All page references are to the French text in the Gallimard Folio edition. All translations are mine.

[4]This lesson not only goes against received wisdom but also, when compared with the moral of Girardin's well-known poem about how lucky it is to be beautiful, "Le Bonheur d'être belle," shows up the difference gender makes.

[5]I find Kelly's short summary of Girardin's life and work helpful ("Delphine Gay de

Girardin"). For information on Girardin and women writers of the time, see Cohen; Ezdinli; Morgan; Schor; and Waller, *Male Malady*.

[6] The students find that physical description occurs in Girardin's novella only when such description is the main key to the story (reactions to Tancrède's beauty), to a character (Mme Poirceau's lack of beauty [155–56]), or to social commentary (remarks on Mme Poirceau's reliance on fashion [155]) or when the object, person, or setting is out of the ordinary (the magical but monstrous cane itself [171]).

[7] For further discussion of the disembodied observer, I suggest assigning some of Girardin's "Courrier de Paris" columns for *La Presse* (1836–48), in which she uses an aristocratic male pseudonym and persona, the vicomte de Launay (*Lettres*). See also Waller, "Disembodiment."

Between Bodies and Texts: A Psychoanalytic Reading of *Le Père Goriot*

Dorothy Kelly

Balzac's texts, their obsession with gender, paternal authority, and decapitation, provide fertile grounds for psychoanalytic readings. They also, in their exploration of the changes wrought by the Revolution, bring to the fore questions of meaning, language, and identity. In response to these aspects of Balzac's themes, my approach to teaching *Le Père Goriot* combines a psychoanalytic reading of the text with a deconstructionist questioning of language.

The way in which psychoanalysis is introduced in a class is an important and delicate matter. If the ground is first prepared through a close reading of the text and an analysis of the major problematics of the work, the psychoanalytic concepts can be introduced somewhat later as a way of enriching understanding of these textual problematics. I have found that students are more convinced of the value of a psychoanalytic reading when psychoanalysis is set up not as some kind of grid through which one reads the text but rather as a meaningful structure that parallels and illuminates our understanding of the already existing and identifiable structures of the text. When teaching *Le Père Goriot,* I assign two psychoanalytic readings. I find that the summaries in *The Language of Psychoanalysis* of the Oedipus and castration complexes are helpful for students (Laplanche and Pontalis 56–59, 282–87). Freud's literary article "The Uncanny" points students in the direction of thinking symbolically about psychoanalytic images. However, I wait to assign these readings until we have had the opportunity to become familiar with Goriot's world.

Thus we begin with a close reading of the opening pages of the novel and use this textual introduction to identify significant themes. The first paragraph is read sentence by sentence, and I invite students to make comments and offer interpretations as we go. We note that the text begins with a woman who has a bourgeois name but who was born "de Conflans" (21; 27). The combination of noble and bourgeois names leads us to identify the first category of themes: the notion of class mobility in the nineteenth century and the reverberations of the Revolution, particularly concerning human identity. The blurring of identity is represented by a word that appears in this first sentence; "entre" 'between' (21; 27). Just as the pension is between the Latin Quarter and the faubourg Saint-Marceau, so Mme Vauquer is between a noble and a bourgeoise. I jump ahead here to parts of the novel students have not yet read to alert them to the fact that the text to come is centered on a character, Rastignac, who must choose between two different paths though he would like to remain on the fence, between, *entre*, the two worlds.

There are several other important themes that make their appearance in these opening pages, the first being the observation—as well as the transgression—of the codes, rules, and laws of social interaction. We learn that there is a coded tradition of this pension: its bourgeois respectability, its rules governing who can live there. However, at the beginning of this story, the long-held tradition disallowing young women has been broken. The code-breaking has to do with gender, yet, since this is such a minor detail, I ask the students if they have noted other bizarre details about gender identity early in the text; usually someone will bring up the "Pension bourgeoise des deux sexes et autres" '*Lodgings for Ladies and Gentlemen, etc.*' (24; 29) for corroboration.

Finally, we note that the story will be centered on a secret, a secret that has to do with a father: "les secrètes infortunes du père Goriot" 'the secret sorrows of old Goriot' (22; 28). I introduce the notion of the *roman d'éducation* and discuss how Rastignac's attempts to uncover secrets are linked to his apprenticeship in the workings of social codes. As Rastignac attempts to learn the secrets both of Goriot and of the women to whom he is drawn, he discovers that secrets and codes lead back to family origins.

It is worthwhile to note at this point that Goriot's secret is described as "épouvantable" 'appalling' (31; 35) and to allow the students to try to guess what horrifying mystery might be related to coded behavior and fathers (their guesses can be very pertinent: incest, parricide [actually mentioned on 34; 37]). Horrible family secrets, fathers, gender, codes and code breaking, betweenness—we review all these themes, and I ask the students if they can tell me the tale of Oedipus, that other story of mysterious paternity and crime. The class can come up with the basic components of the story, which will be important for us in future discussions: killing the father, incest, the sphinx and the riddle, searching for truth and one's origins, being blinded as punishment for incest, codes and laws of human social behavior. I leave the discussion of Freud for the future.

For the next class, I ask students to note the appearance of the word "entre" 'between' in the text and to think about how the concept of betweenness might be important. The word appears a number of times early on (21, 23 [twice], 25, 32; 27, 28 [once], 30, 35) and, significantly, on the last page of the text. The insistent repetition of this word points to its importance and highlights the crucial role of space and, relatedly, of milieu in Balzac. Indeed, the word *entre* not only identifies space as significant (the word is most often used to position an object in the social space of the city) but also introduces the problem of spatial limits—the boundaries between things. These two issues, the influence of the environment and the problem of boundaries, are explored in our first group project, a close reading of the description of the pension Vauquer.

I have found that group work gives students the opportunity to practice their French in smaller, less intimidating circumstances; that students can come up with their own pertinent interpretations when given specific and meaningful tasks; and that the variety of activities breaks up the sometimes monotonous class hour. In groups of three or four, students work on specific questions or parts of the text and then present their findings to the class as a whole. For the first group project, I divide the description of the pension and the introductory pages into a number of sections and ask each group to discuss anything they find important as well as to look for two main themes: first, images of the influence of the environment on the characters; second, images of contagion that relate to permeable boundaries and that thus link fear to the *entre.*

We find, of course, the famous connection between the pension and Mme Vauquer, which we discuss in detail. We also find that the symbiotic exchange between Mme Vauquer and her pension is described as a kind of contagious illness related to crossing borders: "L'embonpoint blafard de cette petite femme est le produit de cette vie, comme le typhus est la conséquence des exhalaisons d'un hôpital" 'The unwholesome plumpness of this little woman is a product of the life she lives here, by the same process that breeds typhoid fever from the noxious vapours of a hospital' (29; 33). The numerous other allusions to illness, contaminated air, contagion, and injury (24, 28, 84; 29, 32, 78) add weight to the image of the danger of contamination brought about by crossing borders, which we discuss as the danger to the self, perhaps the threat of loss of identity, health, meaning, or life.

We proceed next to a group project on Rastignac's social education and his discovery of the two paths between which he must choose: the old world symbolized by Goriot's values and a new world symbolized by Vautrin's. I divide the students into four groups. Group 1 compares Goriot as father with Vautrin as father. Students are asked to summarize Goriot's family situation and to discuss how the family is based on the father's name and on the body, on the physical continuation of the family through blood. Against this "natural" idea of the family, students are asked to study in detail Vautrin's "artificial" paternity in three main scenes (145, 216, 217; 124, 181, 182; see Beizer 125–27; Petrey 90). I also ask students to consider Vautrin's plans to buy slaves in America, slaves that Vautrin considers his "enfants tout venus" 'children ready-made' (154; 131).

Group 2 explores a related theme, that of real emotion as opposed to (artificial) financial liaisons (what Suck analyzes as the "transition from a language of sentiments to one of economic value" [33]). Students first look at examples of real love (Mme de Beauséant, the duchesse de Langeais) (172, 334; 145, 277), then contrast these natural feelings with Ajuda-Pinto's possible financial reasons for marrying Rochefide (108; 97). They also study the metaphor of the pension Vauquer, which is a family based not on natural blood ties but rather on one's artificial, financial status (31–32; 35). Here we note that Vautrin's nickname for Mme Vauquer, "maman," is particularly apt.

Group 3 explores the most basic theme, that of the law. Vautrin's well-known words summarize the two choices offered to Rastignac: "ou une stupide obéissance ou la révolte" 'stupid obedience or revolt' (147; 125). Students study first the side of the law, "obéissance," considering the figure of the police as enforcers of the law of the king (262; 218), and, most important, Goriot's linking of the law with natural paternity (345–46; 286). It is interesting to note in this context that Vautrin calls the police officer "père l'empoigneur" (266; translated in English as "old catch-'em-alive-o" [222] without the use of the term *father*).

Opposed to the law and the state, on the side of "la révolte," is Vautrin, and there are many rich passages to discuss (37–39, 224–25, 250–51, 265–68; 39–41, 187–88, 208–09, 221–23). We note how Vautrin creates a kind of alternative society with its own laws and codes, indeed, how he is a kind of government leader ("leur Bonaparte" 'their Napoleon' [250; 208]).

Group 4 discusses two different conceptions of language in the text. First there is what I outline to the students as a kind of common understanding: that language has a tie to the real, to reality. Words name things; the word *father* names a person who has a real physical tie, that of blood, to his children. As the previous groups have shown, this name of the father is, according to Goriot, also linked to the law and particularly to God (351; 291).

The most interesting link in the novel between fathers and this understanding of the materiality of meaning is in the discussion of the "reading" science of phrenology: Bianchon can read Goriot's body to learn that Goriot is a true father (121; 108), and Mlle Michonneau has the bumps of a Judas (81; 75). Significantly, Vautrin's true nature is linked to undressing the physical body: the police ask Vautrin to disrobe so that they can check for the letters that brand him a criminal. There is a sense that meaning is written on reality and can be deciphered if one knows how to read: "le succès est écrit sur votre beau front" 'success is written on that noble forehead of yours' (279; 233).

The contrary conception of language is outlined by Vautrin. I ask students first to decipher Vautrin's description of law and meaning:

> Il n'y a pas de principes, il n'y a que des événements; il n'y a pas de lois, il n'y a que des circonstances: l'homme supérieur épouse les événements et les circonstances pour les conduire. S'il y avait des principes et des lois fixes, les peuples n'en changeraient pas comme nous changeons de chemises. [. . .] L'on ne trouve pas dans les tribunaux trois juges qui aient le même avis sur un article de la loi. (158)
>
> There are no such things as principles, there are only events; there are no laws, there are only circumstances: the man who is wiser than his fellows accepts events and circumstances in order to turn them to his own ends. If there were fixed principles and laws nations would not change them as easily as we change our shirts. [. . .] There are not three judges in the law-courts with the same opinion about a point of law. (134–35)

Since this is a difficult passage for students, I ask them to think about whether or not Vautrin views meaning as tied to the real. For instance, does the "point of law" that the three judges consider have a real, physical, verifiable meaning? Given that, for Vautrin, there is no grounding of meaning, how does meaning come about?

Here, I try to get students to see that Vautrin believes that meaning is *made* by "the wiser man" ("l'homme supérieur"). To bring this point home, I ask the students to read two more passages. In the first, Vautrin pretends to read Victorine's palm (to read the real as in phrenology) but in fact parodies that kind of reading by *authoring* what he reads in her palm; he has set up the murder of her brother so she will be rich (247; 206).

Thus Vautrin views meaning as something that is made by humankind; laws, principles—all are social agreements constructed by humankind alone, not handed down from the mountain by God or grounded in some real link to the world (see Petrey 83–122). In fact, Vautrin is like a kind of god who controls destiny (157; 134). As he says of the monarchy that supposedly ruled by divine right, kings "se sacrent rois eux-mêmes" 'are crowned kings by their own hands' (217; 182). Finally, we consider his rejection of Collin, the paternal heritage linked to his real father, in favor of his own, artificially created names.

At the end of these four group discussions, we try to summarize the general import of our observations. First, we note that the law supports traditional family structures, in which natural fathers have certain rights and in which law and meaning are grounded in real and verifiable things. Second, we note that this text posits Vautrin as a kind of revolutionary counterpoint to that law, to natural paternity, and to any meaning preexisting humankind's production of meaning. It is important to discuss that the narrative does not decide for us which conception of language and meaning should prevail. Here again, a reminder of the text's betweenness can be fruitful. And it is here where psychoanalysis can help us to negotiate the text's contradictions and allow us to view the text in a new way.

At this point, I ask the students to rethink Goriot's paternity and give them several passages (read in groups) that describe his fatherhood in terms of sexual love: "J'ai bien expié le péché de les trop aimer. [. . .] Mes filles, c'était mon vice à moi; elles étaient mes maîtresses, enfin tout!" 'I have expiated to the full the sin of loving them too much. [. . .] They were my own particular vice; they took the place another man fills with his mistresses, that's the whole story!' (345; 286; see also 127–28, 162, 283; 113, 137, 236). We also look at descriptions of Goriot's excessive pleasure in his daughters (276, 278–83; 230, 231–36). One can end this discussion with the wonderful irony that the *pensionnaires* first think that the women who visit Goriot are his lovers: ultimately the text shows us that the women are.

Now students read Laplanche and Pontalis on the Oedipus and castration complexes and Freud's essay "The Uncanny." We discuss these essays briefly and pay particular attention to the symbols of castration mentioned by Freud: body parts detached and eyes plucked out. I ask students to consider Goriot's excessive and admittedly incestuous love for his daughters and to think of the prohibition against incest not narrowly—as prohibiting incest between son and mother—but rather as a law of civilized society. Discussion can center on attempted definitions of humankind as the only species with a generalized system of law prohibiting certain sexual encounters and on how this symbolic system of law, organized through language and custom and opposed to nature and instinct, can be seen as one of the defining characteristics of human society. The prohibition against incest is the law of humanity.

However, when we then look at the link the text establishes between Goriot and the law, there appears to be a kind of contradiction. What does the coupling of the breaking of the prohibition against incest with Goriot as representative of the law mean? What does this say about the betweenness of the text?

It is now time to ask the students to think about the reasons why Goriot became rich and thus was able to shower his daughters with money. Here we turn to the duchesse de Langeais's sketch of Goriot's life: "Eh bien! ce Loriot, qui vendait du blé aux coupeurs de têtes, n'a eu qu'une passion. Il adore, dit-on, ses filles" 'Well, this Loriot who sold corn to the cut-throats had only one passion, so they say: he adored his daughters' (113; 101; the English version loses most of the reference to the Revolution). After having read Freud on the uncanny, students immediately see the significance of severed heads, particularly in this sentence, in which the guillotine of the Revolution appears alongside Goriot's excessive love for his daughters (Petrey). The link between symbols of castration, the loss of law and king, and incestuous love is established.

A general discussion of the Revolution can set up a parallel between the loss of the law in terms of the beheading of the king/father of France and the resulting lawlessness Balzac sees in French society. Goriot, linked with the beheaders, gains his fortune, as do many other Balzacian characters, with a symbolic oedipal crime (Taillefer is especially interesting in this respect because it is assumed that he got his fortune by beheading a stranger at an inn). Therefore, Goriot is always already on the side of lawlessness. If Goriot represents paternity for Rastignac, then old notions of paternity do indeed disappear in this novel, along with the grounding of law in the real (362–63; 301). The empty carriages that follow Goriot's casket seem like the empty signifiers of the old paternal system (Beizer 139).

To emphasize this point, I give student groups several passages that describe what one could term Goriot's oedipal punishment of beheading and that contain images of castration. The first group looks at Goriot's malady of the head (one can play here with his "folie," too). On his deathbed, Goriot suffers from the sensation that his head is burning and being cut, and he wants it cut off (295, 298, 302, 310, 340, 341, 345, 349; 245 [the English leaves out reference to the head], 248, 251, 257, 281, 282, 286, 289).

The second group can analyze images of fatherhood connected with piercing and cutting bodies: "Madame Vauquer [. . .] en mettant en doute sa paternité, le père Goriot tressaillit comme si son hôtesse l'eût piqué avec un fer" 'when Madame Vauquer [spoke] to him banteringly, implying doubt of his paternal relationship, [. . .] Goriot winced as if she had pricked him with a sword-point' (54; 53–54); Goriot is a "vieux rat sans queue" 'tail-less old rat' (98; 88); Poiret (linked possibly with parricides) has a "culotte presque vide" 'breeches much too big for his shrunken thighs' (33; 37; again the English loses a bit of bite);[1] the word *père* seems to burn Restaud's hand (94; 86).

The third group can look at the image of damaged eyes (an image that should be linked to Freud's essay). Goriot suffers from sick eyes (42–43, 54; 44, 53); his sick eyes are linked to sex (53; 53); he would let his daughters pluck out his eyes (348; 288); Victorine's father is blind to his daughter (36; 39); and, finally, Michonneau, who has inherited a man's money at the expense of his children, has tired eyes (32–33; 36). At the end of this discussion, students are usually intrigued by the parallels between Freud's analyses and Balzac's metaphors.

We next turn to a consideration of how the loss of paternity affects identity. In simple terms, one's proper, family name no longer has meaning, and identity is not grounded in blood and birth. This drift of identity can be studied by three groups looking at three sorts of images.

First, fathers proliferate in this text, but they are never pure (Beizer 132–38). Whether they are incestuous fathers like Goriot; fathers who, like Taillefer, have given up their paternal roles; newly constructed, artificial fathers like papa Vautrin (147, 155, 241; 126, 132, 201); or the police as "père l'empoigneur" (266; 222; the English "old catch-'em-alive-o" doesn't use the term *father*), and even Rastignac (349; 289), there seem to be too many papas. But the most interesting in terms of the cultural construction of identity is the tailor/father: "Eugène rencontra dans le sien [son tailleur] un homme qui avait compris la paternité de son commerce, et qui se considérait comme un trait d'union entre le présent et l'avenir des jeunes gens [. . .]" 'In his tailor Eugène met a man who understood the paternal obligations of his office, and considered himself as a connecting link between a young man's present and his future [. . .]' (138–39 [note the "entre"]; 119). The tailor as father symbolizes the fact that in this new era, the social constructions sewn together by others determine one's identity (Petrey).

Second, gender identity, particularly Rastignac's, is questioned often. Rastignac is "comme une jeune fille" 'like a girl' (147; 126; see also 190, 205–06, 215, 244; 160, 172, 180, 203) or a "maîtresse" 'sweetheart' (274; 228), and in one of Balzac's strangest metaphors, he has the same ardor as "l'impatient calice d'un dattier femelle pour les fécondantes poussières de son hyménée" 'the flowers of the date-palm to receive the fertilizing pollen' (207; 174; the English completely misses the gendered reference here).

The third group of images questioning identity involves monstrosity. Monsters are creatures that blur the distinctions between natural and unnatural, between one animal and another. In this text, monsters are those who break laws and cross boundaries: the Maison Vauquer, in which the father's secret resides and which is itself crossed with Mme Vauquer, is monstrous (34–35; 38); Taillefer (71; 67); his son (248; 206); Rastignac as family money milker (122; 109); monsieur de Restaud (306, 322; 254, 267); de Marsay (212; 178; in the English translation he is merely "inhuman");[2] and Anastasie (309;

256; in the English translation she is a "horrid unnatural creature")—all are monstrous in their untraditional family dealings.

More particularly, the sphinx as monster (a combination of animal and human) arises in connection with Vautrin numerous times (142, 167, 213; 122, 141, 179). In this text of oedipal anxieties, Vautrin as the sphinx with the knowledge is particularly apt. Furthermore, Vautrin's ambiguous sexuality, his going against the law of heterosexuality (71, 147, 226, 243, 246; 67, 125, 189, 202, 205), can be brought in as another meaning of the sphinx (Beizer). Most significant, the word that introduces Vautrin at the beginning of the story is "Entre" 'Between' (37; 39).

We conclude our discussion of the novel with an analysis of how the text views the process of meaning. Goriot's death and his lawlessness seem to call into question the grounding of meaning in God, the world, or things: a father's blood relation no longer defines anything. In fact, what has taken the place of blood is money: significantly, a despairing Goriot asks if "on ne peut donc rien faire de son sang" 'there [is] nothing a man can earn with his flesh and blood' (311; 258). The old ideas of meaning based on the real—on real blood and real emotion—are false and can no longer exist (339; 281). The metaphor of the pension Vauquer, of the family based on money, is truly the sense of this book.

Money has become the universal, floating signifier that can be transformed into anything else: fatherhood is really not the blood that one passes on to one's offspring but the money that is transferred. Once one has no more money to give, one is no longer a father, as Goriot says (311; 258). Money can be equated with just about anything in this text: love (209; 175; in English "fortune" becomes "success"), religion (366; 303), God (204; 171), respect (344; 285), daughters (343; 284), virtue (118; 106; in English "fortune" is once again "success"). Money is even a metaphor for one's appearance: "des faces froides, dures, effacées comme celles des écus démonétisés [. . .]" 'their cold, hard faces were worn, like those on coins withdrawn from circulation [. . .]' (32; 36). Money is a kind of universal shuttle that turns everything into something else; that erases the borders between entities; and that causes, perhaps, that fear of contagion shown in the early pages of the novel.

Goriot's physical and social identity change as he becomes poorer (53–54; 52–53), as his daughters literally sap his paternal being. In a text in which the power of the paternal signifier is thus lost, the phallic power of money appears in an amazing Balzacian metaphor: "A l'instant où l'argent se glisse dans la poche d'un étudiant, il se dresse en lui-même une colonne fantastique sur laquelle il s'appuie" 'Immediately money slides into a student's pocket he feels, in fancy, a pillar rise within him to give him moral support' (139; 119; see Beizer 131; Petrey 96). And Vautrin, the one who knows how to manipulate this new order, describes his own phallic power: "Poussons chacun nos pointes! La mienne est en fer et ne mollit jamais, hé, hé!" 'We may both carry our point—mine is cold steel, and I never yield it, ha! ha!' (218; 183; the English lacks any hints of phallic hardness).

If it seemed that one could read Vautrin's identity as a criminal by reading the letters written physically on his body, if it seems that meaning is anchored in the real, this text shows us that it is humankind that writes the letters on Vautrin, it is humankind that makes the environment that shapes Mme Vauquer and her pension, it is humankind that makes the culture that creates Goriot's paternal "bosse," his phrenological "bump" (121, 108). Meaning comes not from the vertical link between word and reality but from the horizontal linking of signifiers. Rastignac learns by comparing, by reading differences: "*Entre* le boudoir bleu de madame de Restaud et le salon rose de madame de Beauséant" '*Between* Madame de Restaud's blue boudoir and the pink drawing-room of Madame de Beauséant' (105–06; 95; my emphasis; see Prendergast, *Balzac* 74).

One can end the discussion of the novel with the observation of the play of signifiers in this text, which involve, in the most significant cases, semes that relate to gold and value. There is first the wordplay based on transformations of the word for gold, *or*, in the badinage of the Vauquer dinner table: "C*or*" 'Corn' (82–83; 76–77). More important, the names of many of the main characters in the novel have some link either to value or to gold: *Vau*trin, *Vau*quer, G*or*iot, Vict*or*ine. We can interpret this wordplay by affirming that if meaning is no longer grounded in the real, it is grounded in money as signifier. Identity is no longer linked to a body but is rather a product of an exchange between socially contextualized signifiers.

NOTES

[1]Here the link with Zambinella is interesting. Zambinella, the castrato in *Sarrasine,* is described with the same image of empty breeches: "Il portait une culotte de soie noire, qui flottait autour de ses cuisses décharnées en décrivant des plis comme une voile abattue" 'He wore black silk breeches, which floated around his shrunken thighs in folds like a lowered sail' (23; trans. mine).

[2]De Marsay also has an ambiguous gender identity in *La Fille aux yeux d'or.* See Kelly, *Glances* 40–52.

A Queer Theory Approach: Gender and Genre in *Old Goriot*

Lawrence R. Schehr

In this essay, I concentrate on how homosexuality, and specifically that of the character Vautrin, is encoded in Balzac's novel. While elsewhere in this volume Michael Lucey discusses the sociological structure of the family narrative against which homosexuality is set, I take my cues from the narratological aspects of the novel and from the semiotic framework in which homosexuality is articulated. In particular, I examine how homosexuality is literally inscribed in the work.

But an immediate caveat is in order, given that this volume is found in the Approaches to Teaching series. While all approaches to a literary work may be considered polemical, with this approach there is no neutrality or safe haven. To teach *Old Goriot* using gay and lesbian theory is to introduce students to a radical rethinking of the ideas of gender and sexuality as these ideas relate to narrative. Since the field is somewhat controversial, such an approach also means that an instructor needs to engage the students and the texts while realizing that there may exist prejudicial barriers to understanding.

How then to proceed, if students have barriers to understanding? One way is to use their resistance to reading, to a textuality that they may not immediately appreciate. The instructor can use the construction of Vautrin's character to show that Vautrin is not reducible merely to an outlaw homosexual. Vautrin has great personal talents and physical strengths, so the inscription of Vautrin's homosexuality becomes one value among many in a more or less continuous sign system that includes all sorts of characteristics. Another way to proceed, if some students balk, for moral reasons, at the representation of a homosexual character, is to point out the ways in which various other characters react to the revelation or realization of Vautrin's sexuality. Finally, it is clear that a historical context helps students understand. Balzac describes city life in a modern world, but that world is distinct from our own; by stressing the development of each individual in a rapidly modernizing cityscape, the instructor may use these differences between past and present to explore the differences between students' perceptions of public and private matters and those of the characters. In this way, any initial prejudice toward Vautrin may be framed in a literary and historical context and moved away from discussions of morality.

While moving the discussion toward literary considerations, the instructor can use sympathetic points of view offered by students to create a climate in which homosexuality does not appear entirely as an aberration. In each classroom there will undoubtedly be a spectrum of political and moral positions that can be explored as a way of informing reader subjectivity. That is to say, students need to realize that their personal stances are reflected in the way they read. By talking about the role of subjectivity in reading, especially in the light of reading one of the first realist novels, the instructor simultaneously illuminates some of the subjective positions taken in the narrative itself.

A word about homosexuality in Balzac's *La Comédie humaine*. Whether it exists or not, I do not yet know; and I know even less what form that existence might take. Let us hypothetically assume that it does not exist, for, according to some, like David Halperin, homosexuality per se was not to be invented for another quarter to half century. What then do we make of sodomitic characters such as Vautrin; lesbian or bisexual figures such as the girl with the golden eyes; homoerotic subjects like Lucien de Rubempré, Vautrin's catamite in *Splendeurs et misères*; and homosocial beings such as Pons (Berthier; Lucey)? Add to these characters the sexual monsters and mysteries, cynosures and teratological formations, such as the alternately male and female angel Séraphîta and the castrated Zambinella in *Sarrasine*. At least some of these figures, notably Vautrin and Lucien, far exceed the position allotted by social constructivism to the sodomite, a creature who commits a heinous act but whose individual character is not yet that of a homosexual. Indeed, within the fictional world of Balzac's creation, it is easier to assume that homosexuality exists as a separate category, but again, this is only a hypothesis. The whole spectrum of what we now call homosexual and bisexual behavior, be it active or latent, would then fit neatly into a category with which we can feel comfortable.

The question of homosexuality in Balzac begs the larger one that includes two opposing positions in the queer theory debate. One position sees homosexuality as an eternal, transhistorical, essentialist inscription of a same-sex desire. Vautrin would be considered one of a long line of men loving other men, regardless of whether this love is actualized or transformed into a sexual act; in *Old Goriot,* of course, actualization does not occur. Indeed, it is essential to Vautrin that Rastignac remain straight and succeed in heterosexual society. Vautrin is cast as the classic noble pederast, one who loves a younger man and is eager for the young man's success.[1] The other side of the queer theory debate opposes essentialism with what is known as social constructivism. Michel Foucault and Halperin have argued that, because the channeling of desire into certain categories is determined by social organization, it is inappropriate to argue that a person (or character) who lived before the late nineteenth century was homosexual, for the word itself did not exist before the 1860s. Foucault's argument is generous: he sees the early nineteenth century as the period in which what jurisprudence has called "sodomy"—no longer an isolated act—began to be associated with an individual's psychology, existence, social surroundings, and being. Halperin asks us to consider that homosexuality has existed only for about a century: before it had a name, it just did not exist as a concept. The rhetoric of this debate has taken various forms over the years; the social constructivist and transhistorical positions can even be seen in nature-versus-nurture debates: Is homosexuality inborn, or is it learned?

I do not propose solving the debate here and now. But I do think there is a third position, one that synthesizes the other two and that is ultimately far more germane to the novel. While Balzac clearly believes that there is some inborn proclivity to specific sexual behavior, the expression of that behavior is partly determined by social constructs. I would thus propose that Balzac was undoubtedly an essentialist on this matter and that equally undoubtedly he conceived of his strong homosexual characters, like Vautrin, as characters and not just as a set of sodomitic behaviors detached from a persona.

As Gerald Storzer remarks, for Balzac, "natural sexuality—sexuality experienced outside the limitations and repressions fostered by the social order—is the only source of authentic being" (188). At the same time, in Balzac's work, there is a semiotic plane to this being, given his belief and repeated demonstration that naming somehow relates to essence. More pointedly, Balzac presents his readers with the developing image of the homosexual individual, the individual as homosexual in modern society, the social construction that parallels our own. In *Old Goriot,* Balzac shows the modern homosexual evolving as an individual in whom the essentialist and social constructivist models coalesce: Balzac's homosexual characters believe themselves to be individuals. By giving us Vautrin's various incarnations, Balzac helps to prepare for the naming of the homosexual individual fifty years later.

The Vautrin narrative is one of the major arteries of *La Comédie humaine.* His story moves him from a space in which he is considered an arch criminal to, in his last incarnation, the heart of Paris: not as a member of its high society but as the head of the secret police. In part, this movement is a measure of Balzac's cynicism and disgust with the world of Louis Philippe and the bourgeois rewriting of Paris. It is also a means of including several kinds of social and societal outlaws, of which the homosexual is not the most dangerous variety.[2] Vautrin is a metonymy of the changing public space of narrative, a space that moves from a physical insistence in which he and the Maison Vauquer are equally readable (in their own fashion) through a world of misreading in *Lost Illusions* and, finally, to the ironic apotheosis of the scarcely read, barely perceivable traces of an act in which, as the head of the secret police, he operates by clues, bits of information, signs that are far from full speech acts, wispy indices of some hidden truth. Vautrin is endlessly about to become the purloined letter as well as all its possessors and readers. Omnipresent and undecipherable, he remains the quintessential figure of the homosexual in society: invisible insofar as he is not named but visible insofar as he is indicated through signs.

Reading *Old Goriot* from this perspective means entertaining a thorough analysis of the development of the character of Vautrin and his relationships with other characters. The arch criminal Vautrin is simply and astonishingly one of the first major characters in realist narrative whose homosexuality is visible. How does Balzac express Vautrin's sexuality? In *Rendering French Realism,* I have considered the point of unveiling Vautrin for who and what he is in the scene in which Mlle Michonneau, having drugged Vautrin, undresses him, slaps his back, and in so doing reveals the branding that marks him explicitly as an escaped prisoner (Schehr 91-104). This unveiling also marks him implicitly as the homosexual victim of a society whose henchman is the conveniently unsexed Mlle Michonneau. Exposing Vautrin makes the homosexual the property of the state, a public figure with no right to privacy, no right to control his own body; he is there for all to read.

But here let us examine what happens in the exposition of the novel. Balzac is participating in the construction of a set of words, phrases, and half sentences for something or someone who clearly exists but who is not yet named: the homosexual. This novelist offers the reader a logosphere, a linguistic space and a space for representation, in which homosexuality plays a part. Balzac constructs Vautrin's homosexuality obliquely. It is not so much the love that dare not speak its name but the love that *cannot* speak its name. It has no words; it has no language of its own. Balzac writes a voice for that silence.

In the novel's exposition, that voicing begins emblematically, with a set of double signs that tell us that we are going to read something for which we have no name. Our approach to the boardinghouse is illuminated by a literal sign that announces who the residents of the house may be: "Pension bourgeoise des deux sexes et autres" '*Lodgings for Ladies and Gentlemen, etc.*' (24; 29).[3] It is clear which sexes—male and female—these "deux sexes" ("two sexes") are, but the word "autres" ("others") remains a mystery. These others will first seem to be those gathered heterogeneously in a catchall category of misfits: unmarried men and women of various sorts; people of dubious character; people who are not yet, are no longer, or never were members of the set of reproducers of society. This group includes the horrible Mlle Michonneau, the character who will ultimately serve as Judas to Vautrin. Emblematically, Mlle Michonneau is no longer a woman; the narrator asks the rhetorical question: "What acid had consumed the feminine curves of this creature?" (33; 36). The group also includes Vautrin, who occupies a third, outlaw position: he is neither of the male sex, for he does not love women, nor of the female sex, because he is a man. In a world where sex, gender, sexual identity, and physical sexuality are all supposed to jibe, Vautrin is different. He is other.

But if "others" ("autres") exist, who are they? Should we think of Vautrin, Michonneau, and Poiret as some sort of unholy set of those who do not participate in the economy of bourgeois heterosexual relationships? Men, women, and others, says the sign, but these others are a heterogeneous lot.

We do not know what status to give the sign, emblem of the generic or gender distinction that marks those who are neither men nor women. Does the sign merely say something, or does it, by its presence, do something?[4] Does it remark an already existing situation or establish a category? The sign in front of the boardinghouse might be considered a means of establishing a category or set that contains, at least minimally, Vautrin. The sign announces someone already present, Vautrin the sodomite, and thus describes what we will learn about this character. As a device that serves only to remark an already existing class, the sign reinscribes a behavior for which there is no convenient name, a behavior that may or may not include other departures from social norms. The sign may even have the effect of an announcement, not only of the present but also of the future. Like a rainbow flag or a pink triangle, it shows that the house is gay-friendly. Insofar as the sign names what is already known, it names homosexuality by normalizing it into a category parallel to, though different from, the categories of the two sexes. Neither male nor female, these others may be both sexes combined, a third sex, or of no sex at all.

Yet there is another possibility: the sign, by its very existence, may create the category of the third sex, thus classifying Vautrin. Without the sign, Vautrin does not exist. With it, he becomes named, receives a linguistic baptism, and has his locus marked for him. If the sign does something by producing a category, Vautrin becomes derivative of that category; the naming precedes him, making him into the sodomite or homosexual *avant la lettre* that we eventually see him to be.

What does it matter if Vautrin is a homosexual, if he is alone, if he fits in one category or another, if he belongs to the sign or is excluded by it? Everything matters, because our economy of reading depends on understanding his role. The labels *sodomite* (someone given to sodomitic behavior) and *homosexual* (an individual with a full-fledged psychology) derive from a semiotics based on a heterosexual norm. Behavior and existence are always defined against some preexisting ground given as the norm. Balzac manipulates the semiotics here and ironizes heterosexual semiotics such that our convenient models of "deux sexes et autres" are always misreadings, always miscategorizations.

The sign is never alone. In the first pages of *Old Goriot* there are two additional scenes of reading. One is Balzac's apostrophe to a bourgeois man or woman holding the book as he or she sits in a comfortable armchair. We think that this implied reader may be a woman, but we can never be sure (Schuerewegen 15–32). Both the sign and the apostrophe are scenes of misreading, for Balzac predicates his communicational model on a man-to-man and heterosexual system: I am a man whose addressee is another man, who will understand. Such a model erroneously conceives of a female addressee as "merely" a variant of the transparent, zero-degree male.

The sign has no possible addressee who is not an improper variant of some nonexistent neutral position. The sign on the boardinghouse is improperly written and improperly read.[5] And yet it tells us, whoever we are, that there are some others or some remainders not classifiable by gender. If the sign is descriptive, it is improper because it describes something that does not exist within the system. If it does something, it creates something outside the system. Balzac's sign queers the system and makes us wonder to what extent the whole process of signification and semiosis—aside from being subject to a heterosexual, phallocentric law—is itself always already queered.

The third scene of reading on these few pages underscores the impropriety of the sign. There is a statue of Love, with the following inscription on the base: "Qui que tu sois, voici ton maître: Il l'est, le fut, ou le doit être" "Whoe'er thou art, thy master see; / He is, he was, or he should be" (24; 29). Who is addressed?

Men and women certainly, but what about those nebulous others? If the others are not addressed, the "Whoe'er thou art" is wrong, for it includes only some of the possible addressees in the world. If however it includes the others, those mysterious thirds upsetting the bivalent balance of nature and gender, the system itself collapses under the weight of that otherness insisting on finding its mate. Who will love Vautrin? Whom will Vautrin love? And will Vautrin love properly or improperly? We will not know this until much later, when he takes Lucien de Rubempré under his wing. For now, in *Old Goriot,* Vautrin remains in a liminal position, neither fully included nor fully excluded.

Whereas the sign divides the human species in three, the inscription on the base of the statue is inclusive and synthetic: "Whoe'er thou art," your master is love. Here the division in three is not of categories but of tenses: love is, was, or must be—as if in a Kantian obligation—your master. Love is the master of us all, regardless of which category we fit into. Rather than merely contradicting some exclusion on the sign, the inclusiveness confirms that the sign is analytic and not exclusionary. The others are the third sex, subjected to love just as the two usually defined sexes are, even if the third sex is an improper group and even if the others are still defined as improper.

Balzac begins to populate a logosphere for Vautrin, as if creating an image for which there is no word or, from a teleological point of view, not yet any word: Balzac creates an image of the homosexual—with no name but with an identity—emerging from the text where there is not yet proper discourse. From the first presentation of Vautrin, he is enshrouded in mystery. He has secrets, closed-off areas, mysteries that no one may know:

> Souvent une boutade digne de Juvénal, et par laquelle il semblait se complaire à bafouer les lois, à fouetter la haute société, à la convaincre d'inconséquence avec elle-même, devait faire supposer qu'il gardait rancune à l'état social, et qu'il y avait au fond de sa vie un mystère soigneusement enfoui. (38–39)

> He often appeared to delight in scoffing at the law, in lashing society and proving its inconsistency in an outburst of invective worthy of Juvenal, which seemed to show that he held some grudge against the state, and had in the background of his life a carefully buried secret. (41)

What kind of mystery this is we will come to learn only later. In part, it is certainly the fact that Vautrin is a criminal, indeed, the leader of Paris's underworld and a marked man who had been condemned to hard labor but who somehow escaped, changed his identity, and went underground only to emerge in a somewhat less than respectable boardinghouse. The secret world in this novel revolves around two conflated points: on the one hand, the world of the underworld, of police, and, eventually, of the secret police and, on the other, the world of hidden sexuality—that is, of unnameable, if not unknowable, sexual behaviors.

I am still not sure what a homosexual may be for Balzac, even if the word does not exist, even if Vautrin is one of "them" for the author, even if all signs point to him or to homosexuality without naming it. Certainly here and elsewhere, Balzac has set up lots of stumbling blocks. For every analytic study, such as his *Physiologie du mariage,* that depends on a correspondence between signifier and signified and that therefore depends on the stability of generic and gendered markers, there are multiple scenarios in which men are feminine and women masculine, in which, therefore, even the simplest markers of sex or gender are improperly assigned.

Balzac often uses words like *feminine* and *effeminate* to describe his sensitive heroes, whether the future success, Eugène de Rastignac, or the embodiment of noble failure, Lucien de Rubempré. In essence, Balzac has no proper word to describe such men; *feminine* and *effeminate* semiotically drag biologically male characters toward the female sex—and toward the others. Indeed, in Balzac's work, as Martha Moss notes (45), masculine and feminine traits are not necessarily assigned to male and female characters respectively. Again, the sign says two sexes and others. Each character therefore has two different, incompatible alterities: a male character has as his other a female character—a feminine personality—and simultaneously has those nebulous others as some negative image of the self. Two different others, two different directions, two improprieties.

Characters are improperly sexed, improperly signed or assigned as male or female, masculine or feminine. In fact, the only proper addressee might be the most improper Vautrin, he who determines all categories by participating in none of them. But there is more: if each character already evinces some separation between sex and gender, there is always the possibility of some jump or slide. That Balzac has queered the entire sign system away from its enforced heterosexuality is clear. Balzac's structuring of his world of genders and sexualities is complex, and its dynamics are determined by a model of impropriety that fetishizes otherness at its very heart. Paris, Balzac tells us, is "un véritable océan" 'an ocean,' and he advises us: "[J]etez-y la sonde" '[t]hrow in the plummet' (34; 37). I would hasten to add that when you throw in that plumb line, it is, quite simply, never straight and indeed is always queered.

Why read Balzac from a queer perspective? Does such a reading add to or take away from the great humanistic values incarnated in the Western canon? It should be obvious that I think that it adds to our understanding of the complex values and signs that form the canon and of how necessary it is to explore both the overt and the covert signs and systems that realism puts before the reader. Reading Balzac from a queer perspective can show students how the exploration of all the ramifications of a marginalized figure can give us a clearer understanding of the economy of writing, the ways in which reality is understood and represented, and the methods used by Balzac to create his human comedy. And finally, understanding Vautrin means understanding a character whose outlaw status will make him one of the precursors to the antiheroes of twentieth-century literature.

NOTES

[1]Because of Rastignac's rampant heterosexuality, critics have often eschewed this point of view. Lucien de Rubempré, however, with his effeminate side, frequently elicits the homosexual paradigm. Yet Alfred Glauser, a critic who associates Lucien's beauty and feminine character with Vautrin's homosexual desire, also says that this homosexual model would hold "unless Balzac endowed Lucien with these traits in order to find the woman in him, the object of his fundamental desire" (594). I think that in both works, Balzac's ironic take on sexuality, while allowing the possibility for such a heterosexual translation, also deconstructs that possibility at the same time, for the woman within becomes herself the metaphor for the homosexual who cannot yet be named.

[2]Storzer sees the association of criminality and homosexuality as the basis of a paradigm not only for Balzac but also for André Gide and Jean Genet.

[3]Needless to say, the translation does not give the meaning of the all-important word "autres" in the French original.

[4]In technical terms, we would ask whether the sign is constative or performative. A performative utterance, according to J. L. Austin, brings about an act, while a constative utterance makes a statement (5–11). For Austin, a performative must be "reducible, or expandable, or analysable into a form with a verb in the first person singular present indicative active" (61–62). Thus I am using Balzac's words as if they were references to enunciations and, specifically, as if the act of writing and, indeed, the visibility of writing (the sign in front of the boardinghouse and the verse on the statue) were themselves statements either creating an existence by having been said (performative) or asserting an existence as a description thereof (constative).

[5]On the improper reading in another Balzac novel, see Samuel Weber's study of *La Peau de chagrin.*

Kinship, Economics, and Queer Sexuality in Balzac's *Old Goriot*

Michael Lucey

> Les liens du sang qui unissent et qui constituent les familles sont formés par les sentimens d'affection que la nature a mis dans le cœur des parens les uns pour les autres. L'énergie de ces sentiments augmente en raison de la proximité de parenté, et elle est portée au plus haute degré entre les pères et les mères et leurs enfants.
>
> Il n'est aucun législateur sage qui n'ait considéré ces différents degrés d'affection comme lui présentant le meilleur ordre pour la transmission des biens.
>
> —M. Bigot-Préameneu, presenting the articles of the proposed *Code civil* regarding wills to the *corps législatif* in 1804

> The blood ties that unite and constitute families are formed by the sentiments of affection that nature has placed in the hearts of relatives for each other. The energy of these sentiments increases with the closeness of the kin relation, and finds its highest point between fathers and mothers and their children.
>
> There is no wise legislator who wouldn't have considered these different degrees of affection as providing him with the best order for the transmission of property.

> L'enfant conçu pendant le mariage a pour père le mari.
>
> —Article 312 of the 1804 *Code civil*

> A child conceived during the marriage has the husband for father.

In the famous "Avant-propos" to the *Comédie humaine,* Balzac polemically lays claim to a certain antimodernism by stating his allegiance to the family: "I also consider the Family and not the Individual as the true social unit. In this regard, taking the risk of being considered a backwards thinker, I place myself alongside de Bossuet and de Bonald, instead of following modern innovators" ("Avant-propos" [*Œuvres*] 68–69). Yet Balzac's analytic gaze on the family will not confirm the conservative polemics he voices here. Instead, Balzac produces a multifaceted and complex view of what family might be. His novels portray a world in which a family has no clear form, where the concept of family is itself a contested space. The two forces most clearly overdetermining this space for Balzac are the reorganization of civil society undertaken by revolutionary and postrevolutionary governments and the accelerated economic changes concomitant to the onset of modern industrial capitalism. Balzacian novels portray the family as a space in which competing historical and economic interests find their material instantiations. Thus generational tensions, marital strategies, reproductive intents and accidents, sexuality, gender, and emotions and affects all can be seen as in part the overdetermined products of large social forces at work in and on the family. *Old Goriot* exemplifies Balzac's radical social analysis, where economic and historical shifts have particular consequences for both individual and family experiences of kinship, sexuality, and gender.

One common version of family crisis frequently proffered by Balzacian narratives evinces a nostalgia for a prerevolutionary family, putative locus of natural human sentiment. In *Old Goriot,* this nostalgic moment is represented by Rastignac's relationships with his mother and sisters, who were left behind in the provinces when Rastignac came to Paris to get rich quick. In this kind of scenario, true human, family-based sentiment—for which Balzacian narrators often piously advocate—is rapidly being corroded and denatured in the modern economic world:

> His thoughts carried him back to his home and his family. He remembered the pure happiness of his uneventful life there: he recalled the days spent among beings who loved him dearly. Those dear creatures conformed to the natural laws of the domestic hearth, and in so doing found a full and constant happiness there, unmarred by such torments as his. (327; 271)

This narrative of the corrosion and denaturalizing of family sentiment is often mimicked in a certain kind of psychoanalytic account of Balzac's novels that focuses on the perversions of modern sexuality, which are assumed to devolve from a disruption of traditional family structures. Such readings thus could perhaps be taken as uncritical ones in their failure to grasp that the narratives they mimic are themselves ideologically marked, ideologically interested, contestatory and polemical in their original social and historical context, and often contested in the novels themselves.

To put matters another way, any reading of a Balzac novel that casts the social world portrayed in the novel as existing in an unstable moment that can best be read in contrast to an earlier stability—any reading that accepts a version of reality in which the unbridled, perverse, overweening, inappropriate desires and interests of the Balzacian moment are held in contrast to some more grounded, natural moment of properly regulated desire and interest (even if that moment exists only in some utopian or purely theoretical space)—is a reading whose ideology conforms to only one of the ideological positions available in the Balzacian world and obviously a conservative position at that. From such a vantage point it will not be easy to see some of the more challenging thinking about sexuality and family relationships that occurs in and around these novels.

Consider *Old Goriot,* where a wealth of conceptions of the interests embedded in all family structures might be taken as making finally untenable a reading of *any* family structure as presocial, natural, human, disinterested. It is commonplace and sensible to read the novel's protagonist, Eugène de Rastignac, as positioned at the charged crossing of many visions of family structure and interest and as having difficulty choosing among them. There is certainly his nostalgia for his mother, his sisters, and his family's country estate. At least two other discourses of kinship emerge out of the two possible paths to wealth Rastignac considers. Vautrin, knowing that Victorine Taillefer is in love with Rastignac, offers one path, asking Rastignac to become an accomplice in a murder that will make her a rich heiress. This whole scheme is overlaid by a complicated discourse of homoerotic friendship, and indeed kinship, between Vautrin and Rastignac, a discourse I examine in more detail below. The other remaking of kinship would enable Rastignac's insertion into the Goriot family by way of both adultery with a daughter and sentimental devotion to an old man who would be a father-not-quite-in-law. It would be possible to view Rastignac's implied kinship with Vautrin and his links to the Goriot clan as perversions or failures of certain normative models resulting both in and from a moment of general crisis in family structure. Consider one formulation of such a position:

> Despite a certain amount of jealousy, Goriot gives his daughter to Rastignac, indeed entreats him to take her. And Vautrin, as self-appointed guardian of Victorine's hand, bestows it upon the prospective suitor. Here we begin to confront the gaping chaos that the novel desperately seeks to order. For both prospective fathers—Goriot and Vautrin—ultimately abdicate their position, relinquish their authority to say no; whence an unregulated circulation of women, an uncontrolled flow of money, a mad proliferation of familial and social relations. As we begin to look at the perturbed relationships which arise in a frenzied attempt to supplement the missing core, we enter into a truly Yeatsian turmoil. (Beizer 132)

This analysis seems entirely accurate on one level. At the same time, its susceptibility to a discourse of panic (a diagnosis of unregulated, uncontrolled, mad, perturbed, frenzied turmoil) might indicate a susceptibility to, rather than a critical distance from, the conservative polemics of the novel, a polemics that would convince us that panic is an appropriate response to the fearful perversions the novel menacingly reveals to us.[1]

We can read *Old Goriot* differently by keeping firmly in mind that all discourses (even nostalgically normative ones) of family relationships are polemical and that the novel itself both stages the polemics and acts in it. We would thereby be taking seriously the polemical nature of the novelistic project Balzac sets out in the "Avant-propos" and yet noticing that his novels do more than merely voice his conservative polemics. The analytical complexity of *Old Goriot* arises from the way in which the juxtaposition of competing forms of family discourse can be taken to clarify the competing interests of any and all of these discourses.

Consider the situation of Victorine Taillefer, unrecognized daughter of a rich banker. Vautrin concocts a scheme to use her familial situation to enrich both Rastignac and himself. How the relations between "illegitimate" children, "natural" affection, and legal inheritance were to be understood was a subject of great dispute for both revolutionary legislators and the men who drew up the Napoleonic *Code civil* in the first years of the nineteenth century; the novel is clearly referencing this dispute with regard to both Victorine and the children of Goriot's daughter, Madame de Restaud. Vautrin renders Victorine's situation ruthlessly:

> If it were the will of Heaven to take his son from him Taillefer would acknowledge his daughter. He would want to have someone or other to leave his money to, it's a weakness of human nature, and he's not likely to have any more children, I know. Victorine is gentle and sweet, she will soon twist her father round her little finger, and make him spin like a humming-top with the whip of sentiment! (157; 133–34)

The fungible "nature" of family sentiment, the quickness with which family sentiment can be abusively attributed, the different economic interests at stake in the determination of who gains sentimental and legal inclusion in the family are all well understood by Vautrin, as they were by the revolutionary and Napoleonic legislators who argued over how to fix inheritance rights for male and female heirs as well as for legitimate and illegitimate offspring. Victorine's situation is unusual: "Her father believed he had sufficient reason for not recognizing her, refused to have her near him, allowed her only six hundred francs a year, and he had realized his property in order to disinherit her and leave his whole fortune to his son" (38). The translation actually removes some legal complexity from the text: "Son père croyait avoir des raisons pour ne pas la reconnaître, refusait de la garder près de lui, ne lui accordait que six cents francs par an, et avait dénaturé sa fortune, afin de pouvoir la transmettre en entier à son fils" (35–36). Legally, her father cannot *not* recognize her: "L'enfant conçu pendant le mariage a pour père le mari," as the *Code civil* has it. The law is a frank acknowledgment that allowing parents easily to disown children born of adultery would be too disruptive of the order of property in France. Articles 312 to 318 of the *Code* put into place an elaborate set of rules that make it clear that as long as a husband and wife were in rough proximity to each other during the estimated period when the child would have been conceived, the child is to be considered legitimate. It is also not easy for a father to disinherit a child, male or female, by realizing his own property, as long as the property remains recognizably his. In an effort to put a definitive end to primogeniture, the *Code* left parents little control over the share of their estate that went to each child. Thus, as the French text suggests—"[il] avait *dénaturé* sa fortune" (my emphasis)—Taillefer is performing some kind of financial sleight of hand in order to cheat Victorine of a share of his estate.

The direct relation between law and natural family sentiments proposed by the brave legislator M. Bigot-Préameneu in my first epigraph is transparently absent from the actual *Code civil* he is discussing, as it is from the world of Balzac's novel. Indeed, Balzac's image of the humming top spun by the whip of sentiment seems much more enticing and appropriate. Sentiment and a variety of economic interests chase one another's tails. Sometimes sentiment comes in handy after the fact. With the death of her brother, Victorine will be able to put a new spin on her father's previously misogynistic, or stubbornly primogenitural, or genetically suspicious sentiments; she will perhaps renaturalize his relation to his estate and thereby bring him into conformity with the law, which paradoxically has no intention of preserving anything but the appearance of a direct relation between blood ties and the transmission of wealth across generations.

Instead of imagining Vautrin, for whatever reason, as somehow exterior to a system linking in various ways reproduction, kinship, and the transmission of wealth across generations, imagine him as trying to shift the parameters of that same system to suit his own ends, financial and sentimental, as well as reproductive. Vautrin's discourse of homoerotic friendship, combined with his patriarchal slave-plantation fantasy, implies willed kinship relations whose artificiality hardly differs from the more legally willed kinship between Taillefer and Victorine or between Restaud and his wife's children. In one conversation with Rastignac, Vautrin observes:

> I possess at this moment fifty thousand francs, which would give me scarcely forty niggers. I need two hundred thousand francs, for I want two hundred niggers to carry out my idea of the patriarchal life properly. Negroes, you see, are children ready-made that you can do what you like with, without a nosy Public Prosecutor coming to ask you questions about them. (154; 131)

In a later conversation, he continues:

> I mean to leave this country in a few months for America, to go and plant my tobacco [*aller planter mon tabac*]. I will send you the cigars of friendship. If I make money, I will help you. If I have no children (which is likely to be the case: I am not anxious to plant scions of my own stock here [*je ne suis pas curieux de me replanter ici par bouture*]), I will leave you my fortune. [. . .] Is that acting like a friend? (217; 182)

Vautrin is denaturalizing his fortune, assigning and recognizing sentiment where he will, designating his heirs freely. Rastignac, as the designated heir, appreciates this, at least on one level, mentally acknowledging some form of kinship with Vautrin when Vautrin is arrested: "Rastignac lowered his eyes, acknowledging, in expiation of his secret evil thoughts, the kinship [*ce cousinage criminel*] with him that the criminal claimed" (265–66; 221).

When this denaturalized kinship system is rendered consciously affective and erotic, Rastignac violently demurs. The treacherous Mlle Michonneau spins his top for him:

> "This gentleman sides with Collin [one of Vautrin's other names]," she said, scrutinizing the student, with an expression of venomous inquiry on her face. "It's not difficult to understand why."
>
> Eugène sprang forward as if to throw himself upon the old maid and strangle her. The treacherous intention of her look was obvious, and it had let a flood of hideous light into his mind. (269; 224)

What the queer Michonneau does is to suggest publicly Eugène's queerness; in a moment of perfectly modern homophobia she explicitly sexualizes the kinship relation Eugène had tentatively been experiencing between himself and Vautrin. As these two queer denizens of the Vauquer boardinghouse struggle briefly to see which one can be more homophobic than the other, we might notice the family discourse of the novel working to cash in on their struggle by using it to demonize Vautrin and queer kinship, and by creating an affective inclination not to notice that queer and natural kinship systems often work in tandem to reveal each other's structure.

Rastignac's sentimental top will be spun at least one more time, as the novel once again manages to reveal what its surface polemics might seem to deny. The scene in question again specifically links Vautrin to another of the plot's currents, this time to the woes of Goriot's daughter Anastasie de Restaud, who has sold the family diamonds to pay the debts of her lover. Her husband has caught her in her shenanigans and has forced her to reveal which of his children are "really" his ("Answer me this: have I one child which is my own?" [305; 253]) and extorted as well a promise from her to divest herself of her personal fortune in his favor when he asks her to, thereby disempowering her from transmitting her premarital family fortune along her (not his) bloodline.

To make matters worse, her lover still has debts, and since her child by her lover is now likely to require some "extrafamilial" financial assistance at some point, she turns to her father for help in keeping her lover out of debtor's prison, to the tune of twelve thousand francs. Her father has just spent that amount furnishing an apartment for Rastignac and Delphine, where Goriot expects to reside as well, as the odd trio begin to build their own version of an alternative family. Goriot therefore has nothing left with which to help Anastasie, and the two daughters begin a nasty verbal tussle that drives their father to distraction, until Rastignac, listening in the next room, chooses to intervene:

> Eugène, horror-stricken, took the bill he had signed for Vautrin, the stamp on which was sufficient for a larger sum; he changed the figures

> and made it into a proper bill for twelve thousand francs payable to Goriot's order; then he went into the room next door.
>
> "Here is the whole amount, Madame," he said, handing her the piece of paper. "I was sleeping, your conversation wakened me, and so I was able to learn what I owed Monsieur Goriot. This bill clears my debt, and you can convert it into cash. I will pay it off punctually on the proper date." (311–12; 258–59)

Earlier in the novel, Rastignac, owing debts of honor to a couple of aristocratic dandies, was tempted into borrowing some money from Vautrin, signing a note rather than taking on a debt of honor to such a dubious character (215–16; 180–81). That note (Vautrin safely imprisoned and therefore the debt apparently forgettable) is somehow conveniently to hand at this crucial moment. Symbolically, this transaction is thus extremely rich, as the note exists at the outset as a token of Rastignac's kinship with Vautrin and yet here is sentimentally overwritten, as if to forget that relationship. Rastignac provides Goriot with the filial devotion Goriot finds nowhere else, devotion that overcompensates both for Rastignac's now reneged queer openness to Vautrin and for Rastignac's guilt at participating in a world where adulterous couples and their children mix and match in open secrecy with legally regularized families.

Families, *Old Goriot* reiterates, are, in the social world under scrutiny in the novel, only confusedly related to blood; appropriate family sentiment is another structure perfectly capable of being exploited to numerous complex ends, and the relation of sentiment to blood is itself insistently rhetorical. Goriot, attempting to convince his daughter to accept Rastignac's help, exclaims, "But he's my son, our dear child, your brother, your saviour! [. . .] Oh! my child! I will be more than a father to you, I will give you the love of a whole family" (312; 259). This family delirium of Goriot's makes explicit the possibility of taking all family structures as representing social (and not natural) interests that overdetermine and help reproduce certain forms of sentimental and economic dependence as well as certain forms of sexuality. Such a reading necessarily understands that sentiment and sexuality themselves in part enact interests coming from elsewhere.[2]

Vautrin's and Goriot's versions (not necessarily perversions) of kinship structures need not be seen, through some process of degradation, because of some implied excess, or through the structures' homosexual or incestuous possibilities, as revealing in negative a prior stability that, while now elusive, represents some utopian familial normativeness. Instead, by pluralizing and revealing the competition between the versions or visions of kinship and appropriate sentiment available at a given moment, Vautrin's and Goriot's versions could facilitate the development of critical distance on the currents of interest (economic, institutional, reproductive, erotic) that inhere in any of the novel's extant versions of kinship. For instance, one could choose to read the cruel patriarchy of Vautrin's slave-plantation fantasy as offering an implicit critique of the economic exploitation embedded in many heterosexually reproductive structures. One could choose to read in Goriot's affective volatility a critique of the contradictions internal to a family form in which the affective and economic components of paternal interest in daughters dwell in such uneasy proximity.

Analogously, we could learn about the rhetorical construction of a certain homophobia and how homophobia profits from certain forms of family sentiment to sustain itself. When Mlle Michonneau observes homophobically that we all know what Rastignac's relation to Vautrin truly was, Rastignac's homosexual panic is, as much for a polemical reason as for any other, given ample room to express itself in counterbalance to his previous avowal of kinship to Vautrin. This suggests that even the ersatz version of family relationships Rastignac espouses in joining Goriot's family makes use of a hostility to queer sexuality, perhaps in order to hide the dubiousness of its own relation to some putative naturalness. To follow out the continual radical suggestions in Balzac's world of the queerness of all family structures would require us to read both this homophobic hostility and the expression or representation of homosexuality the novel nonetheless provides (precisely in order to harness the concomitant hostility to the novel's own ends) as part of a polemical struggle, thereby not allowing our reading to accept or mimic the polemical forms of panic the novel sometimes invokes to disguise its own insight.

NOTES

[1]Roddey Reid's *Families in Jeopardy: Regulating the Social Body in France, 1750–1910,* especially the introduction and the first chapter, offers a helpful analysis of the uses to which family panic can be put.

[2]See my article "Balzac's Queer Cousins and Their Friends" for further elaboration of this point in relation to other Balzac novels.

A Thematic Approach: Seeing to Learn, Learning to See: Rastignac's Visual Education

John T. Booker

Soon after Balzac's death in 1850, his contemporaries opened the debate as to whether the author should be considered, in Charles Baudelaire's terms, an observer or a visionary. Charles Sainte-Beuve, quoting (and obviously agreeing with) Philarète Chasles, was among the first to deem the novelist a "voyant" (seer) a judgment echoed by Théophile Gautier in 1858 (Sainte-Beuve, "M. de Balzac" 450; Gautier 70). A year later, Baudelaire would make his well-known case for Balzac as "visionnaire, et visionnaire passionné" 'a visionary, and a passionate visionary' (Baudelaire 120; my trans.),[1] which is the view that Albert Béguin, most notably, has promoted in the twentieth century.

Balzac himself had effectively staked out a claim to both titles in his "Avant-propos" to the *Comédie humaine* (1842). Appearing initially to settle for the modest role of "secrétaire" 'secretary' of French society ("Avant-propos" [*Comédie*] 11)—that is, someone who would simply transcribe, as it were, what he could observe happening around him—he went on in fact to set himself a much more active and creative task: "pour mériter les éloges que doit ambitionner tout artiste, ne devais-je pas étudier les raisons ou la raison de ces effets sociaux, surprendre le sens caché dans cet immense assemblage de figures, de passions et d'événements" 'in order to be worthy of the praise for which every artist must strive, should I not study the reasons or reason for those social effects, discover the meaning hidden within that immense collection of figures, passions, and events' (11). Balzac's analysis suggests that the roles of observer and visionary are not so much antithetical as complementary, that they represent two phases of a broad effort to understand reality in all its complexity. As André Allemand has put it: "Tout procède chez Balzac de l'observation et de la vision, et l'une ne va pas sans l'autre. La vision s'empare des faits observés et les organise" 'With Balzac everything proceeds from observation and vision, and the two go together. Vision takes hold of observed phenomena and organizes them' (50).

In the novels of a writer who aspired to uncover the hidden sense of things, it is hardly surprising that visual acuity (or the lack thereof) should be a determining factor in the success (or failure) of so many individual characters. In *La Comédie humaine,* how one fares is often determined by how well one can see—and, just as important, by how effectively one can shield one's own thoughts and emotions from the prying eyes of others. Balzac's world is, in short, one where to see is to know and where knowledge is measured—and regularly expressed—in visual terms. Nowhere is the visual more significant than in the novel that features the education of Eugène de Rastignac. In *Le Père*

Goriot, as Peter Lock has noted, "at times whole scenes are played out by means of gesture and glance. The characters are constantly 'reading' signs, interpreting countenances, intercepting or deflecting the *regard* of others" (41). In the brief period during which Rastignac is formed—in fictional time, from the end of November 1819 to late February 1820—he finds himself in the middle of a visually charged atmosphere, struggling, with mixed success, to learn how to see.

To see, in the fullest sense of the term, is a two-step process (analogous to the double goal Balzac set himself), and both stages are foregrounded in the novel by a visual vocabulary that is remarkably pervasive. There is in the first place physical sight, regularly indicated by the common verbs *regarder* (to look at, watch) and *voir* (to see in a literal sense). Moreover, the force or energy with which a *regard* is projected or received matters a great deal, and a number of stronger verbs—most frequently *jeter* and *lancer* (to throw, fling, cast, flash, dart [a glance])—convey the heightened intensity of a particular scene. But *to see* in a more complete sense also entails what one might call insight, the ability to look beyond what is visible, to see through appearances, to read the true nature of a situation or the state of mind of another individual. This critical capacity is communicated by expressions such as *voir* (to see in the figurative sense of to understand), *voir clair* or *voir juste* (to see clearly, get a clear understanding of), or *lire dans* (to see into, read). These verbs, along with others used on a more occasional basis, create a rich visual fabric that offers the reader, in turn, insight not only into Rastignac's evolution but also into the struggle being played out more generally in *Le Père Goriot* (as in so many novels of *La Comédie humaine*) between weak and strong.

In the fictional world of the novel, the great visionary is of course Vautrin; from first appearance to last, his ability to quickly read a situation and see through other characters is unsurpassed. Early on, for example, after Rastignac returns from a visit to Mme de Beauséant, Vautrin throws him "un de ces regards par lesquels cet homme semblait s'initier aux secrets les plus cachés du cœur" 'one of the penetrating looks with which this man seemed to read the innermost secrets of the heart' (119; 106). Rastignac soon understands the key to Vautrin's strength: "il lui semblait que ce singulier personnage pénétrait ses passions et lisait dans son cœur, tandis que chez lui tout était si bien clos qu'il semblait avoir la profondeur immobile d'un sphinx qui sait, voit tout, et ne dit rien" 'It seemed to him that this strange being examined his feelings every moment and read his inmost heart, while Vautrin himself was so closely sealed that he seemed to possess the still depths of a sphinx, who knows all, sees all, and keeps silent' (142; 121–22). Victorine Taillefer later describes, in more visceral terms, the uneasy feeling of those on whom Vautrin turns his piercing gaze: "il a [. . .] des regards qui gênent une femme comme si on lui enlevait sa robe" 'his looks make you feel as if you had nothing on' (246; 205).

While Vautrin's visual superiority is evident throughout the novel, it is nowhere more apparent, paradoxically, than in the scene of his arrest. Stunned to hear that Mlle Michonneau has been talking about a certain Trompe-la-Mort (Cheat-Death), his "regard magnétique tomba comme un rayon de soleil sur mademoiselle Michonneau, à laquelle ce jet de volonté cassa les jarrets" 'magnetic glance fell like a ray of bright light on Mademoiselle Michonneau, and the old maid's legs seemed to crumple under her as she felt the impact of the man's strong will' (262; 218). But Vautrin quickly sizes up the situation and recognizes the danger: that the police, hoping to provoke a violent response on his part, will use it as a pretext to kill him on the spot. Regaining self-control, he demonstrates "la preuve de la plus haute puissance humaine" 'proof of his possession of a power of the highest order' (263; 219). From that moment, he directs the scene as it plays out, prompting the narrator to see in him "un poème infernal" 'a poet of Hell' (265; 221). Even in handcuffs, Vautrin dominates everyone around him with the force of his defiant glare: "Son regard était celui de l'archange déchu qui veut toujours la guerre" 'He looked about him like the fallen archangel whose only wish was for eternal enmity' (265; 221).

If Vautrin defines visual preeminence, Goriot epitomizes weakness and vulnerability. It is true that, as a shrewd grain trader during the Revolution, he once showed talents that must have rivaled those of Vautrin. The young Goriot, we are told, "avait un coup d'œil d'aigle, il devançait tout, prévoyait tout, savait tout, cachait tout" 'had an eagle's eye, anticipated everything, foresaw everything, knew all, hid all' (126; 112). But the Goriot of 1819 to 1820 bears little resemblance to his former self; he is now little more than the passive—and, again in obvious contrast to Vautrin, transparent—object of the *regards* of others. During the first of the meal scenes that periodically bring the boarders together around Mme Vauquer's table, the name Anastasie de Restaud, mentioned in remarks between Rastignac and Vautrin, jolts Goriot out of his usual torpor: "Le père Goriot leva brusquement la tête, il jeta sur les deux interlocuteurs un regard lumineux et plein d'inquiétude qui surprit les pensionnaires" 'Old Goriot abruptly raised his head and gazed at the two speakers with a look so full of intelligence and anxiety that the lodgers were astonished' (73; 69). As Mme Vauquer marvels at the degree to which the old man's eyes "s'allument" 'are shining' (73; 69), he stares avidly at Rastignac while the latter describes the elegant young woman. But when Vautrin makes disparaging comments about Parisian women like the comtesse de Restaud, "[l]e visage du père Goriot, qui s'était allumé comme le soleil d'un beau jour en entendant l'étudiant, devint sombre à cette cruelle observation de Vautrin" 'Old Goriot's face, which had shone like the sun on a fine day as he listened to the student, clouded over at this cruel speech of Vautrin's' (74; 70).

The demonstrative nature of such reactions marks Goriot as a weak figure in the Balzacian world; his eyes come alive—in a predictable way that actually contributes to his vulnerability—only when it is a question of his daughters. In contrast to the sphinxlike Vautrin, whose eyes continually probe others, prompting meaningful reactions that he can then read to his advantage, Goriot can only react to circumstances over which he exercises no control; his every emotion is immediately visible, putting him at the mercy of others.

In the novel that bears his name, Goriot occupies center stage for only the brief period of his agony and death. By then, his store of visual energy all but exhausted, he struggles just to recognize those around him. When Rastignac comes by to check on him, "Goriot leva sur Eugène des yeux ternes et le regarda fort attentivement sans le reconnaître" 'Goriot raised dull eyes to Eugène's face, and scrutinized him carefully without a sign of recognition' (336; 279). Only Bianchon's mention of Delphine can momentarily bring Goriot's eyes back to life, but they show nothing more than "une activité folle" 'a wild restlessness' (338; 280), as the old man aimlessly scans the room.

One of the dark ironies of this work is that, as physical sight slips away, Goriot finally comes to a moment of lucidity: had he not always indulged his daughters' every wish, they would be there now for him. Such is the cruel truth he acknowledges, in grippingly visual terms:

> En ce moment, je vois ma vie entière. Je suis dupe! [. . .] Oui, je le vois, pour elles, l'habitude de m'ouvrir les entrailles a ôté du prix à tout ce que je faisais. Elles auraient demandé à me crever les yeux, je leur aurais dit: "Crevez-les!" Je suis trop bête. (348)

> Now I see my life whole. I have been duped. [. . .] Yes, I see it now: because I always gave away my whole heart as a matter of course, my gifts were cheap in their eyes. If they had wanted to put out my eyes, I would have told them to do it. I was a fool. (288)

In a sense, Goriot *had* let his daughters "put out his eyes" over the years, had accepted, that is, a kind of voluntary blindness that allowed him to believe (or to pretend) that Anastasie and Delphine really loved him. Unlike the insight that allows Vautrin to understand and adapt to new situations as they unfold, Goriot's is a belated recognition of past mistakes, one that comes much too late to have any bearing on his fate.

By the end, as if to illustrate the fundamental equation of life and sight in this fictional universe, Goriot's very existence is reduced to a desperate effort simply to see his daughters: "Mourir," he tells Rastignac, "c'est ne plus les voir" 'if I die [. . .] I shall not see them any more. That's what death means' (340; 282). A few moments later, in his rambling monologue, he turns the formula around: "Ne pas les voir, voilà l'agonie!" 'Not to see them—there is death's sting!' (350; 290). It seems particularly ironic, then, that one of Goriot's dying gestures is to reach out and seize Bianchon and Rastignac by the hair, mistaking them for his daughters (359; 297).

The contrast between the respective fates of Goriot and Vautrin not only underscores the relation between vision and power in the *Comédie humaine;* it demonstrates as well how little either of those qualities has to do with morality in any conventional sense. On the one hand, Goriot—"ce Christ de la Paternité" 'this Christ-like father' (282; 235)—dies a pitiful death, effectively sightless and deprived of a final glimpse of his daughters. Vautrin, on the other hand, owes his very survival to keen powers of sight and of insight; even in police custody, he remains a triumphant Satanic figure, casting on those around him the unrepentant look of the "archange déchu" 'fallen archangel' (265; 221).

Between the two poles of visual strength and weakness represented by Vautrin and Goriot, other characters occupy intermediate positions determined by individual temperament and by behavior in a given situation. Mme Vauquer, for example, with her "œil de pie" 'magpie's eye' (42; 44), can swiftly calculate "d'un seul coup d'œil le parti le plus avantageux" 'with a single flicker of her eyelids [. . .] which course would be most advantageous to her interests' (270; 225). Mlle Michonneau is similarly opportunistic: left alone momentarily with Vautrin as he lies unconscious in his room, her eyes "semblaient percer les murs" 'seemed to pierce the walls' in search of hidden money (257; 214).

More interesting is Mme de Beauséant, who stands as a transitional figure. Interacting with others, she invariably assumes the stronger role, visually, as Rastignac learns in the course of his first visit. When he casually calls her "Ma cousine," she promptly puts him in his place "en lui jetant un regard dont l'impertinence glaça l'étudiant" 'with a look whose haughtiness froze Eugène' (104; 94). And it is she who teaches Rastignac the secret of success in society: "d'abord ne soyez pas aussi démonstratif" 'you must first learn not to show your feelings so unrestrainedly' (106; 96). At the heart of her admonition lies the principle that explains both Vautrin's strength and Goriot's weakness: "si vous avez un sentiment vrai," she tells her young cousin, "cachez-le comme un trésor; ne le laissez jamais soupçonner, vous seriez perdu. Vous ne seriez plus le bourreau, vous deviendriez la victime" 'if you have any real feeling, hide it like a treasure; never let it be suspected or you will be lost. You would no longer be the executioner then but the victim' (115; 103). So sound is that advice that when she herself fails to heed it, and instead shows the depth of her love for a man who cannot remain true to her, Mme de Beauséant will feel obliged to retire from the social arena. Still, even at that moment of self-imposed exile, with all of high society eagerly watching to see how she will react, she remains every bit as imposing, visually, as Vautrin is; her impenetrable demeanor offers Rastignac one last lesson: "Personne ne pouvait lire dans son âme" 'No one could read her heart' (330; 273).

It is under the influence of Vautrin, Goriot, and Mme de Beauséant that Rastignac learns rapidly how to deal with his world, and his evolution is highlighted in visual terms. Early on, the narrator attributes the very existence of his story to the young man's "observations curieuses" 'observant curiosity' and "son désir de pénétrer les mystères" 'his desire to fathom the mysteries' (31; 35). However curious he may be, the Rastignac we find at the outset is hardly perspicacious. If he takes an interest in the "mysteries" of the boardinghouse, after returning that first evening from Mme de Beauséant's ball, it is because he hears strange noises coming from Goriot's room. Reduced to observing his neighbor's activities through a keyhole, Rastignac cannot understand them any more than he can make sense of the sound of Vautrin's voice, talking with someone else, a floor below. Much the same thing happens when he goes to see the comtesse de Restaud two days later: he is mystified to hear the voices of Goriot and Anastasie, along with what sounds like a kiss, but he doesn't actually see the two of them together. These early scenes in which Rastignac is forced to surmise what is going on primarily from what he can hear, or what he can see only indirectly, illustrate just how ill prepared he is to make much real sense, visually, of the world around him.

At this stage, moreover, Rastignac is regularly overpowered in face-to-face encounters. Arriving on foot at the comtesse de Restaud's, he suffers "le coup d'œil méprisant" 'the scornful glances' of her servants (85; 79). When he persists in imposing himself between Anastasie and her increasingly irritated lover, Rastignac is unable to read Maxime's menacing look, which the narrator readily translates for us (89; 81–82). Nor does he get the message when Anastasie herself throws him "un de ces regards froidement interrogatifs qui disent si bien: Pourquoi ne vous en allez-vous pas?" 'one of those coldly interrogative stares which say so clearly, "Why don't you go?"' (90; 83). He does, finally, experience a moment of insight when he observes the others' change in attitude once his family name has been pronounced: "Une soudaine lumière lui fit voir clair dans l'atmosphère de la haute société parisienne, encore ténébreuse pour lui" 'A sudden light pierced the murky atmosphere of aristocratic Parisian society and he could see, though still but dimly' (91; 83–84).

By the time Rastignac dines with Mme de Beauséant a week or so later, he has already made progress. He can now read the cool reception his cousin initially gives him, preoccupied as she is by difficulties with her lover (166; 140). As the narrator notes, Rastignac has quickly become an "observateur" 'observer' (166; 140); but it will be some time yet before he comes even close to being a visionary. At the theater that same evening, he draws the eyes of everyone present—much as Vautrin regularly commands the attention of those around him—but then he promptly makes the kind of mistake against which Mme de Beauséant had warned him, by staring ostentatiously at Delphine de Nucingen (170–71; 144). Chided for his instant infatuation with the young woman, he reacts "en lançant un regard pénétrant à sa cousine" 'with a searching look at his cousin' (171; 145)—one of the rare instances when a *regard* of Rastignac's is conveyed by a forceful verb (*lancer*). Turning back to Delphine, in a gesture that offers a preview of the novel's denouement, he looks at her "comme un homme insulté regarde son adversaire" 'as a man insulted looks at his adversary' (172; 146). That Rastignac is now less transparent appears to be subtly confirmed the next day, when Vautrin "*semblait vouloir* lire dans son âme" 'stared at the student *as if he would* read his soul' (184; 155; my emphasis); for once, even the keen eyes of the sphinx cannot immediately uncover what the student is up to.

These early sequences provide a good indication of the uneven, irregular nature of what Peter Brooks has called Rastignac's "perceptual progress" (*Melodramatic Imagination* 138; see also Prendergast, *Balzac* 79–80; Rignall 48–49). Periodically, moments of insight allow Rastignac to see (*voir*) clearly, as he does after his lesson from Mme de Beauséant: "Il vit le monde comme il est: les lois et la morale impuissantes chez les riches, et vit dans la fortune l'*ultima ratio mundi*" 'He saw the world as it is; saw how laws and moral judgements are without power among the rich, and found in success the *ultima ratio mundi*' (118; 105; see also 291, 327; 242, 271). Until very late in the story, however, Rastignac continues to find himself visually overmatched. Of the twenty-two exchanges involving him, where the strong verbs *jeter* and *lancer* are used he is the subject of the verb—the active, assertive party—just three times; in all the other encounters, he is the object of the verb, dominated not only by Vautrin and Mme de Beauséant, as one would expect, and by the volatile Mlle Michonneau but also by such unimposing figures as Goriot and Victorine Taillefer and indeed by the servants of both Anastasie and Delphine.

Even as late as Vautrin's arrest, Rastignac is still clearly vulnerable. As he tries to figure out why he fell asleep at the dinner table the night before, Vautrin throws him "le regard froidement fascinateur que certains hommes éminemment magnétiques ont le don de lancer" 'the blood-congealing, mesmeric look that certain men of outstanding magnetic power possess the secret of' (253; 211). After Rastignac returns from a walk taken to reflect and gather his thoughts, his eyes meet those of Vautrin, "dont le regard pénétra si avant dans son cœur et y remua si fortement quelques cordes mauvaises, qu'il en frissonna" 'and he shuddered as he felt that piercing gaze strike home to the depths of his heart, and stir to life its darkest impulses' (261; 218). In the course of the arrest scene, Vautrin's eyes periodically seek out Rastignac (265, 268; 221, 223), who lowers his own in response (265; 221). After Vautrin has been led away, Rastignac is fixed in turn by Mlle Michonneau, who reacts to her own expulsion "en jetant sur l'étudiant un regard venimeux et interrogateur" 'with an expression of venomous inquiry on her face' (269; 224).

It is not until the concluding scene of the novel that Rastignac appears ready to impose his own *regard*. By then, the lessons implicit in Vautrin's downfall, Mme de Beauséant's withdrawal, and Goriot's death have completed his education; now thoroughly disillusioned, he stares intensely at the city spread out below him:

> Ses yeux s'attachèrent presque avidement entre la colonne de la place Vendôme et le dôme des Invalides, là où vivait ce beau monde dans lequel il avait voulu pénétrer. Il lança sur cette ruche bourdonnant un regard qui semblait par avance en pomper le miel, et dit ces mots grandioses: "A nous deux maintenant!" (367)

> His gaze fixed almost avidly upon the space that lay between the column of the Place Vendôme and the dome of the Invalides; there lay the splen-

> did world that he had wished to gain. He eyed that humming hive with a look that foretold its despoliation, as if he already felt on his lips the sweetness of its honey, and said with superb defiance,
>
> "It's war between us now!" (304)

This is the image of Rastignac that is likely to remain in a reader's mind, and it has provoked a good deal of critical commentary. For a character who has been able to show visual strength so infrequently, the force of the verbs—*s'attachèrent, lança, pomper*—points to a remarkable transformation. In one sense, Rastignac appears to have reached "a moment of total understanding" (Prendergast, *Balzac* 79); or, as Brooks puts it, this scene stages a "visionary taking of possession" (*Melodramatic Imagination* 140). It has even been suggested that the protagonist attains at this point a perspective analogous to that of the narrator, who provides a sweeping overview of the capital at the outset of the novel (Prendergast 80; Rignall 49; Brooks 140). Others, however, have stressed the ambiguity inherent in this final scene (Miller 167–69; Rignall 51). As those strong verbs clearly indicate, the view of Paris here is charged with desire, and desire, in the Balzacian world, typically clouds vision. In that sense, Rastignac's position illustrates the irresolvable tension found throughout the *Comédie humaine* between what Max Milner has termed "le voir-désir et le voir-savoir" 'seeing as desire and seeing as knowledge' (Milner, "Dispositifs" 171).

However one interprets this closing tableau, it is clear at least that Rastignac is able now to project his own *regard* with a dynamic force that recalls that of Vautrin. To be sure, he has yet to demonstrate that he will be able to do so on a regular basis in personal encounters; after all, his view at the end is of Paris, and from a distance at that. Still, one can imagine that he now stands poised to take his place among the visually powerful—the *bourreaux* (executioners), to use Mme de Beauséant's unsettling term—of *La Comédie humaine.* The contrast between this Rastignac and the naive and vulnerable figure we met at the beginning is so sharp that it can be difficult to think of them as one and the same person, as Rastignac himself observes late in the story (291; 242). The title of the novel notwithstanding, this is in large measure the story of how a young man comes to learn how to see.

NOTE

[1]The English translations are my own throughout, except when page numbers to the Penguin edition of *Old Goriot* are given.

The Question of Style in *Old Goriot*

Eric Bordas

"Everyone agrees that Balzac wrote badly. On this matter, Opinion does not need to be modified: he wrote badly." Such was Emile Faguet's 1913 pronouncement, written when Balzac's status as a great novelist could no longer be challenged (152–53). For many years this characterization of Balzac as a great novelist but bad writer held sway, allowing one to formulate interesting paradoxes into which, however, it was better not to delve too deeply. The question of Balzac's style, then, is not obvious, since it has for a long time been declared moot. The first thing to ask is: Why such prejudice against the writing of a novelist, a writing judged so clumsy that it was declared to have no style? The answer to this question goes beyond Balzac to a reflection on the general status of novelistic writing in the nineteenth century; at the same time, it raises the issue of stylistics as such (Bordas, "Balzac à l'épreuve," "Scénographie," "Balzac, grand romancier").

The misunderstanding about Balzac's style comes from a theoretical confusion between prose stylistics and poetic rhetoric. One must remember that the promotion of prose to noble style is relatively recent; indeed, it dates from the nineteenth century. Before that, only poetry in verse was deemed appropriate for making ambitious or respectable statements. Prose was for utilitarian discourse or vulgar distractions. But toward the end of the eighteenth century new rhetorical models were developed under the influence of the Revolution's conception of the subject and new discursive praxes for that subject. The ease of prose made it the ideal instrument for these new moral, political, and aesthetic realities. But the change came at a price: a reticent suspicion by rhetoricians who could not allow this democratization of literary speech and who, decade after decade, condemned any prose that did not have the good taste to reproduce poetic models (rhythm, stanza forms, sound, and so forth). For about 150 years the French educational system distinguished between good authors—Rousseau, Bernardin de Saint-Pierre, Chateaubriand, Flaubert—and writers who were to be read with condescension and severity. First among the latter group: the founding father of the modern novel, Balzac.

One consequence of this aesthetic evolution was the replacement, at the end of the nineteenth century, of classical rhetoric by modern stylistics, whose ambitions and limits appear in summary form in Gustave Lanson's *L'Art de la prose* (first published in 1908). At the very moment when stylistics was explicitly theorized as the replacement for obsolete rhetoric, it had nothing to propose other than recasting the standards of poetic meter and sound. Still under the sway of poetic rhetoric, stylistics did not have adequate tools with which to account for the originality of Balzac's novelistic writing. The failure to recognize Balzac's stylistic qualities is tantamount to the admission of the absolute powerlessness of prose stylistics to account for its subject.

Only with developments in linguistics could one learn to see prose as a complex unit of enunciation that, in its diversity and breadth, allows us to read and hear incongruous elements. Thus, Balzacian prose was discovered not as an aesthetic unity but as a set of discourses whose assemblage was often difficult, even brutal, discourses that upset simplistic reading habits. A perfect representative of Balzac's writing, *Old Goriot* contains a number of impurely mixed discourses. And it is in the web of their diversity that Balzacian style is discovered.

One of Balzac's great innovations was to insist on the contextualization of narrative enunciation. This contextualization (or mise-en-scène) is very close to what Dominique Maingueneau describes as "scenography," the situating of the enunciation of a work. Scenography "defines the status of the enunciator and the co-enunciator as well as the space (topography) and time (chronography) from which the enunciation develops" (123). Represented in Balzac's text by dramatized narrative discourses, this novelistic scenography adds another level to the production of meaning of utterances that defines precisely the text's style. There are two principal scenographic matrices in *Old Goriot*. First, on an extrastylistic level of writing as a community's practice of representation, there are sociolectal scenographies. Balzac painstakingly inscribed a variety of specific speech patterns in his work—the ways that duchesses or thieves speak, for example. Second, on an intrastylistic level, there are authorial scenographies. These function as idiolects whose enunciation is part of and contributes to the production of novelistic interest; they thus serve as reference points for the articulation of the writing of a story (narration) and the invention of the novel (fiction). There are two particularly active authorial subscenographies: the inscription of the implied reader (*narrataire*) and the use of metadiscourse.

Critics have long noticed the importance Balzac gave to direct discourse. Characters' speeches are marked by the extreme attention the author paid to the adequation between speaker and statement. As Mario Roques remarks:

> *Old Goriot* has quite rightly been given as an example of the admirable precision with which Balzac differentiates, through language, the characters that life or his imagination bring together. [. . .] Everyone is distinguished by his or her voice, words, or figures of speech: the vulgar speech of the proprietress, the more unpolished speech of her servants, the correct speech of the ex-bourgeois, the jokes of the young, the stupid dignity of Poiret, the ex-salesman, the fearsome *banter* of Vautrin. (254)

Balzac is motivated by a desire for mimetic verisimilitude as well as by the pursuit of diversity as a purveyor of pleasure in reading. The reproduction of discourses seems to manifest the novel's encyclopedism. At the same time, every direct discourse reproduced in a story conveys the ideological codes of a social class (Bakhtin 153). As a translation of the social inscription of the emitter, a discourse is characterized by a specific type of language, a parlance (*parlure*). Each discourse obeys lexical, syntactic, and sometimes morphological rules, all of which signal belonging to a specific social category. Thus enunciation functions as a signal; and in some cases, such as criminal slang, this linguistic attitude can be radicalized so that the signal becomes an intimidating warning.

Worldly feminine parlance is strewn with signs intended to mark distance (the absolute characteristic of all aristocracy). Thus the viscountess de Beauséant and the duchess de Langeais, describing Delphine de Nucingen, née Goriot, multiply indefinite determiners in order to better distance "a" humble origin: "un vermicellier" 'a vermicelli-maker,' "une petite femme" 'a little woman,' "une fille de pâtissier" 'a pastry-cook's daughter,' "un banquier" 'a banker,' "une blonde" 'a blonde' (110–11; 99). They go so far as to devalue proper names: "un baron de Nucingen" 'a Baron de Nucingen' (111; 99). The import of determination becomes almost generic. Metonymy is dear to aristocrats, who are in the habit of referring to others as members of a species rather than as individuals: for example, "ce vieux Quatre-vingt-treize" 'the old '93 man' to designate Goriot (113; 101). Similarly, the duchess de Langeais cannot seem to retain plebeian names, referring to Goriot as Foriot, Moriot, Loriot, and Doriot (112–13; 101–02). Such deformation is an aristocratic and worldly trait, a feigned forgetting of the names of commoners.

The most salient characteristic of the great women of the faubourg Saint-Germain is the recurring use of affectionate apostrophes: "ma chère" takes the lead with eleven uses alone in this novel. Of course context is fundamental for realizing all the perfidy implicit in such ironic protestations of tenderness, which are sometimes the means of allowing the speaker to fire off her most stinging barbs: "Mais, ma chère, Mlle de Rochefide est charmante" 'But, my dear, Mademoiselle de Rochefide is a charming girl' (108; 97), declares the duchess de Langeais about her best friend's happy rival. "Vous êtes bien belle en ce moment, ma chère. Vous avez les plus jolies couleurs que j'aie vues jamais" 'You are very lovely, just now, my dear, I have never seen you with a prettier colour in your cheeks' (114; 102), the duchess says to her friend, while observing the paleness the words have provoked. Balzac reproduces these coded verbal jousts with some pleasure. Such worldly parlance, almost always feminine in *Old Goriot,* is characterized by the quality of a tone elucidated only by the context (Bordas, "Scénographie"). Yet even more than tone, one should speak of voices.

And the voices are plural. For *Old Goriot* is not only the novel of the faubourg Saint-Germain; all sorts of Parisians have their voices heard and participate in realizing this *Scene of Parisian Life.* Like aristocrats, members of the petty bourgeoisie have their own speech, expressions, and pronunciations. But whereas linguistic deformation is more apparent in bourgeois speech than it is in the speech of the aristocracy, context is less fundamental. Phonetic accidents, liaisons, the elision of the silent *e,* and the reduction of consonant groups dot the discourse of the bourgeois characters and provide pseudomimetic indices. Christophe and Sylvie furnish several examples: "monsieur Vautrin, qu'est un bon homme" 'He really isn't a bad sort, you know' (64; 62), "C'te farce!" 'What tomfoolery!' (66, 63), "brouillard qu'est à couper" '[The fog is] that thick you could cut it with a knife' (66; 64); "à c't' heure" 'here and now' 'at this time of day' (120, 145; 107, 123) comes from the mouth of Mme Vauquer. Still, Balzac uses transcription parsimoniously, undoubtedly because of this technique's obvious artificiality. Familiar language is also marked by the suppression of certain pronouns, supposedly to reconstitute spoken language ("ne faudrait rien lui dire" 'you say nothing to her' [65; 62], "faut que j'y aille" 'I'd better go' [66; 63]); by suppression or deformation, which sometimes results in ambiguity ("comme des souches qui sont" 'they're sleeping like logs' [67; 64]); or by the elision of the oppositional adverb ("[Même] que le père Goriot m'a donné un coup" 'and old Goriot gave me a slap' [66; 63]).

Expressivity is here, first of all, a mark of the oral code. Also arising from expressive phonetics, original pronunciations and particular accents play an important role in the characterization of individuals. Popular Parisianisms, often archaisms, punctuate the language. The narrator insists, for example, on what Mme Vauquer "prononce obstinément *tieuilles*" 'persists in calling *line-trees*' (25; 29)—which later become "tyeuilles" 'line-trees' (242; 202). But here the mispronunciation is a personal tic. The whole Vauquer boardinghouse echoes with these popular pronunciations: "Qué baraque!" 'What a hole this place is!' (65; 63); "Qué qui fait donc" 'What do you make of the old codger?' (66; 63), "que nous n'avons néu nos petites passions" 'Have we had our little passions too?' (75; 71); "Eh bien! *monsieurre* Poiret [. . .]. Allons-nous *dinair?*" 'Well, Monsieur-r-r Poiret [. . .]. Are we going to have dinnair?' (80; 74–75); "c'est bon à l'*estomaque*" 'besides being very *stomachical*' (239; 199); "me mener *nune* part" 'to take me *emmywhere*' (243; 203). There are also plays on words, like the gag on *-rama* (80–81, 271; 74–75, 226). In this novel, the reproduction of "authentic" pronunciation is tied to various realist and mimetic motivations. Such motivations generally boil down to designating social belonging, which in turn brings up the question of the place of the individual subject in the context of enunciation in the widest sense of the term (Lane-Mercier).

Remarkably for a story much of which takes place in popular neighborhoods, the author does not overuse lower-class vocabulary. Indeed, Parisian street talk (as opposed to the slang used by Vautrin alone), is rare in *Old Goriot* and limited to forms like "on a voulu m'englauder" '[t]hey tried to pump me' (65–66; 63); " '[. . .] ils ont tous décanillé dès le patron-jacquette.' 'Parle donc bien, Sylvie, reprit Mme Vauquer: on dit le patron-minette' " '"[. . .] they all cleared out at cockerel-crow." "Speak properly, Sylvie," scolded Madame Vauquer, "you should say 'cock-crow' " ' (66–67; 64). And Balzac is prudent as well in limiting the number of morphosyntactic oddities used by the residents of the Pension Vauquer.

The microcosm of the pension Vauquer speaks in a popular language whose most obvious sign is the use of clichés. Goriot's clichés signal the mental alienation of a mediocre man brutally confronted with a passion that exceeds his culture and reaches his deepest feelings. His inability to explain himself except through linguistic stereotypes suggests the absence of individual reflection and the inability to either think or speak without recourse to the language of others. Without a personal language, Goriot has only the elementary use of a popular parlance to lend him expression and reflection. His linguistic alienation is of a psychological order. The materialism of his comparisons, variations on the semes of wealth and poverty, replaces explicit commentary by the narrator. The connotative tenor of such vulgar expressions is not negligible and in it one can see an effect or a process of realist writing. Realism or authenticity? Balzac risks using a language made trite to the point of vulgarity in order better to explain the character—almost an absence of character—of his protagonists.

Both suspect and upsetting for middle-class readers, slang marks the monstrous strangeness of bandits. But at the same time, its insertion in the text should not contaminate or sully the general narrative enunciation: taking its distance through the use of italics, the text protects itself, morally and aesthetically, from what the author denounces. Vautrin uses slang when he is unmasked; then he speaks in the language of the underworld, and his retorts are neither translated nor commented on by the narrator. Only a few words, obviously foreign to everyday language, are placed in italics, and even this device may be interpreted as an indication of spoken emphasis, intended to provoke the boarders witnessing the scene:

> Ça te la coupe, monsieur l'enfonceur, reprit le forçat en regardant le célèbre directeur de la police judiciaire. [. . .] Si j'avais seulement levé la main, dit-il aux pensionnaires, ces trois mouchards-là répandaient tout mon *raisiné* sur le *trimar* domestique de maman Vauquer. [. . . V]ieille cagnotte, tu m'as donné un faux coup de sang, curieuse! En disant deux mots, je pourrais te faire scier le cou [. . .]. Dénichés les oiseaux, envolés d'hier [. . .]. Mes livres de commerce sont là, dit-il en se frappant le front. Je sais qui m'a vendu maintenant. Ce ne peut-être que ce gredin de Fil-de-Soie. Pas vrai, père l'empoigneur? [. . .] il sera *terré* sous quinze jours [. . .]. Ces gens-là ont se faire un plaisir de me traîner un temps infini pour m'*otolondrer*. (264–67)

> "That takes the wind out of your sails, my hopeful blade!" the convict added, looking at the famous detective. [. . .] "If I had so much as raised my hand," he said to the boarders, "I should have been raspberry jam spattered all over Ma Vauquer's sacred hearth. [. . . Y]ou old money-grubber [. . .]. That faked stroke of apoplexy was your work, nosy-parker! I have only to say two words to have your neck wrung [. . .]. The birds are flown; they left the nest yesterday [. . .]. My business books are here," and he tapped his forehead. "Now I know who sold me, it must have been that blackguard Fil-de-Soie. That's who it was, isn't it, old catch-'em-alive-o?

> [. . .] he'll be pushing up the daisies in a fortnight [. . .]. These people will get some fun out of making me cool my heels till the end of time." (220–22)

Gutter slang is isolated in these lines. Favored by the absence of any enunciative warning, the effect is that of a wild, brutal eruption. Thus slang, though episodic, plays a double role: it guarantees the realism of the description and contributes to the construction of Vautrin's character and of the web of relations in the fictional world whose center, or master, Vautrin is becoming. His speech is imposed with such force that any metatextual precaution becomes impossible. Enunciation here is submitted to linguistic violence (Vautrin's slang) in order to better represent this violence as a novelistic theme (Bell; Mitterand, "Artiste?" 142–43). Slang is a strange and foreign speech, with all the aggression and incommunicability that such an alterity implies. The insertion of slang in novelistic language brings about a redistribution of enunciative roles, which once again calls into question the relation between literature and the real.

While characters, through the style of their speech, show their membership in a class and thus contribute to the "realism" of the novel, authorial scenography marks the space not of fiction but of the literary enunciation of fiction. Thus fiction is inscribed in a specific context by the social class, geographic location, political milieu, and so on of fiction readers. In general, Balzac is fond of explicitly inscribing the recipient of narrative discourse, who justifies and thus legitimates the discourse (subscenography: the addressee [*narrataire*]) and of developing the enunciation codes of the grammar of the story (subscenography: metadiscourse).

The Balzacian narrator doesn't speak to just anyone. If the signals he disseminates in his text for the benefit of his addressee are often either neutral or indifferent, he usually determines the identity of the one to whom he tells the story. This determination is first done on a completely concrete referential level: the narrator specifies the social, geographic, and moral situation of his addressee (topography and chronography). Indeed, one could say that Balzac creates a census profile of the addressee that makes the latter one of the characters of the novel.

It is logical that a novelist as taken with women as Balzac was would turn toward them when he thinks of his public, and everyone has interpreted these famous lines in that way:

> Ainsi ferez-vous, vous qui tenez ce livre d'une main blanche, vous qui vous enfoncez dans un moelleux fauteuil en vous disant : Peut-être ceci va-t-il m'amuser. Après avoir lu les secrètes infortunes du père Goriot, vous dînerez avec appétit en mettant votre insensibilité sur le compte de l'auteur, en le taxant d'exagération, en l'accusant de poésie. (22)

> And you will show the same insensibility, as you hold this book in your white hand, lying back in a softly cushioned armchair, and saying to yourself, "Perhaps this one is amusing." When you have read of the secret sorrows of old Goriot you will dine with unimpaired appetite, blaming the author for your callousness, taxing him with exaggeration, accusing him of having given wings to his imagination. (28)

For the majority of critics, this reading contract is addressed to a female reader. But doesn't reading these lines as an address by a successful novelist to his usual public merely confuse author and narrator, reader and addressee? Certainly the female-reader hypothesis is plausible in terms of literary history, but this hypothesis nevertheless confuses ends and means, and has led to a number of misreadings of this act of reading. "How could one not deduce from this white hand the femininity of the desired reader, as well as her elegance?" writes Jean Rousset (27). Indeed, if truth be told, the index is thin: why would a white hand be more feminine than masculine (Schehr, "Homo-diégèse" 138)? What is fairly certain is the social class of the implied reader: during the July Monarchy, working-class people rarely had either white hands or "softly cushioned armchair[s]" and, in any case, could scarcely read. Everything in Balzac's description, including the abundance implied by a dinner eaten with appetite, implies an aristocratic or bourgeois reader.[1]

Doubtful about the sensitivity of the addressee, the narrator also wonders about the intelligence of that addressee. As far as *Old Goriot* is concerned: "Sera-t-elle comprise au-delà de Paris? le doute est permis. Les particularités de cette scène pleine d'observations et de couleurs locales ne peuvent être appréciées qu'entre les buttes de Montmartre et les hauteurs de Montrouge" 'Will it be understood outside Paris? One may doubt it. Only between the heights of Montmartre and Montrouge are there people who can appreciate how exactly, with what close observation, it is drawn from life' (21–22; 27). Here is a preface that works like a reading code. Knowledge of Paris is obligatory. The addressee tends to acquire an original individuality, and this, in the interest of the story itself. Thus the marks of characterization function as criteria of selection that exclude everyone who does not conform. Indeed, as Franc Schuerewegen remarks, "the more precise the image of the inscribed reader is, undoubtedly the easier it is, for the empirical subject, to contradict the inscription and to refuse the role imposed by the text" (19). But at the same time, the more precise the proposed or imposed image is, the more lively the reader's act of rejection is and the more effective that image is in the illocutionary perspective developed by the writer for his narrative strategies. As Gérard Genette remarks, when reading the beginning of *Old Goriot* "I have the right to object (mentally) that my hands are not that white or that my armchair is not that softly cushioned, which means that I take this apostrophe as legitimately directed to me" (*Nouveau discours* 91). Thus the novelist has reached his goal: if I claim to escape the text, I belong to it. Every implied reader implicitly supposes his or her negation, which itself remains another mode of reading. The

Balzacian text never stops playing with this double-bladed selection in order to bring into focus the plurisemic image of an ideal addressee.

The speeches to the addressee that run throughout the Balzacian text trace a reception that is also a production. In postulating a middle-class and superficial reader, for example, the text produces statements that are answers to that reader's expectations and that can be read as a discursive silhouette of the addressee. Enunciation, articulated by *one* (the narrator), is motivated by the *other* (the addressee). This motivation conditions and orients the production of the text, so that the responsibility for that enunciation, unified by being cast in the third person, must be divided between the two productive agents. All these inscriptions of the addressee, figuring the act of reception of the text, can and must be read as metadiscursive statements by which the discourse takes charge of the story, explains it, makes it explicit, justifies it, comments on it, and thus makes it possible. Unlike digressions, which can treat any subject, the metadiscursive statement is exclusively concerned with the poetics of the story and is never a rupture in the narration, since its function is to take control of the narration. Having an enunciative function, metadiscourse is thus a statement that has its own codes of expression and meaning.

The function of some metadiscursive statements is to organize narration, to assure its coherence and especially its clarity when the story risks getting confusing. The narrator intervenes in an explicit fashion to name, announce, refute, and organize. The metadiscursive statement can warn the addressee or anticipate future events:

> Le lendemain devait prendre place parmi les jours les plus extraordinaires de l'histoire de la Maison-Vauquer. Jusqu'alors l'événement le plus saillant de cette vie paisible avait été l'apparition météorique de la fausse comtesse de l'Ambermesnil. Mais tout allait pâlir devant les péripéties de cette grande journée, de laquelle il serait éternellement question dans les conversations de madame Vauquer. (252)

> The next day was to take its place in the annals of the Maison Vauquer as one of the most extraordinary it had ever known. Until then the most startling event in its peaceful existence had been the meteoric apparition of the false Comtesse de l'Ambermesnil. But everything was to pale before the catastrophes of this great day, which was destined to furnish matter for conversation to Madame Vauquer to the end of her days. (210)

This prolepsis creates suspense. The narrator excites the curiosity of the addressee and implicitly designates the pages that follow as something to be savored. Eminently dramatic, the enunciation that constitutes the metadiscourse is a staging of the act of narration itself as it designates a framework for valorizing the text and foresees the text's reception.

As the organizer of narration in the enunciative act that defines narration, metadiscourse can also distribute the story's statements along the chronological axis of the story according to what is deemed essential. This type of manipulation is most often admittedly direct when it anticipates and controls the relation of the addressee to the narration. The addressee can even be the direct subject of the metadiscursive statement: "Chacun comprendra mieux l'espèce particulière à laquelle appartenait Poiret, dans la grande famille des niais, après une remarque déjà faite par certains observateurs, mais qui jusqu'à présent n'a pas été publiée" 'If one considers what has already been noted by certain observers, although nothing has been published on the subject yet, one may understand better the particular species Poiret belonged to in the great family of fools' (220–21; 184). As the director of the novel, the narrator judges what is indispensable or superfluous in the story: "enfin une foule de circonstances *inutiles à consigner ici,* décuplèrent son désir de parvenir" 'In sum, a multitude of circumstances *it is unnecessary to detail here* made him long to distinguish himself, and his ambition to succeed increased tenfold' (57; 56; my emphasis). Thus, the redoubling of the text by the metadiscourse allows for dispensing with certain developments in the story.

This examination of several kinds of discourse in *Old Goriot* is, needless to say, not exhaustive. In particular, it should be followed by a study of the statements of morality and ethics, of the techniques of humor, of the poetic valorizations that characterize the tone and style of the Balzacian narrator (Bordas, *Balzac*). With such a study, the full meaning of this novelistic prose, which draws its power to represent from the effects of contextualization, would take shape in all its richness. The scenographic dimension of the Balzacian story, in its varied deployment, reveals a refusal of the nonproblematized adequation of form and idea, within whatever limit, starting with the rhetorical limit of the sentence (Schehr, *Rendering* 90–146; Paris)—an unacceptable scandal for generations of readers fervently attached to a fetishism of the word, of the sign, and of a meaning to be understood.

NOTES

This essay was translated from the French by Lawrence R. Schehr.

[1]The first version of the text was more precise: "vous qui tenez la REVUE DE PARIS d'une main blanche" 'you who hold the PARIS REVIEW with a white hand.' It is only after the first Werdet edition that the title of the review that had first published the novel (14–28 December 1834) was replaced by the anonymous deictic "this book." See the variants in the Gallimard-Pléiade edition of the novel in *La Comédie humaine* (1221). We should also remember, as Stéphane Vachon points out in his edition of *Le Père Goriot,* that Pierre Larousse, in his *Grand Dictionnaire universel du XIXe siècle* (1865–76), includes the following definition for the expression "Ecrire de sa main blanche" 'Write with the white hand': "Ecrire soi-même, de sa *propre* main. Détestable équivoque sur les mots blanche et propre" 'Write oneself, with one's own hand. A distasteful equivocation on the words white and clean or own' (370; my trans.). Philological precision reminds us that the readings proposed here are interpretations.

SPECIFIC COURSES

Teaching *Old Goriot* in a Course on French Culture: Balzac's Myth of Paris Revisited

Catherine Nesci

In the opening of his book *Paris and the Nineteenth Century,* Christopher Prendergast imagines a scene of reading in *Madame Bovary* in which the heroine's fantasy of Paris is nourished by her bulimic devouring of Balzac's urban fictions. In Prendergast's supplement to Flaubert's 1857 great novel, Emma is reading *Old Goriot,* Balzac's Parisian novel first published, like *Madame Bovary,* in installments in the trendy periodical *La Revue de Paris.* For Emma, Prendergast writes, "Paris is 'Paris,' a magical proper name ('Comment était ce Paris? Quel nom démesuré . . .'), around which fantasy and desire fluctuate in direct proportion to her feeling of local entrapment" (1).[1] From Emma's perspective in provincial Normandy, Paris represents excess and enormity and promises a life full of mysteries and revelations. Coming from a rural background, Emma is a petite bourgeoise without any professional experience or social knowledge; she is quite vulnerable to the sociocultural models offered by the fascinating "capital of the nineteenth century," to use the title of Walter Benjamin's famous 1935–39 essays on Paris.[2] Seduced by the urban and social myth, Emma transforms Paris into an imagined center around which she builds her vision of the metropolitan *là-bas,* the "over there" and "elsewhere" that negates her provincial surroundings.

As Italo Calvino has observed, the entire novelistic energy of Balzac's work is sustained by, and condensed into, the foundation of a mythology of the modern metropolis (151–52). To a certain extent, Emma Bovary's Paricentric vision of the world dramatizes the apotheosis of Paris that Balzac stages in *Old Goriot,* an apotheosis Flaubert will later dismantle in his 1869 novel, *Sentimental Education.*[3] What are the characteristics of the urban and social myth exemplified in Balzac's novel? This essay addresses this question through the social and moral topography of *Old Goriot*'s Paris. Starting with the city as context and then considering it as text, I will examine the mapping of the urban space and the intersection of social spheres. I will demonstrate that "more than a background, the city provides the terms of the narrative itself" (Ferguson, *Paris* 2). Insofar as *Old Goriot*'s Paris embodies modern rites of passage, it helps us better apprehend—and better teach—the nature of the modernity expressed in Balzac's literary vision.

Focusing on the realistic representation of Paris in *Old Goriot* in the context of a course on French culture provides the opportunity for a thorough introduction to modern France and the development of urban capitalism. Some revealing statistics on the urbanization of France help students understand how nineteenth-century French society reacted to the deep crisis generated by two phenomena central to economic modernity: the demographic revolution and the industrial revolution. Between the eighteenth and the twentieth centuries, France's population grew twofold, while the population of Paris multiplied by twenty. While the Parisian population had increased slowly between 1675 and 1788, between 1801 and 1851 the number of Parisians doubled, primarily through emigration from the provinces. The newcomers were principally young males. Until 1817, more than half the Parisian population were women. Between 1817 and 1836, however, the percentage of female city dwellers decreased; in 1836, there were only ninety women for every one hundred men in the thirty- to forty-year-old age group. As a result of this dramatic population shift, women became increasingly rare and thus more precious (Marchand 7–13).

These demographic changes deeply influenced the shape of Balzac's plot of ambition and desire as early as 1829, when the author published the *Physiology of Marriage,* a cynical essay dealing less with marriage than with the sociology of adultery in high society. Presenting himself as deeply committed to the knowledge of Paris, Balzac dramatizes this knowledge through his analysis of the mercenary approach to happiness taken by young men eager to succeed by trafficking in a rare and precious species—the married women of the wealthy bourgeoisie and aristocracy. This view of women as commodities is given a satirical illustration in chapter 3 of the *Physiology,* "The Honest Woman," in which Balzac provides a complete and forceful portrait of the artist-flaneur, of the artist as prowler: "To wander through Paris! Truly a delightful, an adorable existence! Strolling [*flâner*] is a science, a feast of the eye. Walking [*se promener*] is vegetating; strolling is life." This portrayal of the artist-flaneur, also depicted as "a foot-soldier of Paris" (930; 32), is inserted as a euphoric digression from the dialogue of dandies chatting about their rich mistresses. Positioned on the boulevard as the invisible man eavesdropping on the passing dandies' plots of seduction, the essayist of the *Physiology* transforms the words of the passersby into a fantasy of control of the urban space. Whereas the dandies assume privileged access to the desirable women of high society, figured as essentially available despite their married status, the artist-flaneur visualizes the capital as a source of ready satisfactions and knowledge. Seen from the perspective of the flaneur and his mobile, penetrating gaze, Paris thus becomes an object of desire at the same time as it is an object of sensual knowledge and intellectual mastery (Ferguson, *Paris* 90–93). This passage thereby foreshadows the terms of Eugène de Rastignac's conquest of wealth and prominence in Parisian high society: like the sophisticated, knowing flaneur of the *Physiology of Marriage*, whose life is "full of desires, fully realised" (32), Eugène must first become a kind of "foot-soldier" and observer of Paris in order to master the art of seduction and urban knowledge.

But why was it so important for a young author writing in the 1830s to establish the necessity of a mastery of urban space? Priscilla Parkhurst Ferguson provides a relevant answer by placing the Balzacian novel in the political and historical framework of postrevolutionary France, and, as well, in the context of the "aesthetics of integration" that the nineteenth-century novel so convincingly epitomizes ("Reading" 59). Nineteenth-century Paris "illustrated the patterns and complexities of modernity," especially in the multifaceted process of the centralization and concentration of France's riches, intellectual energies, and cultural institutions. The city, Ferguson observes, "defined the age because it symbolized the experience of change"; it was a "laboratory for social change" ("Reading" 47). Ferguson's analysis of the symbolic ramifications of the Revolution of 1789 and the execution of Louis XVI provides an enlightening background for the historical allusions disseminated throughout Balzac's urban novel:

> The successful contestation of authority opened the city to definitions from every quarter. The execution of one king, the defeat and subsequent flight of his successors in 1814, 1815, 1830 [. . .] bespoke the fragility of political authority. With no center, the urban symbol system was in disarray. ("Reading" 52)

The intense crisis of legitimacy, begun with the Revolution of 1789, was reinforced by a deep anxiety surrounding the urban space, making that space the object of ethnographic examination: knowing to whom the city belonged required knowing the city, this object appearing as suddenly foreign to city dwellers and visitors alike. Following the model of Mercier's eighteenth-century *Tableau de Paris*, numerous literary guidebooks prospered in postrevolutionary France, feeding an avid readership with images of Paris and Parisians. But these publications reproduced the diversity and disorientation of urban life without achieving any coherent vision of the city (Ferguson 54–60). In Balzac's work, however, all the parts of the city cohere: they form a whole in which metonymy plays an organizing role. The Balzacian narrator appropriated for himself "the authority of definition" of the capital city (60).

From the *Physiology of Marriage* to *The Human Comedy,* Balzac's portrayal of Paris testifies to "a new sense of the city as a total dynamic entity and way of life, a total horizon bounding one's perception and one's life, beyond which was the unthinkable darkness of the provinces," in the words of Peter Brooks ("Text" 7). In *Old Goriot,* the most puzzling definition of Paris is given by the chief of police, the character in charge of representing the law and the king: "Paris is Paris, can't you see. This word explains my life" (251).[4] The chief's tautological statement partakes of the myth of Paris as a "total horizon" needing no further explanation. On the contrary, all the other characters, along with the narrator, have a vision of, or a theory about, Paris; they speak of and define Paris and Parisian women and young men, thus doubling the narrator-observer's acute discourse on Paris. The characters' rhetorical activities, their grids of perception and self-representation betray their desire to belong to the theater of Paris, be it in person or vicariously, like Vautrin and Goriot. Everyone wishes to be a part of Paris or even to possess it as a whole, like Rastignac in control of his newly acquired gold: "The whole world belonged to him. [. . .] Paris belongs to him" (138–39).

A valuable way to explore how *Old Goriot*'s Paris presents its readers with a "total dynamic entity and way of life" is to ask students how the novel communicates an experience of the urban space. As we know from the opening description, written in the present tense until Mme Vauquer's portrayal is completed (21–29), and from Balzac's use of authentic geographic details throughout the novel, *Old Goriot* assimilates the fictional space with that of historical Paris. But the novel does not serve as a tourist's guide; it presents its readers with a social as well as a moral guide to Parisian society. When we follow Eugène de Rastignac as he acquires a knowledge of the capital, a knowledge he will try to use in his conquest of high society, we gain a moral understanding of the city. The reader's experience of the city is thus structured through Eugène's ascent of the social ladder and his seduction by the "enchantments" of Paris (170); his wanderings through urban sites intersect with the different stages of his Parisian education. In its spatial orientation, our vision of Paris is at the beginning of the novel limited as well: the opening description locates the drama between the Latin Quarter and the faubourg Saint-Marceau. The narrator insists that the story, which takes place within the walls of Paris, may be understood between the heights of Montmartre (in the north) and the hills of Montrouge (in the south); however, outside the walls of Paris, the story risks being misunderstood (21–22). Understanding the story and accepting the specifically Parisian nature of the tragedy requires that readers be converted into Parisians. Readers become virtual inhabitants of the space inscribed between the walls and the heights that circumscribe the artificial and natural boundaries of the city.

Often the students, aware of the narrative logic by which, as readers, they are invited to take on the identity of Parisians, notice that this topographical experience is tightly linked with the history of postrevolutionary France. The experience is as oriented and limited, as close and distant, in time as it is in space. Restoration society and its immediately preceding history are portrayed through a precise and accurate location of social spheres on the Left and Right Banks. Balzac's deployment of authentic topographical references and his invocation of historical, financial, and material details "beguile his readers into suspending their disbelief and treating imaginary characters as if they were real," as David Bellos puts it (67); such details also organize the spatial as well as temporal enclosure of the drama characterized as essentially Parisian. But what about the division of the urban space along two different axes of social segregation (vertical for the Vauquer lodging house, according to divisions of wealth, and horizontal, according to a class principle)? The Paris of 1819, in which the drama unfolds, is at first presented as a strictly hierarchical space. Asking students which kinds of hierarchies are mapped onto the Parisian labyrinth usually leads to many fruitful discussions on the roots of distinction and power in *Old Goriot's* post-Napoleonic society. In what follows, I propose a reading of the relation between urban space and social hierarchization that demonstrates how the unfolding of the narrative dramatically challenges the social and moral hierarchization of the capital.

With regard to the Parisian topography of the novel, readers enter the Paris of *Old Goriot* from the southeast, on the Left Bank, through the in-between zone bordering the faubourg Saint-Marceau and the Latin Quarter, the district inhabited by French students such as Rastignac, a law student, and Bianchon, a medical student who observes Paris essentially from the Jardin des Plantes and the Jardin du Luxembourg; the young men eat at the Vauquer lodging house, where Rastignac is a full boarder.[5] Also on the Left Bank, we follow Rastignac to the Beauséant mansion (*hôtel* in French, which means implicitly *hôtel particulier* [private residence]), on the rue de Grenelle, located in the midst of the faubourg Saint-Germain, the stronghold of the aristocracy of the ancien régime. Presided over by Mme de Beauséant, Rastignac's distant cousin, the Beauséant residence and the faubourg where it is situated represent "a kind of sacred city" of inherited class privilege within the secular city.[6] This representation of the exclusive faubourg Saint-Germain underlines the moral distance the aristocrats want to preserve between themselves and the rest of the capital, as the duchesse de Langeais explains: "the world is a quagmire, let's try to remain above it, on its heights" (114). Mme de Beauséant, "the last daughter of the virtually royal house of Burgundy" (329), rises above social evil and embodies the utmost distinction; her values and manners are depicted as superior and genuinely different from those of the other characters in the novel.

On the Right Bank lies the new quarter of the Chaussée d'Antin, where the two Goriot daughters live. This is a world inhabited by aristocrats less selective than those living in the faubourg Saint-Germain and by the bankers and the nouveaux riches whose main desire is to be admitted into the salons of the faubourg Saint-Germain, as Mme de Beauséant reveals in a striking assertion:

"Delphine de Nucingen would lap up all the mud between the rue Saint-Lazare and the rue de Grenelle to be admitted to my salon" (116). M. de Restaud, despite his name (Restaud/Restoration) and his belonging to hereditary aristocracy, lives in the Chaussée d'Antin because of his marriage to the rich but bourgeois Anastasie Goriot. Also on the Right Bank runs the boulevard des Italiens, where almost all the characters go to be entertained. The new aristocracy of the Chaussée d'Antin and the old aristocracy of the faubourg Saint-Germain mingle there less to socialize than to scrutinize each other; they all demonstrate that they belong to high society, in order to reaffirm their social position. M. de Beauséant's social habit takes him to the Variétés theater in the company of his mistress (169), whereas his wife has a permanent loge at the Italiens, where she too reigns as a kind of queen, admitting only highly selected visitors, in addition to her lover, Marquis d'Ajuda-Pinto. In describing these social spheres, the instructor can introduce the students to Restoration society and to the interaction between the legitimist Parisians living in the noble faubourg Saint-Germain—aristocrats whose coveted distinction is founded on their names—and the financiers of the Chaussée d'Antin, whose materialist and degraded values are based on wealth (see, e.g., Baron de Nucingen's illegal real estate speculations, 300).

The students' reading tour thus takes them from the Left Bank to the Right Bank, from the Paris of the past to the new Paris. On the Right Bank, students learn about Goriot's history of speculations on the rue de la Jussienne, east of the Palais Royal; they also penetrate the two sisters' mansions (one on the rue du Helder, the other on the rue Saint-Lazare). It is revealing that Mme de Restaud's mansion and Rastignac's new apartment, prepared in secret by Delphine and Goriot on the rue d'Artois, are both located on streets that cross the boulevard des Italiens: the Chaussée d'Antin is thus shown as contiguous to the new center of entertainment and leisure that will soon displace the faubourg Saint-Germain as the center of the most exalted and fashionable Parisian society. Rastignac is only a footstep away from the Italiens, where he can join Delphine in her loge. The advantageous location of his new lodging symbolizes his surrender to the Paris of seductive but illusionary appearances. The stages of Eugène's Parisian education foreshadow the increasing asymmetry between the two banks of the Seine and the shifting of the center of elegant life to the northwestern parts of Paris on the Right Bank. The novel also describes the rise of the new boulevard culture whose cafés, theaters, and Opéra will soon destroy the Palais Royal's supremacy as a center of cultural attraction. Rastignac goes to the Palais Royal only to win the money necessary to Delphine's secular salvation, as she tells him dramatically: "you have saved me from shame and death" (199); his gains clearly symbolize the monetary triumph that will give him entrance into Delphine's heart. It is therefore interesting that at the close of the novel the ambitious young man challenges high society by standing at the top of the Père Lachaise cemetery, in a position of dominance vis-à-vis the Right Bank; but he is only able to do so after Mme de Beauséant has exiled herself from Paris. The symbolic death of the faubourg Saint-Germain's queen jeopardizes the supremacy, even the very survival, of the social group to which she belongs; her self-imposed exile inaugurates an eclipse of the values she embodies and the concomitant triumph of the profane values of the Chaussée d'Antin. No wonder that Rastignac leaves the cemetery to have dinner at Delphine's mansion.

That aristocratic and bourgeois spheres coexist and intersect in the novel is emphasized in the opening sentence of *Old Goriot.* Here a family name is coupled with an aristocratic one in a biological way—"Madame Vauquer, born *de* Conflans" (my emphasis)—revealing the noble origin behind the bourgeois name, which thus receives a mark of respectability. The lodging house's owner will later utter her noble maiden name to reiterate that she is a reputable person (286). In the narrative, dishonorable or disavowed parent-child relationships (between Goriot and his daughters, between Victorine Taillefer and her father) and acknowledged ancestries connect the different quarters of Paris. Because Eugène de Rastignac shares his noble ancestry with Mme de Beauséant, the petty noble from the southern provinces and boarder at the Vauquer lodging house is admitted into the sacrosanct faubourg Saint-Germain, goes to the Italiens and moves to the Chaussée d'Antin. The twenty-one-year-old hero even demonstrates his inherited superiority when he teaches Delphine how to repay de Marsay; Delphine characterizes his ideas as "pure Beauséant" (201). In *Old Goriot,* genuinely noble names correspond to authentic, recognizable addresses taken by Balzac from the real Parisian toponymy and topography. When an anonymous but knowing coachman tells Rastignac about the two Beauséant addresses and determines which one the ignorant young man must go to, the coachman displays a real command of Paris: not only a topographical one but a social one as well (97). Although Rastignac's aristocratic connections open the door of Mme de Restaud's residence and ensure M. de Restaud's benevolence, Rastignac precludes his own admission to the Restaud mansion when he pronounces the bourgeois name and derogatory nickname of old Goriot. The intersection of aristocracy and bourgeoisie is therefore dramatized by Eugène's wanderings and his access to the Parisian salons. Eugène's conquest depends largely on learning how to read Paris, a skill that entails unveiling the city's biological, sexual, and financial secrets as well as learning how to differentiate between a bourgeois woman and an aristocratic one and how to unravel the origins of a name. Basically, the young man learns a double equation: both Mme de Restaud and Mme de Nucingen are "born Goriot"—a truth the eponymous father confesses and one that no boarder of the lodging house believes.

The shifting intersections of social spheres are an important component of the urban experience *Old Goriot* communicates. Each world possesses its assigned viewpoints, from which it observes the others. For example, after being dismissed from the Restaud mansion, Eugène visits Mme de Beauséant and learns from her and from Antoinette de Langeais about Goriot's past and about the sibling rivalries of Goriot's daughters. The two authentic aristocrats speak contemptuously of the Chaussée d'Antin and the social behavior of Goriot's daughters, with whom the aristocrats must share not only public spaces, such as the Italiens, but also the semiprivate spaces of their own salons. The two aristocrats assert the superiority of the faubourg Saint-Germain, the world of "assigned" identities, over the Chaussée d'Antin, the world of "achieved" and thus exchangeable identities (Brooks, "Text" 7). As Mme de Beauséant explains, women from the bourgeoisie hope to ape authentically distinguished manners by wearing the same hats as noblewomen—a useless gesture according to the aristocrat, who sees in this fashion mimicry a process of merely borrowing identities (116–17). But her haughty perception that the Chaussée d'Antin possesses spurious values is defeated in the cruelest way, when everyone witnesses her fall following the desertion of Marquis d'Ajuda-Pinto (324–25).

Students' comments on the implications of this episode revolve around two questions: Can the distinction between the faubourg Saint-Germain and the Chaussée d'Antin retain its validity after Mme de Beauséant's exile? To what extent does her exile signal a feeling of loss and uncenteredness for the new urban life represented by the Chaussée d'Antin? The most significant consequence of Mme de Beauséant's dramatic departure, however, is her voluntary abandonment of her Parisian identity at the same moment that her cousin Eugène sheds his provincial skin (291) and crosses the Parisian Rubicon (290), thus converting himself into a Parisian. Does Rastignac respect the contract made with his cousin, who lends him her name provided that he return it "white," unsullied (117)? His knowing acceptance of the values of the Parisian hell (evidenced in his signing of a bill of exchange to save Mme de Restaud [312–13]) degrades the world of assigned identities that is his birthright. In spite of his refusal to participate in Vautrin's assassination plot, Eugène's subsequent complicity with Baron de Nucingen's financial schemes, related in *La Maison Nucingen* (1838), foreshadows the destruction of the hereditary aristocracy by the rule of money.

Thus, by linking high society with the low society of the lodging house, the novel challenges the hierarchization of Parisian society. Furthermore, the lodging house and the rue Neuve-Sainte-Geneviève are constituted as places of death, announcing the real and symbolic deaths society fosters in this novel. Eugène's itinerary through this social hell leads ultimately to Père Lachaise, from where Eugène deciphers society in its totality. His panoramic view of Paris encompasses the symbolic cohesion of the novel. The images of the Catacombes and the metaphors of Paris as hell, quagmire, and labyrinth thus figure the themes of modern damnation (Gengembre 43). When Delphine likens the attendees at Mme de Beauséant's last Parisian appearance to a crowd gathering for a public execution (324–25), she registers the symbolic charge of the social death of the woman Rastignac views as a goddess from the *Iliad* (331).

In conclusion, to summarize what the myth of Paris represents in *Old Goriot*, the following questions are useful: Is high society the object of desire par excellence? Is that the place to make one's mark? Or is it revealed as the place where women, gold, and money circulate and are made available to ambitious young men? I usually ask students to relate these questions to the weakening of the social contract and of family ties, on which Eugène's itinerary is based (Nash 2–5). I then lead students to discuss such topics as the role of individualism, the various forms of ambition and desire, the relation between time and the quest for gratification, and the search for gold and money. Students are also asked to consider the various deaths accorded the characters in the novel and the many illusions Rastignac loses.[7]

All these themes are expressed by, and through, the myth of Paris, as figured in Balzac's revolutionary vision of the postrevolutionary world. *Old Goriot's* Paris, this boundless name- and desire-producing machine, will become an object of nostalgia when Baron Haussmann restructures the city in the 1850s. In *Madame Bovary* Emma intoxicates herself with what is for readers in 1857 the myth of a dead city. Revisiting Balzac's urban and social myths reveals the material as well as the spiritual aspects of modernization and its daunting psychic costs.

NOTES

I would like to thank Ann Jensen Adams, Abigail Solomon-Godeau, Michal Ginsburg, and Elizabeth MacArthur for their generous help.

[1]The passage in *Madame Bovary* reads: "How was this Paris? What a boundless name!" (91; my trans.).

[2]In his unfinished project on nineteenth-century industrial culture, the *Passagen-Werk* (Arcades project), Benjamin notes that topography is the key to Balzac's myth of Paris (*Paris* 108).

[3]On Gustave Flaubert's rewriting of Balzac's myth of Paris, see Peter Brooks, *Reading for the Plot* 172–74; Ferguson, *Paris as Revolution* 80–114. Franco Moretti recently proposed a refreshing view of Balzac's "plural city," which he describes as "a true mosaic of worlds, where the social division of labor seems to have literally stamped itself upon the urban surface" (*Atlas* 87).

[4]For quotations from *Old Goriot,* the page numbers given refer to the French edition; all the translations are mine.

[5]Throughout the course, I use the maps in Marchand 18, 46; in Gengembre's edition of *Père Goriot,* 4–5; in Guichardet 86–93; and in Moretti, *Atlas* 87–99. Moretti uses Norah Stevenson's "demographic plan" of the *Human Comedy,* elaborated in the 1930s.

[6]The expression "a kind of sacred city" is taken from an anonymous text, *Le Rôdeur des Faubourgs* (1829), describing the faubourg Saint-Germain as "a truly privileged city" within the city, a place, removed from the agitation of the rest of the capital, in which the peacefulness of a provincial town reigns (qtd. in Bertaut 43; Gengembre 121).

[7]Students' paper assignments have included the following: Discuss the myth of *la Parisienne* in *Old Goriot;* illustrate your analysis with images from nineteenth-century popular print culture. Analyze the disjunction between rural and urban experience in *Old Goriot.* Characterize the meaning and economy of the *quartier* in *Old Goriot.* For the last two topics, I ask students to read Nash 8–9.

Nuance in the Novel: Teaching *Le Père Goriot* in the Context of a Course on French or World Literature

Laurence M. Porter

The hardest task for a teacher of literature is sensitizing students to what is being said indirectly. Meaning often depends on allusion. How many times our class remains silent when we ask what made them laugh or what they found ironic in a passage of the text. The barrier of a second language makes recognizing connotation even more difficult, and literature, a language within a language, is particularly rich in connotation. *Le Père Goriot* provides an ideal opportunity for teaching nuance: thematically it is a subtle work, but several of the most influential interpretations of it—be they psychoanalytic, Marxist, or melodramatic—risk presenting Balzac's novel as a monolithic struggle between two unnuanced opposing forces: desire and repression, workers and privileged classes, moral good and evil.

Initially I prepare students to read one text at a time; historical surveys flood them with information that has not yet become relevant, and that discourages independent investigation. I save synthesis for the end. First the instructor must make students aware of how the novel can say things: directly, figuratively, and by implication. We treat each of the four sections of *Le Père Goriot* in turn. To begin, students are asked to summarize the assigned section in two sentences: one conveys their understanding of the essence of the plot; the other conveys the version of the plot suggested by Balzac's section titles. For instance:

1."Une pension bourgeoise" The ambitious young nobleman Rastignac is stuck in a shabby middle-class boardinghouse, emblematic of his poverty and unworthy of his rightful social station.

2."L'Entrée dans le monde" With the help of his distant cousin, Mme de Beauséant, Rastignac succeeds in entering high society.

3."Trompe-la-Mort" Vautrin is unmasked and arrested.

4."La Mort du Père" Having sacrificed everything for his daughters, Goriot dies without them, having only Rastignac and Rastignac's fellow student Bianchon at his bedside.

To begin the final class, students alerted in advance are asked to characterize in a sentence the relations between and among the four sections. For instance, Balzac uses the age-old device of the inn to assemble his characters in section 1, and to disperse them in section 4. As the story progresses, each of Rastignac's three main protectors departs in turn, finally leaving Rastignac alone to face Paris with only Delphine's money and his wits. The chiasmatic arrangement of the words in the titles of the last two sections, however

("Trompe-*la-mort*" and "*La Mort* du Père"), reminds us that the central reality for everyone is death.

During the first class, I prepare for later discussions of implication and nuance by introducing the contrast of homodiegetic (within the main story) and heterodiegetic (outside the main story) elements. The most straightforward commentary typically emerges in apparent digressions: authorial asides, metaphors, and allegory. Indirect commentary appears notably in intratextuality (implied connections between two parts of a work) and intertextuality (implied connections between one work and another). The trope of syllepsis, a condensed form of equivocation, frequently provides a junction between the direct and indirect. The technical terminology above, already glossed on a handout, is graphically and leisurely illustrated in the classroom. The first paragraph or so of the target text is highlighted in colors on an overhead projection. The students are asked to seek their own examples as they read on. Syllepses (hard for a second-language learner to recognize) appearing later in the text are identified, but without comments; the students will provide the comments when the time comes.

In Balzac's first paragraph (3–4), the text could be unpacked this way (items 1 and 2 are indirect [in these instances, anticipatory] comments; 3 to 5 are direct): (1) In the description of the boardinghouse, "[c]e respectable établissement" '[t]his respectable establishment' is an antiphrasis, that is, it says the opposite of what it means.[1] Its irony will gradually emerge throughout the story as several boarders are unmasked in turn as a confidence artist (la comtesse d'Ambremesnil); a master criminal (Vautrin); and a police spy (Mlle Michonneau). The irony is compounded and redoubled because the persecution of Goriot by the other boarders is, ethically if not legally, equally reprehensible. (2) In the episodic mention of "une pauvre jeune fille" 'a poor young girl,' "pauvre" carries the sylleptic meanings of "impoverished" and "afflicted" (both owing to her father's cruelty). Victorine is the "right" woman for Rastignac, but she will be passed over by him when he becomes a successful gigolo. Her story is textually echoed by *La Peau de chagrin*, where the hero Raphaël de Valentin, an *unsuccessful* gigolo despite Rastignac's coaching, finally finds blissful but self-destructive happiness with the right woman, who had secretly helped him survive in a benign counterpart to Mme Vauquer's malign boardinghouse. Such contrasts imply that Rastignac's story does not exhaust all the possibilities of Balzac's imagination. (3) Should one use the word "drame" for this novel? Balzac asks. The term implies a Romantic ethos in which feelings and the imagination may be more momentous than historical events—and by extension implies a bourgeois rather than an aristocratic literature. (4) Metaphors present Paris as a vale of tears and society as a juggernaut that crushes the weak. Students should be asked to look for restatements of this theme by some of the characters, later in the work. (5) Balzac attacks the insensitivity of the reader, who dismisses the novel as a fantasy, whereas it is actually "true" (a syllepsis, here referring to the truth of feelings as opposed to the truth of history): he writes "All is true" in English (4), to suggest the shift of context from facts to moral truths.

Once the long initial description of the boardinghouse has ended, students should be apprised that the point of view has decisively changed. The implied author continues to intervene frequently with metaphors and with authoritative generalizations concerning human nature (e.g., "le bonheur est la poésie des femmes" 'Happiness is what makes women seem poetic' [11]); he remains a controlling presence. Students should be asked to find some examples of such intrusions. Nevertheless, the italics, which until this point were used to highlight erudition (phrases in Latin and English, titles of literary works), now convey clichés representing the limited vision or blindness of the characters, rather than the privileged vision of the author (e.g., "femmes qui ont eu des malheurs" 'women who have had misfortunes,' "bonne femme au fond" 'a good woman deep down' [8]). The italics serve to mark either privileged or deficient knowledge, as they do later in Flaubert. The twofold notation of misapprehension and reality will later be increasingly condensed into syllepses such as "vos filles" 'your whores' or 'your daughters,' a phrase used by those who believe Goriot is exploiting young women when he is in fact being exploited by them (23); Vautrin's "je vous aime" 'I love you' to Rastignac, meant homosexually but understood and intended to be understood homosocially as 'I like you' (78, 122); and "le monde" 'high society' or 'the world,' a term reflecting the delusions of those ambitious or complacent people who consider high society to be all that matters.

As the story unfolds, intratextuality—echoes of the phrases or plans of one character by another in different circumstances—implies further moral commentary by the author. At the two extremes of society, the duchesse de Langeais and Vautrin agree that society is a "bourbier" 'quagmire' (37, 60). The police agent Gondureau proves more cynical than Vautrin, arousing our sympathy for the latter's social revolt: the detective echoes the criminal's sentiments—"il est d'un homme supérieur de se mettre au-dessus des préjugés" 'a superior man knows how to place himself above moral conventions' (144)—but after arresting Vautrin he plans to have the unarmed criminal bayoneted at the slightest pretext. In contrast, Vautrin arranges the murder of Victorine's brother with a trick fencing lunge, but at least the young man dies while fighting a duel, sword in hand (132). Finally, "à nous deux!" 'it's between the two of us now' (79), the preamble to Vautrin's suggestion that Rastignac give him a commission in exchange for the murder that will restore to Victorine her rightful inheritance and make it profitable for Rastignac to marry her, anticipates Rastignac's challenge to the city of Paris at the conclusion: "A nous deux maintenant!" (216). That this phrase functions as a syllepsis implying first complicity and then defiance suggests that Rastignac cannot participate in the social struggle without compromising himself.

Insensitivity to nuance leads many readers astray when they evaluate Rastignac's last utterance. To read this next-to-last sentence as a triumphant affirmation of full moral maturity falsely infers Balzac's moral endorsement of his character's attitudes, for the author ironically introduces his hero's words as "grandiose" (216). It is easy to forget that fiction often has two endings: one for the protagonist and another for the implied author. At the conclusion of *Les Liaisons dangereuses,* for example, after Choderlos de Laclos has lovingly depicted his supremely immoral Marquise de Merteuil duping one person after another, she is suddenly and improbably disfigured by smallpox, denounced, impoverished, disgraced, and forced into exile in the country. With the tacked-on ending, Laclos seems to be saying, "That looks like fun . . . but I probably couldn't get away with it." Balzac's own authorial ending, his last sentence tellingly isolated as a separate paragraph, reads "Et pour premier acte du défi qu'il portait à la Société, Rastignac alla dîner chez madame de Nucingen" 'And as the first act in his challenge to society, Rastignac went to have supper with Madame de Nucingen' (216). Rastignac, forgetting his mistress's cruelty toward her father, whom he has just buried, resolutely embarks on a career as gigolo and social parasite. That he mentally compares himself to Napoleon here (ask students to find out how) creates a glaring anticlimax that makes him at least faintly ridiculous.

How then can one integrate *Le Père Goriot* into a survey of the novel? We might begin with these hypotheses:

1. Authors in all periods repeat themselves, telling a story more than once within a single work (often with different characters) and in a series of different works; retelling a story reveals its subjective importance for the teller. As the preceding clause suggests, what is repeated always adds an implied meaning to what was said first: repetition occurs in a new, self-created context. For instance, the first time the wealthy miller's daughter Delphine tries to penetrate high society, she is rejected by her unnatural sister Anastasie, who could open doors for Delphine but chooses not to do so; Delphine's devoted father cannot help. On her second attempt, Rastignac makes it possible for her to achieve her goal; thus he becomes in a sense more than family. This repetition with a difference makes Delphine's infatuation with Rastignac overdetermined.

2. Fictional characters have trouble learning things, so for them such repetition is necessary. Before Rastignac can fully accept this knowledge, he must be told and shown again and again—by instructors from both social extremes—that society is a jungle. His cousin Mme de Beauséant and Vautrin lecture him, and their teaching is confirmed for Rastignac when he observes that neither son-in-law, although enriched by Goriot, is willing to help pay for Goriot's simple funeral; when he overhears how both his cousin and her best friend, the duchesse de Langeais, have been betrayed by their lovers; when, after Goriot's death, he has to stop Mme Vauquer from stealing Goriot's treasured locket containing pictures of Delphine and Anastasie. The relative obtuseness of the character produces insight, since repetition by the author suggests generalizations about human nature.

How can Balzac sympathize with a protagonist whose "education" is complete when he has learned to believe in nothing? Balzac's response is nuanced. The narrator must intervene in a curious attempt at rescue. He dictates cynical calculations (in free direct discourse) to Rastignac, but then says that as yet they are not spelled out in Rastignac's mind; they are like hazy clouds. As if to hold Rastignac back, the narrator then condemns the slippery slope of moral compromise, praising Molière's self-righteous Alceste of *Le Misanthrope* (as did Rousseau) as a model of moral integrity. Finally the narrator himself begins to slide, admitting that the struggles of an ambitious, worldly man to succeed without getting deeply involved in evil might furnish an aesthetically beautiful if not morally admirable subject (98).

3. As a novel develops, repetitions modulate increasingly into variations on a theme. In *Le Père Goriot,* for example, Balzac often creates character doublets in order to contrast two ways of playing one social role: a heartless daughter (calculating Anastasie or heedless Delphine); an ungrateful son-in-law (disdainful Count Restaud or greedy Baron Nucingen); a poor student (idealistic Bianchon or Rastignac, becoming steadily more cynical); a criminal (the gang leader Vautrin or the solitary confidence woman called "la comtesse d'Ambremesnil"); a loving younger sister (the steady Agatha or the imaginative Laure); and an unscrupulous financier (the flinty, cautious Gobseck or the wildly speculative Nucingen).

4. As *the* novel develops, time becomes increasingly chopped up: the epic's roast becomes the realist's stew, then the postmodernist's hash. Balzac adopts a transitional realist-Romantic mode: flashbacks fill in various characters' histories, and we find several anticipations of the future, including a clear allusion to Rastignac's later success. However, Balzac's time disturbances are local (episodic, segmental), not pervasive (supersegmental).

5. In the evolving novel, ever more space is claimed by the landscape of thought until it blends with the landscape of action. (Time permitting, evoke the counterexample of the *Iliad* here in order to challenge the myth of literary "progress": most of Homer's long text is stretched over only four days, and persuasion in various forms—counsel, supplication, exhortation, inner debate—occupies far more space than the fighting does. Achilles's outstanding verbal gifts as much as his brawn are what give Achilles real substance and distinction as a fictional character [see Martin 59, 138, 141–43, 191–92, 231–38].) Parastories (unrealized possibilities) proliferate: Vautrin's daydreams of living as a slaveholder in America (83); Rastignac and Bianchon's shared fantasies concerning whether either would make his wishes come true by willing the death of a mandarin in China (103).

The major transition from thought to deed in Balzac (inspired, perhaps, by Goethe's *Faust*) occurs through temptation. Bianchon never yields; Vautrin sees all temptation merely as opportunity. Rastignac is the star of the story because, unpredictable, he remains suspended between vice and virtue.

Like Rastignac, Balzacian symbolic descriptions occupy an ambiguous site between thoughts and actions. As Goriot's room becomes more denuded, the language that describes it becomes more luxuriant. His pauperization progressively limits his possibilities for action, while simultaneously increasing Balzac's opportunities for pathos. The longer the description (authorial action), the less free the character, if only as measured by the relative proportion of text space the character occupies.

In a term-long course on the novel, I devote two or three hours each to introduction and conclusion and five to nine hours each to anywhere from five to seven works. In the first session we discuss the questions What is a story? Does it differ from a novel? What do you like about stories? What do you tell stories about? The contrast between routine and privileged moments is explored. The second session presents Charles Baudelaire's "Le Voyage," the poem that concludes *Les Fleurs du Mal* in the 1861 edition, as a story frame without content. The nameless, disillusioned travelers in the poem are driven by restlessness and dissatisfaction (here one could invoke Lockean "uneasiness" [see, e.g., Locke, esp. 272–87]); raw curiosity impels the would-be audience.

Throughout literary history, fictional characters' failure to learn generates narrative repetition. In tablets 9 through 11 of *The Epic of Gilgamesh* (74–108), as in Baudelaire—and with strikingly similar language—dissatisfaction drives the story. The hero, horrified at seeing his best friend Enkidu die and decay, desperately seeks immortality. The three people he meets in turn all immediately ask: "Why is your heart so wretched, your features so haggard? Why is there such sadness deep within you? Why do you look like one who has been traveling a long distance so that ice and heat have seared your face?" (84, 87, 90). In the Old Babylonian version of the epic, Siduri the Tavern Keeper urges Gilgamesh to accept and enjoy the transient pleasures of food, music, a mate, and children (85n1). The hero cannot listen and pursues his fruitless quest. Why is a person who cannot learn—for example, the protagonist in ancient Greek tragedy, or the warrior Roland—so often the hero? Agonizing over mistakes may give the hero a richer inner life.

When introducing a chronological series of individual works, I follow a conceptual arrangement that can be presented as developmental if one wishes: episodic structure, dramatic structure, character development, social development, naive authorial intervention (self-consciousness), covert authorial intervention (artistic elaboration and unreliable narrators), and complex authorial intervention (ludic structures). Here I suggest, space lacking, only one French and one other example for each category.

1. Episodic structure: picaresque novels and satires (Voltaire, *Candide*; *Lazarillo de Tormes*). Folly and social corruption (rather than Gilgamesh's counterphobic activity) compel the characters to remain in motion. A steady chronological progression and clear focus on a central hero compensate for causal discontinuity.

2. Dramatic structure: introduction, complication, decision, climax, and resolution (Lafayette, *La Princesse de Clèves;* Goethe, *The Sorrows of Young Werther*). Since in such stories the landscape of thought has been developed, motivation may be guided either by disillusionment (knowledge that disables) or by enlightenment (knowledge that empowers).

3. The bildungsroman: a young person learns about life and finds a place in

society (Balzac, *Le Père Goriot*; Dickens, *Great Expectations* [which also has an escaped convict as protector]). Balzac introduces a melancholic rhetoric of insight. Revelations are given to, not sought by, the characters (in contrast, say, with Nemours's successful but futile voyeurism in *La Princesse de Clèves*), but the characters usually learn too late (ask students to look for examples). The complement of belated awareness is self-destructive ignorance in Goriot, both his daughters, Mme de Beauséant, the duchesse de Langeais, and even the omnicompetent Vautrin (he learns that he cannot insult Mlle Michonneau with impunity; she learns that she would have received twice as much money for a warning as she received for a denunciation). Even the flinty Mme Vauquer is duped in her homosocial trust in a sham countess. Balzac dissociates tragic blindness from nobility of character, which becomes a sufficient but not a necessary precondition for the former.

In Balzac's Darwinian struggle for life, the only ostensible moral may be that "les belles âmes ne peuvent pas rester longtemps dans ce monde" 'noble souls can't endure long in this society' (198). What conduct, then, does the author advise? *Le Père Goriot* does not necessarily represent a melancholic resignation to corruption once we place it in the broader context of *La Comédie humaine.* With guidance, ambitious students can trace the story of one of the recurring characters to key passages from another work such as *La Maison Nucingen* or *Le Médecin de campagne,* "L'Auberge rouge" or *Gobseck.*

Balzac's introduction of recurring characters in *Le Père Goriot* may imply a partial retreat from omniscient narration: one cannot learn everything about another person all at once. Time permitting, I teach Marcel Proust's *La Prisonnière* (*The Captive*) here. In it one can continue to trace the motifs of concealment, mystery, voyeurism, and bootless insight that were introduced with *La Princesse de Clèves* and reencountered in Balzac.

4. Chronicle: the rise and fall of a family or milieu, characterized by great social density (the rich, vivid representation of characters of both genders and of all ages) and by nostalgia. Such stories often represent a collective elegy for a bygone order, as in Sir Walter Scott, a major influence on Balzac. I recommend Driss Chraïbi's *Oum-er-bia: The Mother of Spring,* which allows one to discuss Islam, and Alessandro Manzoni's *The Betrothed,* especially popular with students.

5. Self-conscious narrative: writing about writing, or the audience, or both. Denis Diderot's *Jacques le fataliste* provides a challenging example from the ironic tradition going back to *Don Quixote* and beyond. Ask students to comment on the meaning of the main plot line, a journey: does it suggests aimlessness, a quest, or both? The paradox of Diderot's self-assertive servant reflects a dialogical rather than an essentialist view of character. Laurence Sterne's *Tristram Shandy* presents a contrasting self-conscious mode—the refusal of motion or event while relating a military and an amorous siege, the latter with genders reversed. Here one can explore how the intense self-consciousness of traditionally realist authors such as Stendhal or Balzac differs so greatly from that of Diderot or Sterne—it shuts interpretation down rather than opens it up.

6. Paranoid-schizophrenic narrative, or the mimetic fantastic. Like inmates

taking over an asylum, here the alien inner story of self-conscious narrative devours its frame, erasing all ironic distance beyond that implied by exaggeration and internal contradictions. Such tales are strongly organized by the delusional perceptions of a deranged protagonist who cherishes ideas of reference, of being the center of the world. The protagonist's benign egotism contrasts with the malign egotism of the totalitarian social setting. Michel Tournier's *Le Roi des Aulnes* (*The Ogre*) and Gunter Grass's *The Tin Drum* are exemplary.

7. Postmodernist narrative. Self-conscious and playful in rapidly shifting among different times, settings, and characters, it lacks the stabilizing counterweight of a fixed set of interlocutors. Characters' obsessions reflect their basic disengagement (which is diagnosed rather than recommended by the implied author). Georges Perec's *La Vie mode d'emploi* (*Life: A User's Manual;* the careful index guides the instructor to the major plot lines, from among which a reading assignment can be conveniently tailored) and Julio Cortázar's *Rayuela* (*Hopscotch,* from which parts 1 and 2 of 3 can reasonably be selected) are ideal illustrations. Both novels play a game of hopping by the numbers (Perec structures his story to conform with the knight's tour in chess but played on a ten-by-ten-square board); both use description to subvert novelistic structure; and both prove to be self-canceling artifacts. Cortázar's hero, as his lover Polia says in other words, resembles a universal solvent.

A natural sequel, as life imitates art in today's wealthy societies, is the passive spectator of the flickering image. In the electronic age, from the humanistic point of view the landscape of thought seems to have become overwhelmed by the landscape of action (for this distinction see Bruner, Goodnow, and Austin). Technological progress seems to move pari passu with intellectual regress. But we teachers need not yield to despair on witnessing Victor Hugo's dire prophecy "ceci tuera cela" (text will kill images [198–211]) being fulfilled in reverse. Students' extensive experience with images can be exploited by asking some students to tell which scenes from *Le Père Goriot* they would illustrate and why. Others might analyze how a film remake of a novel (such as Claude Chabrol's *Madame Bovary*) can present time shifts and the landscape of thought. Still others might examine a French studies Web site to explore how electronic communication remains dependent on text for conveying its message. Best yet, cultural critique provides a jujitsu that can subdue the monster (see Bourdieu). We literature teachers should not fear but face the competition, exploring the relations between image and word—not as all but as part of what we do—with the same zeal we have always brought to exploring the relations between statement and story.

NOTE

[1]All references to *Père Goriot* are to Peter Lock's 1968 edition (St. Martin's); translations are mine.

You Can't Judge a Book by Its Cover: Teaching *Le Père Goriot* and Modernism

Janet Beizer

In an undergraduate survey course on nineteenth- and twentieth-century French literature, I like to emphasize continuity as we move from Romanticism to postmodernism—though the temptation to focus on change is great. The students' limited exposure to aesthetic and cultural history; the sweeping passage, in just fourteen weeks, over almost two hundred years; and the necessarily skeletal reading list all contribute to an impulse to adopt a schematic approach that would situate the two centuries oppositionally. When we begin the semester with *Le Père Goriot,* we can extract from the novel (and from the century it is taken to emblematize) the seeds of modern rupture and fragmentation. *Goriot* introduces the old order against which contemporary disorder may be set, but it presents this old order as inherently unstable. To open the course with this novel is then to open the possibility that the modern evolved over time and, specifically, that it was already present, at least already latent, in the early nineteenth century. Part of my goal is to circumvent a binary reading—of *Le Père Goriot* and of the nineteenth and twentieth centuries—that would set up the nineteenth century as foil to the twentieth.

I owe to the back cover of the penultimate Garnier-Flammarion edition of the novel the serendipitous discovery of a quotation from Albert Thibaudet that conveniently frames the reading from which I want to depart:

> "Quand j'ai été père, dit Goriot, j'ai compris Dieu." Voilà un mot extraordinaire qui nous met aux sources de la création balzacienne. La présence de Dieu, le consentement à Dieu sont aussi évidents, aussi nécessaires, aussi absolus dans l'œuvre de Balzac, pleine comme un jour de la création, que l'absence, l'inexistence de Dieu dans l'œuvre de Proust, procès-verbal d'un monde qui se détruit.[1]

> "When I became a father," said Goriot, "I understood God." That is an extraordinary idea that places us at the source of Balzacian creation. The presence of God, and the acceptance of God, are as evident, as necessary, as absolute in Balzac's works, which are as full as a day of creation, as are the absence and the inexistence of God in Proust's works, which constitute the record of a world on a course toward destruction. (my trans.)

This eulogy of Balzac's world, a world Thibaudet contrasts to a latter-day Proust-identified godless universe, sets up a series of polarities that begin to structure a reading—but simultaneously a questioning—of *Le Père Goriot.* When he places Balzac's works in contradistinction to Marcel Proust's, Thibaudet aligns with the two authors two contrasting series of characteristics. Balzac and the nineteenth century, the father, God, creation and creativity, totalization, presence, linearity, and order exist in opposition (only partly explicit) to Proust and the twentieth century, the missing father, godlessness, sterility (biological and literary), absence, fragmentation, and disorder.

When we turn to the novel, we find that the reading suggested by Thibaudet's oppositions is instantly and constantly challenged. In what follows I show how, concentrating on broad narrative structures of the novel and details of the opening scene.

Why start with a citation from an outmoded critic? Thibaudet's oppositional analysis is invaluable, even when we disagree, because it presents Balzac's novel—succinctly—in much the same way Balzac does. Echoing the novel's alibi in summary form, the citation might be said to represent the novel's "cover," even when it does not appear on the outside of the book: it covers for the novel's subversive elements. It serves as paratextual pendant to the title, which also presents the novel under the sign of the father. Balzac's title and Thibaudet's commentary, authorial pretext and critical posttext, respectively announce and recall the novel in the father's name.

But let us look more closely at this name. If the role of Goriot's name in the title, played out in the novel, is central, it is nonetheless qualified: *le père* precedes the proper name not only to designate the significance of the paternal function but also to denigrate the worth of the person who fills it. In French, to refer to someone who is not a religious father as "le père" something or other is to disrespect his station and to depreciate his stature.[2] So from the very beginning, even before the first paragraph takes form, the father's centrality is simultaneously posed and undermined.

The novel's ambivalence about the father whom the title names Goriot extends to his very identity. Although the title identifies a very precise focal point, this designated spot will be progressively decentered—thematically and, we will later see, formally—as the plot unfolds. If Goriot represents paternity of the most obvious (that is to say, biological and sentimental) sort, both Vautrin and Rastignac vie with him, admittedly in very different ways, for the reader's attention in matters of paternity. Vautrin's paternity is of course always metaphorical, given his delicately stated but always intimated sexual preference ("Pour moi qui ai bien creusé la vie, il n'existe qu'un seul sentiment réel, une amitié d'homme à homme" '[F]or me, and I have turned life inside out, only one real sentiment exists—friendship between man and man' [218; 182–83]). Vautrin sees himself as a patriarch rather than as a pater, his vision of fatherhood displaying itself most moderately through the desire to authorize Rastignac's young life. "[J]e vous connais comme si je vous avais fait" '[. . .] I know you as well as if I had made you myself,' he tells him (145; 124). More extremely, however, his paternal vision spins out exotic American plantation scenes in which he is featured as slave-owner "father" to a brood of slave "children":

> J'ai besoin de deux cent mille francs, parce que je veux deux cents nègres, afin de satisfaire mon goût pour la vie patriarcale. Des nègres, voyez-vous? c'est des enfants tout venus dont on fait ce qu'on veut. (154)

> I need two hundred thousand francs, for I want two hundred niggers to carry out my idea of the patriarchal life properly. Negroes, you see, are children ready-made that you can do what you like with. (131)

In both cases, paternity, for Vautrin, is manifestly related to a puppeteer-like power to animate dependent lives—an authorizing capacity not entirely distinguishable from an authoring function: "Je suis un grande poète. Mes poésies, je ne les écris pas: elles consistent en actions et en sentiments" 'I am a great poet. My poems are not written: they are expressed in action and in feeling' (154; 131). The text here provides a suggestive juncture between Vautrin and Goriot. For Goriot, the ultimate fatherhood involves an authorship based not only on engendering but also on puppeteering a daughter's life: "C'est moi qui suis l'auteur de ta joie, comme je suis l'auteur de tes jours" 'It was I who authored your happiness as I authored your life,' he tells Delphine after effectively scripting Rastignac in her life and casting him in her bed. (278; 231; trans. modified). So although we may distinguish between the father's affect as presented by Goriot and the father's force as displayed by Vautrin, both affect and force are in the end variants of an ethos of paternal power.

Rastignac plays son to Goriot as father, and to Vautrin. Reborn in a world whose very laws of existence he must learn, he seeks alternative models for the aristocratic but impoverished father he has effectively abandoned back home.[3] Although the "family values" Goriot incarnates ostensibly orient Rastignac's quest, the choice between Goriot and Vautrin ultimately depends on which one will allow Rastignac the greatest and most rapid access to the father's domain: women, money, social authority.

Each of the three male protagonists represents a plot that vies for dominance. Any one of the three plots could potentially take over and determine the novel's course. If we read from Goriot's or from Vautrin's point of view, the novel represents the father's quest for a child who might affirm (his) paternity (on a personal and an institutional level). If we follow Rastignac's plot, we read a similar story from a different perspective: a filial quest for a paternal figure who could properly serve as model. Though the titular father might seem to privilege a reading for and from the father's point of view, the fact remains that the novel is at least in part a bildungsroman, narrated from the point of view of the son—albeit ironized by the narrator. The three rival plots coexist in a state of unresolved tension, a state that speaks not only to the vexed circumstances of family relationships in this novel but also to a formal irresolution, to which we shall return.

The multiplication of paternal plots in itself serves to put in question the father the novel names as central. When we consider each of the novel's paternal-filial relationships, the father's name is further weakened. For despite a proliferation of players, not one can be found to fill the role adequately—not even among the bit-part fathers whose shadows momentarily cross the stage. The comte de Restaud, husband to Goriot's daughter Anastasie, is father to only one of the three children she has borne. Victorine de Taillefer, in one sense Goriot's inverted counterpart, is a disinherited daughter less interested in financial than in emotional acceptance by the father who has lingering doubts about his wife's fidelity and, consequently, his own paternity. The novel's quest for a father extends even to the walls of the Maison Vauquer, hung with a paper that depicts scenes from Fénélon's version of the son's archetypal odyssey, *Télémaque* (26; 31).

All father-child relationships founder in this novel; all paternal variants fail. This is not entirely surprising given the premise on which the novel is built. Rastignac's quest for paternal privilege (in the guise of power, money, women) originates after all in lack. He rejects the father who has endowed him only with a name—a name signifying little but past privilege. It is the very *absence* of the desired father (the father as source of privilege and power) that motivates Rastignac's relocation to Paris.

Rastignac's search is doomed ever to reproduce its founding void. Though his noncompliance with Vautrin's authority is less a matter of resistance than it is an accident of fate (which casts a more expeditious success in his path, in the form of Goriot's Delphine), the result is to estrange Rastignac's narrative line from Vautrin's. In more abstract terms, Vautrin's paternity, as it is played out in his role of guardian banker to a society of convicts, is, perhaps perversely, closer than any other in the novel to the traditional paternal ideals of strength and protection and loyalty. In other ways Vautrin veers sharply from tradition: this new-style father, master of disguise, bears no fixed identity or address. The name of the father as embodied by Vautrin/Collin/Trompe-la-mort (etc.) moves us away from all stabilizing notions of the paternal.

The shortcomings of the ostensibly quintessential father do not entirely surprise when they are replaced in the general context of paternity in this novel. Goriot is not simply a victim of filial rejection but a father both weak and excessive, unable to regulate the reigning chaos of relationships that surrounds and includes him. His love for his ungrateful daughters, measured out in currency, is from the beginning of the novel depicted as figuratively incestuous, a lover's passion displaced at the death of his wife.[4] As the narrative continues, Goriot stages a virtual ménage à trois to facilitate both Delphine's access to her lover Rastignac and her father's own access to her (232–33; 194–95). Goriot's passion is further displayed in caresses and scenes of jealousy (276–84; 230–36).

By the novel's close, unbounded paternal love has swelled into a generalized loss of limits. In the rhetoric of Goriot's deathbed ravings the text places supreme reason. In fact, as Nicole Mozet has argued, it is the recognition of truth that kills Goriot: "Il meurt alors de savoir [la vérité] et d'être obligé de confesser qu'il savait" 'He dies from knowing the truth, and having to admit that he knew it all along' (*Balzac* 80; my trans.). The febrile image of the madly regenerating shreds of a father's heart are a just measure of the excess associated with paternity: "Mon cœur est grand, il peut tout recevoir. Oui, vous aurez beau le percer, les lambeaux feront encore des cœurs de père" 'My heart is big enough to hold all your troubles. Yes, even if my heart is broken each piece will make a father's heart again' (306–07; 254). In the legend provided by Goriot's end, more is clearly translated as less. Fatherhood has become a "vice," in Goriot's own words: "Mes filles, c'était mon vice à moi; elles étaient mes maîtresses, enfin tout!" '[My daughters] were my own particular vice; my mistresses, in fact, everything!' (345; 286; trans. modified). Paternity has become a potential source of crime, and Goriot, a latent criminal: "Si je savais où aller pour voler, mais il est encore difficile de trouver un vol à faire" 'If I only knew where to go to steal the money, but it is so hard to find a place to rob' (311; 258).

Goriot's fantasized theft for love evokes another petty theft inspired by family love: Rastignac's (successful) request to his sisters, mother, and aunt to send him money unbeknownst to his father (121–23; 108–10). Together these transgressions suggest a broader infraction of the father's law. A state of lawlessness reigns in a world where the father is either robbed or robber, victim or martyr. Anarchy is repeatedly expressed by an overcoding of family relationships, as when Goriot defends Rastignac's knowledge of delicate family matters to Anastasie: "Mais c'est mon fils, notre enfant, ton frère, ton sauveur. [. . .] Oh! mon enfant! Je serai plus qu'un père pour toi, je veux être une famille" 'But he's my son, our dear child, your brother, your saviour! [. . .] Oh! my child! I will be more than a father to you, I will be a whole family' (312; 259; trans. modified). In narrativized kinship terms, more is not simply less; it is confusion, commotion, disorder, a kind of semantic incest.[5]

I want to pause here to reflect on the remarkable resemblance of Balzac's nineteenth-century tale of the father to Thibaudet's ostensibly antithetical description of Proust's modern godforsaken world, "procès-verbal d'un monde qui se détruit" 'record of a world on a course toward destruction' (221). The fullness of creation that Thibaudet attributes to Balzac's work ("pleine comme un jour de la création") sounds, to this reader's ear, strangely hollow. For the death of Goriot figures not merely an individual father's demise but also the passing of fatherhood as an institution—with all the attendant cultural and philosophical complications that poststructuralism has detailed.[6] Well before the poststructuralists, Balzac grasped the implications of the death Goriot symbolically foretold, phrasing in Goriot's last gasps the prediction-cum-lament: "La patrie périra si les pères sont foulés aux pieds. Cela est clair. La société, le monde roulent sur la paternité. Tout croule si les enfants n'aiment plus leurs pères" 'The country will go to ruin if the fathers are trampled underfoot. The thing is clear as day. Society, the whole world, turns on fatherly love, everything falls to pieces if children do not love their fathers' (345–46; 286).[7]

Everything falls to pieces. *Le Père Goriot* is early evidence of a massive crumbling, not just of paternal flesh and bones to dust but also of social, cultural, and narrative structures. This is a huge subject that obviously exceeds the scope of my essay but one that we can at least begin to approach by noting some of the ways in which Goriot's death reverberates to the edges of the novel, affecting formal narrative patterns.[8]

I alluded earlier to a formal irresolution attached to the competing plots of three protagonists who vie for centrality. At stake are issues that juxtapose (in not simply oppositional ways) traditional family mores and changing social value systems, old and new, good and evil, reproduction and production—and also the shape of the narrative that embodies all such issues. The decentering of Goriot's plot suggests not only that the father's name is uncertain and the hero's identity undecidable but also that plot itself may no longer be central. When the center is askew, opposing points may not hold and linearity may be an illusion.

Although the linear structure of *Le Père Goriot* is apparent, it is not untroubled. The narrative unfolds the lives of its major protagonists from a given point in time forward; that much goes without saying. However, the point from which everything unfurls and develops—the opening scene at the Maison Vauquer—occupies an inordinate amount of time and space in the novel, arguably disrupting the temporal line. Also, the very device that is often cited as evidence of the overarching unity of Balzac's work—the use of characters that reappear from novel to novel—might well also be taken as a sign of alinearity, discontinuity, and disunity within this novel (Kanes 16–17).

I want to argue not that *Le Père Goriot* is a postmodern novel but rather that it prefigures postmodern narrative. It is betwixt and between the traditional and the modern, order and disorder, and is prone to excesses in both directions. So that we may look in more detail at the often simultaneous exaggerations of unity and disunity in this novel, I now turn briefly to their manifestations in the novel's opening.

Moving in domestic circles inward in his human comic version of Dante's infernal rings, Balzac takes us slowly from the walls of Paris to the dining room of the Maison Vauquer, coming finally to rest on the rotund body of the pension's owner. In his classic analysis of this scene, Erich Auerbach has emphasized its "stylistic unity," created by the harmonic representation of person and milieu that he names "atmospheric realism" (470–73). He mentions too, however, in passing, "the lack of order and disregard for the rational in the text" (471), which he attributes partly to Balzac's haste but also, more importantly, to Balzac's obsession with a demonic significance not readily assignable to specific objects and persons.[9]

Without disputing Auerbach's thesis of stylistic unity, I want to bring into sharper focus the disorder and irrationality to which he alludes. It is remarkable that what is consonant on every concentric level of Balzac's description is a dissonance of detail. Squalor, dirt, crumbling, flaking, decay, clutter, disparity, and disarray are the qualifying terms of harmony and order.

Let me cite quickly an assortment of examples indicative of a pervasive descriptive form that can be followed at greater length. The narrator immediately situates the tale that is about to unfold in a Paris qualified as "cette illustre vallée de plâtras incessamment près de tomber et de ruisseaux noirs de boue" 'a valley of crumbling stucco and gutters black with mud' (22; 27). In the next circle inward, we are shown the *quartier*, the gloomy, tomblike founding site of the novel, compared to the Catacombs (23; 28). From here we are introduced to the exterior of the house: the trompe-l'oeil arch painted on the wall over a chipped, scaling statue of Cupid (24; 29) and a facade that features some fifteen windows, all of which have blinds "dont aucune n'est relevée de la même manière, en sorte que toutes leurs lignes jurent entre elles" 'all drawn up to different levels so that the lines are at sixes and sevens' (25; 30). Behind the house is a yard "où vivent en bonne intelligence des cochons, des poules, des lapins" 'inhabited by a happy family of pigs, hens and rabbits' (25; 30). When next we are moved from the heteroclitic exterior into the house, we face a motley array of mismatched, clashing objects, odors, and persons (26–29; 30–33). The multiple layers of paint and grease and stains on the walls and furniture and kitchenware give heterogeneity a temporal as well as a spatial empire.

The clutter is centered in the person of Mme Vauquer, whose unkempt, frittered, scattered appearance speaks oddly to a larger harmony:

> Son jupon de laine tricotée, qui dépasse sa première jupe faite avec une vieille robe, et dont la ouate s'échappe par les fentes de l'étoffe lézardée, résume le salon, la salle à manger, le jardinet, annonce la cuisine et fait pressentir les pensionnaires. (29)

> Her knitted woollen petticoat dipping below the refurbished old dress which forms her skirt, its wadding escaping from rents in the ripped material, expresses the essence of the sitting-room, the dining-room and the little garden, makes you realize what the kitchen must be like, and foreshadows the boarders. (33)

But if this passage leads us to expect some definition, some centering, or some further delineation of Mme Vauquer through the presentation of her boarders, disappointment must follow; she prefigures and exemplifies them *in her very state of dispersion and discordance.* The boarders of the Maison Vauquer—"ces êtres rassemblés par le hasard" 'these persons [brought] together [by chance]' (32; 35)—are alike only in their utter disparity: "Une réunion semblable devait offrir et offrait en petit les éléments d'une société complète" 'Such a gathering should contain a sample of all the elements that make up society, and this one did so' (40; 42).

In Auerbach's reading, disunity is recuperated by its layered repetition. I take this consonance of dissonance less as a defeat of disorder than as a sign of irresolution. Balzac's text seems painfully torn between unity and fragmentation, unable to find stasis either way—much as it is torn between a stabilizing, regulating idea of fatherhood and the dethroning of this idea. When we locate within *Le Père Goriot*—for many, the traditional novel par excellence—a struggle among thematic, cultural, and formal forces that are more often split binarily, into traditional and modern pairs, it becomes easier not only to discuss the nuances of this particular novel but also, more generally, to teach the nineteenth and twentieth centuries as an extended cultural period with perceptible continuities as well as discontinuities. The nineteenth century then becomes not an idyllic prelapsarian foil to the twentieth but rather a time preparatory to our own. Reading the nineteenth century through *Le Père Goriot,* one is tempted to believe that the father would not have been so tenaciously sought if he hadn't already been lost.

NOTES

[1] The passage originally appeared in Thibaudet's *Histoire de la littérature française de 1789 à nos jours* (221), and it was reprinted on the back cover of Pierre Citron's Garnier-Flammarion edition of *Le Père Goriot* from 1966 to 1995.

[2] Sandy Petrey remarks that "when Mme de Langeais dismembers the second component of *père Goriot* [by referring to him indiscriminately as Loriot, Poriot, Doriot, Moriot, and Goriot], she merely does to the father's proper name what the novel has done to his common name from its opening words" (88). See Petrey's Lacanian-Austinian reading of the fate of the father's name in *Le Père Goriot.*

[3] "Ses illusions d'enfance, ses idées de province avaient disparu. Son intelligence modifiée, son ambition exaltée lui firent voir juste au milieu du manoir paternel, au sein de la famille" 'His childish illusions, his provincial ideas, had gone. His increased knowledge, his kindled ambition, had opened his eyes, so that he saw things clearly back in his father's house, in the family circle' (57; 56; trans. modified).

[4] "Dans cette situation, le sentiment de la paternité se développa chez Goriot jusqu'à la déraison. Il reporta ses affections trompées par la mort sur ses deux filles [. . .]" '[A]s things were, paternal feeling developed to the point of mania in Goriot: the wealth of affection which death had frustrated was transferred to his two daughters [. . .]' (127–28; 113).

[5] For an elaboration of this argument, see Beizer 132–39.

[6] See Said, for example.

[7] I agree in part with Roddey Reid's Foucauldian argument that the notion of families in jeopardy in fact operates nostalgically to create the idea—the ideology—of the nineteenth-century family: "Now, once 'lack' is considered as a discursive technology for inscribing 'family' in the social body, in turn, it becomes difficult to conceive the domestic family household in any straightforward empirical or realist sense. [. . .] I want to argue that we must entertain the very real possibility that 'family' [. . .] has always been a moment in strategies of governance [. . .] and that it has existed only to the very extent that it was constructed by discourses and institutional practices that were invested by a political and social imaginary, which, in a circular fashion, these same discourses and institutional practices helped construct in the first place" (7–8). Nonetheless, however discursively constructed the traditional family was, it existed, again discursively, in lockstep with a panoply of cultural discourses and practices whose lack or loss or waning was no less empirically felt despite (or because of) their status as discursive technology.

[8] For a more fully developed exposition of these issues in *Le Père Goriot,* more generally in Balzac, and most generally in nineteenth-century narrative and culture, see Beizer.

[9] See Brooks (*Melodramatic Imagination*) for the best extended analysis of the tension between what Auerbach names a demonic significance (472) not easily pinned down and a more orderly representation of objects and affect and being.

Teaching *Old Goriot* across the Disciplines: Mapping Social and Urban Space

Sharon Marcus and Vanessa Schwartz

How can we show students that *Old Goriot* maps urban space and social relations? And how can we tailor that point to different disciplinary perspectives—for example, those of literary criticism, urban studies, and French history?

An assignment we have found to be effective demonstrates this claim by taking mapping literally. We ask students to list the novel's urban references, then locate some of these references on a map of Paris. In assigned questions and classroom discussion, we then ask what students learn from comparing how the novel and the map represent Paris.

Here's a prototype of the exercise: "As you read *Old Goriot,* make as complete a list as possible of the novel's references to places in Paris. On a map of Paris, preferably from between 1819 and 1848, locate at least ten of these places." The exercise lends itself to many variations. For example, the teacher can calibrate how independently the students work with the map—from asking them to locate maps and street atlases themselves to putting maps on reserve to handing out copies of maps that have already been partially annotated. Students can work in pairs or larger groups, on the novel as a whole or on specific sections of it.

In class, pool information so that students can annotate their individual maps more fully, either by asking groups to exchange information or by annotating a map yourself on an overhead projector. If everyone is consulting a different map (if, for example, one group's map comes from an 1835 guidebook, another's from a historical atlas of Paris), reconciling all these maps to one another can be unwieldy and time consuming. You can streamline class time by distributing blank copies of a map that then becomes a common reference point.

We'd advise, however, not to emphasize a smooth classroom experience that results in everyone's sharing a tidy, comprehensive map. This exercise is more about process than about product. The students should have a map clear enough to help them understand the novel's urban setting, but the exercise's interest also resides in struggling to find a map and read it; in seeing how maps of the same place differ in scale, format, and content; and in questioning how and why we can correlate the novel to a map at all.

A written assignment should accompany the exercise so that students do not fixate on sheer mechanics. You can pose an open-ended question: What did the list and map teach us about the novel or about a particular theme of the novel (urban relations, the structure of Restoration society)? You can also provide more pointed questions and topics for discussion: What spaces and places appear throughout the novel? Certain characters seem associated with certain places. Give examples of this. Who appears where? Why? Now that we have a map of Paris in its entirety, we can see that the novel does not represent all of

Paris. Which sections of the city does it include? exclude? What principles of selection do these choices imply? The novel makes much of the social distances separating certain neighborhoods—for example, between the faubourg Saint-Germain and the Chaussée d'Antin and between Père Lachaise and central Paris. Locate these areas on the map. Does social distance correspond to physical distance? Does the map help to explain the social standing of a neighborhood? For example, what kinds of institutions are present or absent in the three neighborhoods cited above? In a course that focuses on Paris, you can ask students to write brief reports on the different theaters, parks, and *quartiers* that appear in the novel and on the map. Ask students to compare how the two types of text represent these places. What significance does the novel assign to these places? How does the novel use language and narrative sequence to assign significance? What kind of significance does the map assign to these places, and how does it use visual cues and graphic design to rank the relative importance of place?

We develop answers to some of these questions below, but before doing so, we want to highlight how this exercise's form yields as many pedagogical rewards as its content does. First, the list alone encourages students to engage more carefully with *Old Goriot*'s unfamiliar elements. When reading in translation, students often gloss over foreign names and phrases; when reading about Paris, a place that they usually will not have experienced firsthand, they tend to blur the realist details that are supposed to convey a transparent urban view. When we ask students to write down every Parisian place-name they encounter, attentive curiosity can replace the reflex to skip over French references that seem interchangeable in their incomprehensibility.

When students then undertake the challenging task of locating the listed places on a map, they experience the novel as an interpretive puzzle and get caught up in the frustration and satisfaction of solving it. Most get grumpy about the difficulties of finding a map and locating the places on it—and it is difficult, especially if they're using French books but don't know French or are trying to locate streets and *quartiers* but have never before seen a map of Paris. When they do find what they're looking for, however, they feel triumphant. The exercise thus not only informs students about *Old Goriot*'s setting but also makes them identify with Eugène's urban education by subjecting them to the confusion and clarification that Eugène undergoes as he navigates the city. As a result, when you address how *Old Goriot* combines Eugène's individual development with his education in the system of urban signs, the discussion will be enriched by the students' experience of reading the novel and executing the assignment.

The map also lends itself to teaching *Old Goriot* across the disciplines. Below, we show how you can use the list and the map to discuss the novel from several perspectives. While we have provisionally distinguished among literature, urban studies, and history classrooms, we assume that these sections overlap and that teachers in one discipline will be attuned to issues raised in others.

The Literature Classroom: Readers and Realism

Old Goriot immediately differentiates its readers by location and genre; the narrator declares at the outset that, as a drama, the novel will affect readers "*intra muros et extra*" but, as a realist text, will probably not be understood outside Paris: "Only between the heights of Montmartre and Montrouge are there people who can appreciate how exactly, with what close observation, it is drawn from life" (27). The assignment bears out the implication that only a reader familiar with Paris can understand *Old Goriot;* after compiling a list whose sheer length testifies to the proliferation of Parisian references in *Old Goriot*, students see clearly how the novel assumes knowledge of the city.

Once you have established that the novel seems to require previous knowledge of Paris, you can begin to refine that point by focusing on the different types of knowledge encoded in a novel and in a map. What kind of knowledge of Paris does the novel require? Topographical? social? historical? The maps of Paris contain knowledge of Paris in a concentrated form; how does that knowledge help to explicate the novel? What additional information would help to explain the novel's Parisian references? Despite its claims to rely on the reader's previous familiarity with the city, doesn't the novel sometimes provide, even impose, the knowledge it requires? For example, the novel clearly conveys the differences between the Maison Vauquer and the Hôtel de Beauséant (cf. 30–32 with 142). Even when the narrator does not explain the history and meaning of places—the Palais Royal, the various theaters attended by the characters—the actions that occur in them and the type of people who frequent them help the reader infer the meanings associated with those sites.

The narrator is thus somewhat disingenuous when he says that readers outside Paris may not understand *Old Goriot*. By using casual name-dropping to refer to real places and by describing fictional locales in detail, he can solicit readers both knowledgeable and ignorant, inside and outside Paris, in part by uniting the Parisian and provincial readers under the rubric of "everyone" (28) but also by teaching outsiders about Paris over the course of the novel. The very process of reading the novel places readers "between [. . .] Montmartre and Montrouge," no matter what their actual locations. The novel is a vehicle for transporting readers to Paris.

The novel's opening also invokes the issue of realism. What specific capacity does the narrator ascribe to Parisian readers? They can verify the novel's veracity—indeed, only they can "appreciate how exactly" the novel "is drawn from life." This comment defines realism as transparent referentiality—as an open window onto a real space, an undistorted view that can be objectively verified. The map exercise seems to confirm this definition by demonstrating that the novel's references to Paris correspond to the real city charted on the map. It is very important to intervene in this confusion of realism and referentiality, even in a history or urban studies classroom where you want to use the book as documentary evidence. The grounds of this intervention are familiar. Realism consists of representational decisions and choices, but the conventions that govern those choices have been so naturalized that we no longer perceive them. Far from being a slice of reality that transcends any particular perspective, realism is a historically specific movement, dependent on developments (materialism, individualism, bourgeois liberalism, sexual differentiation) that had their apotheosis in the nineteenth century. You can make these points in terms of the critical definitions of realism generated by Auerbach, Barthes, Watt, and others.

You can also illustrate the differences between realism and reference by showing that both the novel and the map depend on representational conventions and choices. If your class knows little about realism and issues of representation, start with some basics. Ask them to define realism using examples from the text. What aspects of the novel seem realistic? Students will probably mention the novel's extensive use of exhaustive description, its precise evocation of material details, its frequent references to real places, and the overall impression of objectivity these techniques produce. You can problematize the novel's referentiality by looking closely at the descriptive passages and discussing how they are filtered through subjective consciousnesses, saturated with judgments, and shaped by social norms. Furthermore, you can point out that the novel's realist technique of detailed, objective description is deployed primarily when the narrative focuses on fictional places, not real ones. The conjunction of realist technique and fictive locations suggests that realism emerges as a supplement to fiction, not as a direct transcription of reality.

You can also encourage students to question the referential status of the map. Students may adduce the map to bolster their claims about the novel's referentiality by arguing that the map proves that the novel consistently refers to real places. Turn their attention to their assumptions that the map is a standard of reality. If the realist novel works by formally producing reality effects, how do maps produce such effects? Maps approximate reality by being exhaustive, by using a consistent, single scale to represent all objects, and by effacing any overt traces of the map's makers. You can challenge the maps' referentiality by asking students to compare the different maps they found. Analyzing the variations between maps (in scale, detail, labeling) shows that maps follow conventions, make choices, and mediate reality rather than mirror it (to develop this, see Monmonier).

You can then shift discussion to an analysis of the different representational conventions that distinguish the novel and the map; each form highlights the selective protocols of the other. While the map represents Paris as a totality, the novel excludes whole sections of the city and pays disproportionate attention to particular sites. On the map, for example, the trajectory from the rue du Helder to the Bouffons to the Pont-Neuf to the rue Neuve-Sainte-Geneviève necessarily includes all the places in between, while the novel elides any mention of intervening places (169–70). In other respects, however, the novel is more inclusive than the map. Ask students to look at their lists and identify some of the locations and place-names that appear only in the novel, not on their map.

For the most part, these will be either places outside Paris or private residences—the Hôtel de Beauséant, the Maison Vauquer. Why are the residences not on the map? The obvious explanation is that they are fictional; but they are also absent because they are private spaces. To the extent that the novel represents these spaces, it provides a more inclusive perspective than does the map. While most maps represent only public streets and buildings, the realist novel portrays both public and private spaces; *Old Goriot* defines Paris as a continuum of private and public, interior and exterior spaces (see Marcus).

The Urban Studies Classroom

Old Goriot can vividly illustrate the importance of the city in nineteenth-century western Europe, the centrality of Paris as a capital city, and ways of interpreting urban form and meaning.

The novel attests to the existence of an active urban culture whose participants were eager to read about themselves and about the city. As the novel's opening pages suggest, being Parisian is defined not only by one's physical location in the city but also by a reflexive process in which knowledge of Paris confirms one's membership in it. For Eugène, knowledge of the city also spurs development as an individual. After defining the bildungsroman as a novel of education, which charts an individual's confrontation with and accommodation to society, you can propose that *Old Goriot* is an urban bildungsroman that links Eugène's development to his negotiation of Paris (see 55–60, 83–84, 92, 95, 104, 242, 278). Eugène's character illustrates the interdependence of urban knowledge, self-knowledge, and social mobility, whose imbrication in this 1834 novel anticipates later studies of the nineteenth-century affinity between the city and modern bourgeois male subjectivity (charted by writers like Green, Simmel, Benjamin [*Baudelaire*, "Work"], Clark, Harvey, Wolff, Wilson, and Walkowitz). The novel's statements about the differences between Parisian and provincial characters can also help to identify the qualities Balzac ascribes to urban culture.

Old Goriot's emphasis on the division between Paris and the provinces illustrates the importance of Paris as a capital city. Absolutist state building and revolutionary centralization gave Paris a long, only occasionally interrupted history as a center of government, finance, culture, and education. How do the map and the novel illustrate Paris's status as a capital city? The map shows the schools, exchanges, monuments, and assemblies that made Paris a capital. In the novel, Bianchon articulates both the necessity of contact with the capital (its centrality within the nation) and the division between Paris and the provinces (157–58). Like the other students in the Maison Vauquer, Bianchon must come to Paris for his professional training, but he intends to return to his provincial home. Eugène's determination to conquer Paris signals that his ambition is greater than Bianchon's precisely because Paris is the nation's center of power and status and because, as we discuss below, the distribution of power and status remained relatively fixed in the provinces but became much more mobile in Paris (a point Balzac also makes in *Lost Illusions*).

Read in tandem with a map, theories of urban morphology, and histories of Parisian architecture and urbanism, *Old Goriot* also illustrates methods for classifying urban space. For example, students can list and define the units of space the novel generates: the house, the street, the arrondissement, the *quartier*, the faubourg, the city. Are these formal, administrative categories? colloquial ones? both? The novel differentiates various districts, most notably the Chaussée d'Antin, the faubourg Saint-Germain, and the vicinity of the Maison Vauquer. How does the novel distinguish among them? Does the map differentiate and demarcate these areas as clearly as the novel does? Next, students can examine subdivisions within larger units. For example, the novel differentiates between types of housing: the pension, the apartment, the *hôtel*. How do these types of housing correspond to the novel's sociological classifications? What kinds of people live in each housing type? What architectural features characterize each type? (For the pension, see 28–36 and 151–52; for a banker's house, 161; for the aristocratic *hôtel*, 90; and for the bachelor's apartment, 230. You can supplement this discussion with slides and with readings from Loyer and Sutcliffe.)

If you want to use the novel to enrich students' understanding of concepts in urban theory, consider assigning excerpts from Kevin Lynch's *The Image of the City* (1–13 and 46–49). Both *Old Goriot* and *The Image of the City* emphasize the necessity of reading urban form, of making it legible. Lynch's emphasis on the city as an ordered aesthetic object (2) helps explain urban affinities to an aesthetic form like the novel. You can compare Lynch's account of how we come to form images of the city (2–8) with the novel's account of how Eugène learns about Paris.

Lynch's anatomy of the elements that constitute an image of the city (46–49) can serve as an interpretive grid for the novel. "Districts" correspond to the novel's neighborhoods. "Paths" describe Eugène's numerous trajectories, on foot and by coach. "Landmarks," national and personal, appear throughout the novel. "Nodes" provide a helpful rubric for the sites in *Old Goriot* where people collect and collide: theaters, parks, and residences. The example of parks in *Old Goriot* both illuminates and extends the definition of nodes as "strategic spots," "intensive foci," "concentrations," and sites of the "crossing or convergence of paths" (48–49). References to and episodes in the Jardin des Plantes and the Jardin du Luxembourg illustrate the function of the *jardins* as sites where different paths converge (see 184 ff, 156 ff).

While Lynch emphasizes how physical form identifies a particular node or district, the novel underlines how what Lynch calls "social meaning" defines the elements of urban space. For example, the parks cited above also had symbolic and historical meanings that explain why the novel associates them with specific characters, classes, and neighborhoods. The Jardin des Plantes, an educational park based on Enlightenment ideals and fueled by bourgeois desires for self-improvement, becomes associated with the medical student Bianchon and with Poiret, Michonneau, and Gondureau, the participants in a police surveillance mission. The Jardin du Luxembourg, laid out according to a classical plan on a site originally developed for Marie de Médicis, is associated with aristocratic characters and aspirations. The Champs-Elysées, frequented by the wives of newly rich bankers and of notables, partake of the novelty and spectacular display that Balzac attributes to these classes.

Old Goriot does not simply exemplify Lynch's theory of how we form images of the city. The novel also generates its own theory of urban morphology. As we have seen above, while Lynch emphasizes the formal coherence of urban spaces, Balzac places heavy stress on how social meanings make urban images cohere. Where Lynch emphasizes general processes over individual differences (7), Balzac focuses on the heterogeneity of city dwellers and the images of the city they develop. You can ask your class, for example, to compare Mme Vauquer's extremely localized image of the city to Goriot's personalized image and to Vautrin's global one or to compare Eugène's image of the city at the novel's outset to the panoramic one described at its end. Finally, where Lynch includes in his image of the city only those elements visible from the public, exterior space of the street, *Old Goriot* shows that images of the city and urban knowledge also encompass private, residential interiors, such as the rooms of the Maison Vauquer and the antechambers and boudoirs of Mme Nucingen and Countess Restaud.

The History Classroom: Mapping the Social in Postrevolutionary Paris

When used in a course on the history of modern France, the mapping exercise can serve several functions. First, students will gain a familiarity with an urban context that will appear throughout the semester, not only in discussions of the city's redesign at mid-century but also in reference to the major revolutions of the nineteenth century (in 1789, 1830, 1848, and 1871), in which upheaval in the streets of Paris features prominently. Students become literally oriented to the city's early-nineteenth-century geography, which will serve as a useful contrast to the subsequent changes wrought by Haussmannization, such as the new boulevards and the expansion of the city into the adjacent suburbs. In 1819, Eugène can stand in Père Lachaise and be at the city's edge. By 1860, he would have been well within the city limits.

The use of an actual map also offers students a means to visualize the ways that social life in postrevolutionary France became conceived on the model of a map. In this context, students will move from using a map to imagining the map in metaphoric terms as a model of the social order. If the pyramid in ancient Egypt materialized a deeply hierarchical society with a very narrow top, the map became the model for an increasingly uniform postrevolutionary society. The Revolution embraced Enlightenment principles of transparency; maps claim transparency by serving as models of what they purport to represent. The Revolution abolished feudal privileges and ushered in an era of radical equality through the application of general law; maps employ a single standard of measurement and thus rely on notions of universal equivalence. Revolutionary society inaugurated the centrality of normative standards through which every object or subject was systematically defined by its relation to another; maps plot sites in relation to one another according to a consistent uniform scale. Finally, students can also use the map to understand a key transformation in social life after the Revolution: society became a web of fluid and interconnected spaces, putatively open to talent and merit. Once the Revolution destroyed the feudal regime, the neatly demarcated and static hierarchy of a society of fixed orders disappeared as well.

Looking at the map in the context of the history of modern France also requires students to become familiar with the political and social changes associated with the complicated settlement of the Restoration. The restoration of the Bourbons to the throne, first in 1814 and then again in 1815 after Napoleon's definitive defeat at Waterloo, has been depicted by historians as a failed counterrevolution because it staged an aristocratic reaction without challenging many of the fundamental gains of the Revolution. Although Louis XVIII came to the throne, he had to accept that he would govern with a charter (a term used to avoid the revolutionary connotations of a constitution). The charter maintained the revolutionary principles of general law—liberty and equality before the law for all French people, regardless of title and rank. That said, the Old Regime nobility and the new Napoleonic nobility (appointed by Napoleon on the basis of wealth and military accomplishment) were both recognized as legitimate. Without a system of legal privilege, however, nobility became purely titular.

The charter also reinforced other revolutionary gains. Although Catholicism was declared the state religion, religious toleration was maintained. The new government validated the revolutionary sale of church lands by asserting the inviolable right of existing property. The king shared power with a bicameral legislature: a chamber of peers, consisting of hereditary appointments made by the king, and an elected chamber of deputies, whose qualifications ensured that wealth served as the basis for political participation. The charter's curtain of forgetfulness meant that Napoleonic appointees could be incorporated into the newly regal state. The Restoration and subsequent July Monarchy have thus been called "la France des notables"—a world run by elites whose status no longer resided exclusively in their birth, but a world in which power was not quite yet achieved through the anonymity and democracy of industrial capitalism (Jardin and Tudesq).

Balzac's novel, set in the middle of the Restoration, contrasts the power of the social changes wrought by the Revolution to the failure of aristocratic reaction and does so by contrasting the practices of a mobile and newly monied elite to a static and gatekeeping traditional aristocracy. Although the metaphor of the ladder also emerges in postrevolutionary France (one cannot help being reminded of the many ladders Stendhal's Napoleonic Julien Sorel climbs in *Le Rouge et le noir*), *Père Goriot* signals the victory of the map over the ladder and highlights the foolishness Balzac ascribes to the gatekeeping practices of Restoration elites.

Historians have examined the Restoration's aristocratic sociability by looking at the era's demarcation of distinct social spaces, typified in Balzac's novel in the "gilded salons" of the faubourg Saint-Germain (58). Balzac's contemporary, the writer and salon hostess Sophie Gay, explained the existence of these salons: "No sooner has the law equalized all ranks than Society differentiates them" (48). During the Old Regime, aristocratic women held salons as an alternative court society that dictated taste and manners. The salon functioned as a gated social space, and the architecture of the *hôtel particulier,* with its elaborate doorways and courtyard, materialized this. Balzac's novel accurately depicts the reappearance of the salon as an important institution during the Restoration and emphasizes that its literal gatekeeping function now constructed rather than mirrored social hierarchy. Whereas the salon once supposedly stood for a social order already delineated by birth, the postrevolutionary salon would have to create social distinction.

The novel poses in spatial terms the problem of a revivified aristocratic sociability in a postrevolutionary social order. For example, it frequently contrasts two neighborhoods: the faubourg Saint-Germain and the Chaussée d'Antin. The faubourg Saint-Germain, on the less densely populated Left Bank, was an almost exclusively residential neighborhood associated with the traditional aristocracy since their exodus from the Marais in the eighteenth century. In what is now the seventh arrondissement (dipping slightly east into the sixth), the faubourg Saint-Germain ran from the boulevard des Invalides up to the rue de Sèvres to the rue du Four and the rue de Seine. Readers are reminded that the neighborhood is densely occupied by aristocrats when Eugène climbs into the hackney coach and asks to be taken to the Hôtel de Beauséant only to be questioned by the driver about which Beauséant he wants to visit—the count on the rue de Grenelle or the marquis on the rue Saint-Dominique (88).

The novel also evokes the contrasting neighborhood of the Chaussée d'Antin, that area on the Right Bank north of the boulevards from the Madeleine to the boulevard des Italiens, bounded roughly by the rue Saint-Lazare to the north, the rue de Caumartin to the west, and running east to the rue le Peletier. This neighborhood, whose construction began during the reign of Louis XVI, became the favorite area for bankers during the Directory and Consulate. During the Restoration they, along with other notables and celebrated artists, contributed to the neighborhood's growing popularity. Here live Goriot's daughters: Anastasie de Restaud on the rue du Helder and Delphine de Nucingen on the rue Saint-Lazare, both residing squarely in a neighborhood that symbolizes new money.

The two neighborhoods are explicitly compared throughout the novel: "[. . .] to open a door in the Faubourg Saint-Germain a banker's wife would stick at nothing" (159); "At the Chaussée-d'Antin Madame de Restaud had the smart cabriolet of a young man of six-and-twenty in her court. At the Faubourg Saint-Germain a carriage which thirty thousand francs could not have bought awaited the pleasure of a great nobleman" (89). Beyond the specific contrasts, students might compare the various descriptions of *hôtels*. (For the vicomtesse, see 90 and 142; for Mme de Restaud, 79–82; for Mme de Nucingen, 161 and 168–69; and for Eugène's rooms on the rue d'Artois, 230–32.)

The novel emphasizes that the social distance between the faubourg Saint-Germain and the parvenu culture of the Chaussée d'Antin corresponds to the spatial distance that separates them. As Eugène goes back and forth between the two, worrying about his means of transport and trying not to muddy his clothes, readers are reminded that though these neighborhoods face each other, there is a significant distance between them—as also described, rather graphically, by Delphine's willingness to lap up the mud between the rue Saint-Lazare and the rue de Grenelle to be admitted to the salon of the vicomtesse (104).

Although *Old Goriot* uses spatial distance to represent social differentiation, it also invokes the model of the map to show that spatial mobility, not spatial segregation, is the means to social mastery in postrevolutionary France. In this way, the social order is imagined more as a map than as a ladder, and social navigation rather than social climbing becomes the key to success. The novel thus negatively contrasts those characters who are geographically fixed to those who are mobile. No character in the novel is as incapable of moving around the city as is the vicomtesse de Beauséant, a consummate gatekeeper. Her self-imposed exile toward the novel's end indicates that in the contemporary social scene spatial exclusion of others no longer ensures social power. She departs, saying, "I shall never see Paris or this world again" (275). By this, she announces more than her own exile; she hails the defeat of the Restoration's attempt to reintroduce old-fashioned notions of vertical and fixed hierarchy—epitomized in her milieu, the salons of the faubourg Saint-Germain. Unsympathetic characters such as Poiret and Madame Vauquer are also geographically fixed. He goes only to the nearby Jardin des Plantes; she leaves the boardinghouse only once, to go to the theater with Vautrin.

Those characters, by contrast, who recognize the power of mobility are more sympathetic and successful. Goriot embodies the postrevolutionary achievements associated with the upward social mobility of a ladder and accomplished through the power of wealth. Aware that money was remaking the world (see, e.g., 101, 284), he is limited by his failure to grasp fully that money relies first and foremost on the mobility of circulation rather than the upward verticality of social climbing. Vautrin, the novel's closest approximation to a Napoleonic hero (his amazing talents even earn him the nickname Cheat-Death), is a master of mobility—equally adept in the semirespectable society of the Maison Vauquer and as banker to the criminal underworld. The police refer to his "counter-detective" system (187), investing him with great surveillance powers. Yet

Vautrin is ensnared by the superiority of a police force that effectively enlists the sticks-in-the-mud, Poiret and Michonneau, to help them trap him. And Vautrin's fantasy of escape to the New World to live the plantation life of "a monarch" (131) suggests the strain of the authoritarian backwardness of Bonapartism.

True victory belongs, instead, to Eugène, who passes in and out of the aristocracy's gates, turns down the crass fortune hunting advocated by Vautrin, and instead weaves a web of interconnections, learning to successfully navigate the postrevolutionary city. Eugène inhabits the Maison Vauquer, situated in the "grimmest quarter of Paris" (28), a neighborhood "where there's never a cat stirring" (238), but links the boardinghouse through his movements to other places in Paris. Students should pay careful attention to the vast number and variety of places Eugène visits: the Maison Vauquer; the School of Law; the gambling house; the houses of the vicomtesse de Beauséant, Madame de Restaud, and Madame de Nucingen; the Hôtel Rochefide; the Tuileries; the Italiens; the Jardin du Luxembourg; his rooms on the rue d'Artois; Père Lachaise. His mobility is evidence of the novel's message that unless one circulates through the city one literally and figuratively goes nowhere.

The final image of Eugène standing on the highest point of Père Lachaise, surveying the space between the Place Vendôme and the dome of the Invalides at first seems a final confirmation that his ability to map the city assures his success (304). But the novel does not neatly close Eugène's coming-of-age story, since at the end we are not sure if Eugène will have Delphine or money, both or neither. Rather, the reader's sense of his final triumph comes from his attainment of the point of view that has been the reader's throughout the novel. After all, it is the reader, conjoined to the narrator, who has the only truly panoramic view in the novel. Only the reader knows more than even Eugène does, for example, when watching the police set up Vautrin's capture (184–91). Ultimate empowerment comes to Eugène when he seemingly gains the reader's all-encompassing perspective on the city—when he can stand outside the city and survey it as he would a map. The reader's Paris, like Eugène's, is a map that can be studied and negotiated through the creation of a horizontal web of social relations. Mastery in this system mimics success in the terms of a capitalist economy: circulation is essential. If *Old Goriot* depicts the triumph of a society where money and mobility count, Eugène's successful education in movement through the city by the novel's end presciently anticipates the city's mid-nineteenth-century redesign, organized around the increased possibility of the circulation of people and goods.

SURVEY PARTICIPANTS

Listed below are the names and affiliations of the scholars and teachers who generously agreed to participate in the survey of approaches to teaching *Old Goriot*. The information they provided was invaluable in preparing this volume.

Ruth Amossy, *Tel Aviv University*
Janet Beizer, *University of Virginia*
David F. Bell, *Duke University*
John T. Booker, *University of Kansas*
Margaret Cohen, *New York University*
Dean de la Motte, *Belmont Abbey College*
Polly Rimer Duke, *Columbia University*
David R. Ellison, *University of Miami*
Graham Falconer, *University of Toronto*
A. Gruzinska, *Arizona State University*
Oscar A. Hall, *State University of New York, Stony Brook*
Dorothy Kelly, *Boston University*
Claudia Brodsky Lacour, *Princeton University*
Eric Le Calvez, *Georgia State University*
Rosemary Lloyd, *Indiana University, Bloomington*
Michael Lucey, *University of California, Berkeley*
Sharon Marcus, *University of California, Berkeley*
Catherine Nesci, *University of California, Santa Barbara*
Allan H. Pasco, *University of Kansas*
Jorge Pedraza
Catherine Perry, *University of Notre Dame*
Laurence M. Porter, *Michigan State University*
Gerald Prince, *University of Pennsylvania*
James H. Reid, *Illinois State University*
Lawrence R. Schehr, *University of Illinois, Urbana*
Vanessa Schwartz, *University of Southern California*
Armand E. Singer, *West Virginia University*
Margaret Waller, *Pomona College*

NOTES ON CONTRIBUTORS

Ruth Amossy teaches French literature and the theory of literature at Tel Aviv University. She is the author of several books on Julien Gracq and on Salvador Dalí as well as on stereotypes in contemporary culture (*Les Idées reçues: sémiologie du stéréotype* [1991], *Stéréotypes et clichés: langue, discours, société* [1997]). Among her many publications, several articles and book chapters are devoted to Balzac, specifically to his use of clichés and of genres (in *Eugénie Grandet, La Peau de chagrin, Melmoth réconcilié, La Cousine Bette, Sarrasine*) and to feminist issues (in *Les Chouans* and *La Femme de trente ans*). Her current work focuses on argumentation.

Janet Beizer is professor of French at the University of Virginia. Author of *Family Plots: Balzac's Narrative Generations* (1986) and *Ventriloquized Bodies: Narrative of Hysteria in Nineteenth-Century France* (1994), she is currently writing *Vicarious Lives*, a book about women's autobiographical biography. Her teaching and research interests include narrative and narrative theory, psychoanalysis and literature, gender studies, and cultural studies.

David F. Bell is professor of French and director of the Center for European Studies at Duke University. He is the author of *Models of Power: Politics and Economics in Zola's* Rougon-Macquart (1988) and *Circumstances: Chance in the Literary Text* (1993); he is coeditor of Michel Serres's *Hermes: Literature, Science, Philosophy* (1982) and of a special issue of *Substance, Reading Violence.* His interests include nineteenth- and twentieth-century French literature and culture, literature and science, and literary criticism. He is currently working on a book treating technologies of communication in nineteenth-century France.

John T. Booker is associate professor of French at the University of Kansas. His teaching and research interests include the French novel of the nineteenth and twentieth centuries and first-person narrative in general. He is coeditor of *The Play of Terror in Nineteenth-Century France* (1997) and has published articles on Constant, Balzac, Stendhal, Gide, and Mauriac. He is working on a book dealing with the French first-person novel from the eighteenth century to the twentieth.

Eric Bordas is maître de conférences at the Université de Paris III. His main teaching and research interests are linguistics and stylistics. He is the author of *Balzac, discours et détours: pour une stylistique de l'énonciation romanesque* (1997) as well as articles on Balzac, Sade, and Stendhal. He is currently preparing an edition of Balzac's *Recherche de l'absolu,* for Livre de Poche and editions of several other novels for the first complete edition of Balzac on CD-ROM.

Dean de la Motte is academic dean and associate professor of comparative literature at Belmont Abbey College. He is coeditor of *Making the News: Modernity and the Mass Press in Nineteenth-Century France* (1999) and of *Approaches to Teaching Stendhal's* The Red and the Black (1999). His main interests are nineteenth-century narrative and culture, francophone studies, and contemporary France. He is currently at work on a book dealing with narratives of progress in nineteenth-century France.

David R. Ellison, professor of French and chair of the Department of Foreign Languages and Literatures at the University of Miami, is the author of *The Reading of Proust* (1984), *Understanding Albert Camus* (1990), and *Of Words and the World: Referential Anxiety in Contemporary French Fiction* (1993). He is interested in the modern and contemporary French novel, literary theory, comparative literature of the modern period, and postmodern philology. His book *From the Sublime to the Uncanny: Ethics and Aesthetics of European Modernism* will be published in 2001.

Michal Peled Ginsburg is professor of French and comparative literature and chair of the Department of French and Italian at Northwestern University. She is the author of *Flaubert Writing: A Study in Narrative Strategies* (1986) and of *Economies of Change: Form and Transformation in the Nineteenth-Century Novel* (1996). She is currently completing a book on the Israeli novelist David Shahar.

Dorothy Kelly is professor of French and chair of the Department of Modern Foreign Languages and Literatures at Boston University. She published *Telling Glances: Voyeurism in the French Novel* (1992) and *Fictional Genders: Role and Representation in Nineteenth-Century French Narrative* (1998) and is currently working on a book entitled *Constructing Women: Fiction and Reality in the Nineteenth Century.* Her research and teaching interests are nineteenth-century French literature and literary theory.

Claudia Brodsky Lacour is professor of comparative literature at Princeton University and directeur de programme, Collège International de Philosophie, Paris. She is the author of *The Imposition of Form: Studies in Narrative Representation and Knowledge* (1987) and *Lines of Thought: Discourse, Architectonics, and the Origin of Modern Philosophy* (1996) and coeditor of *Birth of a Nation'hood* (1997). Her research and teaching interests include literature and philosophy from the Enlightenment to the present; critical, literary, and aesthetic theory; and representation and architectural form. She is currently at work on a book entitled *Writing and Building* that deals with the latter topic.

Eric Le Calvez is associate professor of French at Georgia State University. He is the author of *Flaubert topographe:* L'Education sentimentale: *essai de poétique génétique* (1997) and coeditor of *Texte(s) et intertexte(s)* (1998). Interested in the nineteenth-century novel, narratology, genetic criticism, poetics, and intertextuality, he is currently preparing a book entitled *Description et narrativité dans les manuscrits de* L'Education sentimentale.

Michael Lucey, associate professor of French and comparative literature at the University of California, Berkeley, is the author of *Gide's Bent: Sexuality, Politics, Writing* (1995). His teaching and research interests include queer studies and nineteenth- and twentieth-century French, American, and English literature and culture. He is currently completing a book entitled *The Misfit of the Family: Balzac and the Social Forms of Sexuality.*

Sharon Marcus is associate professor of English at the University of California, Berkeley. She is the author of *Apartment Stories: City and Home in Nineteenth-Century Paris and London* (1999) and of an introduction to a recently reprinted translation of Balzac's *Physiology of Marriage* (1997). Her teaching and research interests are the nineteenth-century French and British novel, urban and architectural history, and feminist and queer theory.

Catherine Nesci is associate professor of French and women's studies at the University of California, Santa Barbara. She is the author of *La Femme mode d'emploi:*

Balzac, de la Physiologie du mariage *à* La Comédie humaine (1992) and coeditor of a special issue of *Paragraphes, L'œuvre d'identité: essais sur le romantisme de Nodier à Baudelaire.* She is currently working on two book projects: one on women and urban experience in nineteenth-century France and the other dealing with heritage and gender in postrevolutionary France.

Laurence M. Porter teaches French studies, comparative literature, critical theory, and African studies at Michigan State University, where he received a distinguished faculty award in 1995. He is currently writing *Happening, Knowing, and Telling: How Stories Work in Life and Art.* He edited the MLA Approaches volumes on Flaubert and Baudelaire. Other books have treated Romanticism, symbolism, and Hugo, and he has published over a hundred articles and book chapters on topics ranging from the Middle Ages to the present and from Shakespeare to Dostoevsky, Thomas Mann, Aimé Césaire, and García Márquez.

Gerald Prince is professor of Romance languages at the University of Pennsylvania. A specialist in narrative theory and in nineteenth- and twentieth- century French literature, he published *Métaphysique et technique dans l'œuvre romanesque de Sartre* (1968), *A Grammar of Stories* (1973), *Narratology: The Form and Functioning of Narrative* (1982), *A Dictionary of Narratology* (1987), and *Narrative as Theme* (1992). He is currently writing Le Petit Prince*: guide du roman de langue française au vingtième siècle.*

James H. Reid is associate professor of French at Illinois State University. His research and teaching interests include Proust, Beckett, and critical theory. He published *Narration and Description in the French Realist Novel* (1993) and is currently completing a book on lying and forgetting in Proust and in Beckett's trilogy.

Lawrence R. Schehr is professor of French at the University of Illinois, Urbana. A specialist in nineteenth- and twentieth-century French narrative, critical theory, and gay studies, his most recent books include *Parts of an Andrology: On Representation of Men's Bodies* (1997), *Rendering French Realism* (1997), *Alcibiades at the Door: Gay Discourses in French Literature* (1995), and *The Shock of Men: Homosexual Hermeneutics and French Writing* (1995). He is currently at work on two books: *Realism and Its Others* and *Straight Lines: Proust, Gide, Cocteau.*

Vanessa Schwartz is associate professor of history at the University of Southern California. She is the author of *Spectacular Realities: Early Mass Culture in Fin-de-siècle Paris* (1998) and coeditor of *Cinema and the Invention of Modern Life* (1995). Her teaching and research interests include French cultural history; the history of visual culture, with an emphasis on film; and urban history. She is currently preparing a book-length study on the commodification of Frenchness in post–World War II France and America.

Margaret Waller is associate professor of French at Pomona College and the author of *The Male Malady: Fictions of Impotence in the French Romantic Novel* (1993). Most recently she coauthored an introduction to *Ourika* and published an essay entitled "Disembodiment as a Masquerade: Fashion Journalists and Other 'Realist' Observers in Directory Paris." Her current project is a book-length study of the culture of the visible and the politics of identity and difference in postrevolutionary France.

WORKS CITED

Allemand, André. *Unité et structure de l'univers balzacien.* Paris: Plon, 1965.

Auerbach, Erich. *Mimesis: The Representation of Reality in Western Literature.* Trans. Willard R. Trask. Princeton: Princeton UP, 1953.

Austin, J. L. *How to Do Things with Words.* Cambridge: Harvard UP, 1962.

Bakhtin, Mikhail. *Esthétique et théorie du roman.* Paris: Gallimard, 1987.

Balzac, Honoré de. "Avant-propos." Balzac, *Comédie* 1: 7–20.

———. "Avant-propos." *Œuvres complètes.* Vol. 1. Paris: L'Honnête Homme, 1956. 63–75.

———. *Le Colonel Chabert.* Balzac, *Comédie* 3: 311–73.

———. *Le Colonel Chabert.* Pref. Pierre Barbéris. Paris: Librairie Générale Française, 1984.

———. *La Comédie humaine.* Ed. Pierre-Georges Castex. 12 vols. Paris: Gallimard-Pléïade, 1976–81.

———. *Gobseck.* Trans. Katherine Prescott Wormeley. Boston: Little, 1906.

———. *Gobseck. Gobseck [and] Une Double Famille.* Ed. Philippe Berthier. Paris: Garnier-Flammarion, 1984. 71–128.

———. *Old Goriot.* Trans. Marion Ayton Crawford. Harmondsworth: Penguin, 1951.

———. *Le Père Goriot.* Ed. Thierry Bodin. Pref. Félicien Marceau. Folio. Paris: Gallimard, 1971.

———. *Le Père Goriot* [in English]. Ed. Peter Brooks. Trans. Burton Raffel. Norton Critical Eds. New York: Norton, 1998.

———. *Le Père Goriot.* Ed. and pref. Pierre-Georges Castex. Classiques Garnier. Paris: Garnier, 1966.

———. *Le Père Goriot.* Ed. Pierre Citron. Introd. Philippe Berthier. Paris: Garnier-Flammarion, 1966.

———. *Le Père Goriot.* Ed. and pref. Gérard Gengembre. Lire et voir les classiques. Paris: Pocket, 1989.

———. *Le Père Goriot.* Ed. Peter W. Lock. New York: St. Martin's, 1968.

———. *Le Père Goriot* [in English]. Trans. Henry Reed. Signet Classics. New York: Signet-NAL, 1962.

———. *Le Père Goriot.* Ed. and pref. Françoise van Rossum-Guyon. Paris: Livre de Poche, 1983.

———. *Le Père Goriot.* Ed. and introd. Horatio Smith. New York: Scribner, 1958.

———. *Le Père Goriot.* Ed. Stéphane Vachon. Paris: Livre de Poche, 1995.

———. *La Physiologie du mariage.* Balzac, *Comédie* 11: 903–1205.

———. *Physiology of Marriage.* Introd. Sharon Marcus. Baltimore: Johns Hopkins UP, 1997.

———. *Sarrasine.* Sarrasine *suivi de Michel Serres* L'Hermaphrodite. Paris: Garnier-Flammarion, 1989. 9–66.

———. *Les Secrets de la princesse de Cadignan.* 1839. Paris: Gallimard, 1980.

———. *Splendeurs et misères des courtisanes.* Paris: Garnier-Flammarion, 1968.

Barbéris, Pierre. *Le Monde de Balzac.* Paris: Arthaud, 1973.

———. Le Père Goriot *de Balzac: écriture, structure, signification.* Paris: Larousse, 1972.

Barthes, Roland. *Mythologies.* Trans. Annette Lavers. New York: Hill, 1972.

———. *S/Z.* Paris: Seuil, 1970. Trans. Richard Miller. New York: Hill, 1974.

Baudelaire, Charles. "Théophile Gautier." *Œuvres complètes.* By Baudelaire. Ed. Claude Pichois. Paris: Gallimard-Pléiade, 1976. 103–28.

Béguin, Albert. *Balzac visionnaire.* Paris: Skira, 1946.

Beizer, Janet L. *Family Plots: Balzac's Narrative Generations.* New Haven: Yale UP, 1986.

Bell, David. "Marque, trace, pistes: Balzac à la recherche d'une science des indices." Mahieu and Schuerewegen 107–12.

Bellos, David. *Honoré de Balzac:* Old Goriot. Cambridge: Cambridge UP, 1987.

Benjamin, Walter. *Charles Baudelaire: A Lyric Poet in the Era of High Capitalism.* Trans. Harry Zohn. London: Verso, 1989.

———. *Paris, capitale du XIX*[e] *siècle: le livre des passages.* Ed. Jean Lacoste. Paris: Cerf, 1989.

———. "The Work of Art in the Age of Mechanical Reproduction." *Illuminations.* Trans. Harry Zohn. Ed. Hannah Arendt. New York: Schocken, 1969. 217–51.

Bertaut, Jules. Le Père Goriot *de Balzac.* Amiens: Malfère, 1928.

Berthier, Patrick. "Balzac du côté de Sodome." *L'Année balzacienne* (1979): 147–77.

Bible. King James Version.

Bordas, Eric. "Balzac à l'épreuve de la stylistique (ou la stylistique à l'épreuve de Balzac?). Historique d'un préjugé." *L'Information littéraire* 3 (1995): 34–46.

———. *Balzac, discours et détours: pour une stylistique de l'énonciation romanesque.* Toulouse: PU Mirail, 1997.

———. "Balzac, grand romancier sans être grand écrivain?" Herschberg-Pierrot 113–31.

———. "Scénographie du dialogue balzacien." *MLN* 111 (1996): 722–33.

Bourdieu, Pierre. *Sur la télévision.* Paris: Raisons D'Agir-Liber, 1996.

Brooks, Peter. Introduction. Balzac, *Père Goriot* [Brooks] vii–xiii.

———. *The Melodramatic Imagination: Balzac, Henry James, Melodrama, and the Mode of Excess.* New Haven: Yale UP, 1976.

———. *Reading for the Plot: Design and Intention in Narrative.* New York: Vintage, 1985.

———. "The Text of the City." *Oppositions* 8 (1977): 7–11.

Bruner, Jerome S., J. J. Goodnow, and G. A. Austin. *A Study of Thinking.* New York: New York Sciences, 1956.

Calvino, Italo. *La Machine littérature.* Paris: Seuil, 1984.

Caron, Jean-Claude. *Générations romantiques: les étudiants de Paris et le Quartier Latin, 1814–1851.* Paris: Colin, 1991.

Clark, T. J. *The Painting of Modern Life: Paris in the Art of Manet and His Followers.* Princeton: Princeton UP, 1984.

Cohen, Margaret. "Women in Fiction in the Nineteenth Century." *Cambridge Companion to the French Novel: From 1800 to the Present.* Ed. Timothy Unwin. Cambridge: Cambridge UP, 1997. 54–72.

Crawford, Marion Ayton. Introduction. Balzac, *Old Goriot* 5–24.

Des œuvres de jeunesse au Père Goriot. Spec. issue of *L'Année balzacienne* ns 7 (1986): 9–416.

The Epic of Gilgamesh. Trans. and ed. Maureen Gallery Kovacs. Stanford: Stanford UP, 1989.

Ezdinli, Leyla. "*La Canne de M. de Balzac:* Parody at the Intersection of Politics and Literature." *L'Esprit Créateur* 33.3 (1993): 95–103.

Faguet, Emile. *Balzac.* Paris: Hachette, 1913.

Ferguson, Priscilla Parkhurst. *Paris as Revolution: Writing the Nineteenth-Century City.* Berkeley: U of California P, 1994.

———. "Reading Revolutionary Paris." *Literature and Social Practice.* Ed. Ferguson et al. Chicago: Chicago UP, 1989. 46–68.

Flaubert, Gustave. *L'Education sentimentale. Œuvres complètes.* Ed. Bernard Masson. Paris: Seuil, 1964. 7–163.

———. *Madame Bovary.* Paris: Garnier-Flammarion, 1966.

Foucault, Michel. *Discipline and Punish: The Birth of the Prison.* Trans. Alan Sheridan. New York: Pantheon, 1977.

Freud, Sigmund. "The Uncanny." *On Creativity and the Unconscious.* New York: Harper, 1958. 122–61.

Gaudon, Jean. "Sur la chronologie du *Père Goriot.*" *L'Année balzacienne* (1967): 147–56.

Gautier, Théophile. "Honoré de Balzac." *Ecrivains et artistes romantiques.* Paris: Plon, 1933. 48–150.

Gay, Sophie. *Salons célèbres.* 1837. Paris: Levy, 1864.

Genette, Gérard. *Narrative Discourse.* Trans. Jane E. Lewin. Ithaca: Cornell UP, 1980.

———. *Nouveau discours du récit.* Paris: Seuil, 1983.

———. "Vraisemblance et motivation." *Communications* 11 (1968): 5–21.

Gengembre, Gérard. Introduction. *Balzac:* Le Père Goriot. Textes et contextes. Paris: Magnard, 1985.

Girard, René. *Deceit, Desire, and the Novel: Self and Other in Literary Structure.* Trans. Yvonne Freccero. Baltimore: Johns Hopkins UP, 1965.

Girardin, Delphine Gay de. "Le Bonheur d'être belle." *Œuvres complètes.* Vol. 1. Paris: Plon, 1860–61. 211–12.

———. *La Canne de M. de Balzac. Nouvelles.* Ed. Arlette Michel. Paris: Slatkine, 1979. 135–72.

———. *Lettres parisiennes du vicomte de Launay.* 2 vols. Paris: Mercure de France, 1986.

Glauser, Alfred. "Balzac/Vautrin." *Romanic Review* 79 (1988): 585–610.

Goethe, Johann Wolfgang von. *Faust: Der Tragödie Erster und Zweiter Teil; Urfaust.* Ed. Erich Trunz. Munich: Beck, 1975.

Green, Nicholas. *The Spectacle of Nature: Landscape and Bourgeois Culture in Nineteenth-Century France.* Manchester: Manchester UP, 1990.

Guichardet, Jeannine. *Balzac archéologue de Paris.* Paris: SEDES, 1986.

Halperin, David. *"One Hundred Years of Homosexuality" and Other Essays on Greek Love.* New York: Routledge, 1990.

Hamon, Philippe. *Introduction à l'analyse du descriptif.* Paris: Hachette, 1981.

Harvey, David. *Consciousness and the Urban Experience.* Baltimore: Johns Hopkins UP, 1985.

Hemmings, F. W. J. *Culture and Society in France, 1789–1848.* Leicester, Eng.: Leicester UP, 1987.

Herschberg-Pierrot, Anne, ed. *Balzac et le style.* Paris: SEDES, 1998.

Hobsbawm, E. J. *The Age of Revolution: Europe, 1789–1848.* London: Little, 1977.

Hugo, Victor. *Notre-Dame de Paris.* Paris: Garnier-Flammarion, 1967.

Jardin, A., and A. J. Tudesq. *La France des notables.* Paris: Seuil, 1973. Vols. 6 and 7 of *Nouvelle histoire de la France contemporaine.*

Kanes, Martin. Père Goriot*: Anatomy of a Troubled World.* New York: Twayne, 1993.

Kant, Immanuel. *Critique of Practical Reason.* Trans. Lewis White Beck. New York: Macmillan, 1956.

Kelly, Dorothy. "Delphine Gay de Girardin." *French Woman Writers.* Ed. Eva Martin Sartori and Dorothy Wayne Zimmerman. Lincoln: U of Nebraska P, 1991. 188–97.

———. *Telling Glances: Voyeurism in the French Novel.* New Brunswick: Rutgers UP, 1992.

Lane-Mercier, Gillian. *La Parole romanesque.* Ottawa: PU Ottawa; Paris: Klincksieck, 1989.

Lanson, Gustave. *L'Art de la prose.* Paris: Annales Poétiques et Littéraires, 1908.

Laplanche, Jean, and J.-B. Pontalis. *The Language of Psychoanalysis.* New York: Norton, 1973.

Larousse, Pierre. "Progrès." *Grand Dictionnaire universel du XIXe siècle.* 1866–79. Genève: Slatkine, 1982.

Le Hir, Marie-Pierre. *Le Romantisme aux enchères: Ducange, Pixerécourt, Hugo.* Amsterdam: Benjamins, 1992.

Lévy-Leblond, Jean-Marc. *L'Esprit de sel: science, culture, politique.* Paris: Seuil, 1984.

Lock, Peter. *Balzac:* Père Goriot. Studies in French Lit. 11. London: Arnold, 1967.

Locke, John. *An Essay Concerning Human Understanding.* Ed. Peter H. Nidditch. Oxford: Clarendon, 1975.

Lotte, Fernand. "Le Retour des personnages dans *La Comédie humaine.*" *L'Année balzacienne* (1961): 227–81.

Lough, John, and Muriel Lough. *An Introduction to Nineteenth Century France.* London: Longman, 1978.

Loyer, François. *Paris: Nineteenth Century: Architecture and Urbanism.* Trans. Charles Lynn Clark. New York: Abbeville, 1988.

Lucey, Michael. "Balzac's Queer Cousins and Their Friends." *Novel Gazing: Queer*

Readings in Fiction. Ed. Eve Kosofsky Sedgwick. Durham: Duke UP, 1997. 167–98.

Lukács, Georg. "Narrate or Describe." Lukács, "*Writer*" 110–48.

———. "*Writer and Critic" and Other Essays.* Ed. and trans. Arthur D. Kahn. New York: Grosset, 1971.

Lynch, Kevin. *The Image of the City.* Cambridge: MIT P, 1960.

Mahieu, Raymond, and Franc Schuerewegen, eds. *Balzac ou la tentation de l'impossible.* Paris: SEDES, 1998.

Maingueneau, Dominique. *Le Contexte de l'œuvre littéraire: énonciation, écrivain, société.* Paris: Dunod, 1993.

Marchand, Bernard. *Paris: histoire d'une ville: XIXe–XXe siècle.* Paris: Seuil, 1993.

Marcus, Sharon. *Apartment Stories: City and Home in Nineteenth-Century Paris and London.* Berkeley: U of California P, 1999.

Martin, Richard P. *The Language of Heroes: Speech and Performance in the* Iliad. Ithaca: Cornell UP, 1989.

Miller, D. A. "Balzac's Illusions Lost and Found." *Yale French Studies* 67 (1984): 164–81.

Milner, Max. "Les Dispositifs voyeuristes dans le récit balzacien." *Balzac: une poétique du roman.* Ed. Stéphane Vachon. Paris: PU Vincennes, 1996. 157–71.

———. "La Poésie du mal chez Balzac." *L'Année balzacienne* (1963): 321–35.

Mitterand, Henri, ed. *Le Dix-Neuvième Siècle.* Introd. Pierre Nora. Littérature: textes et documents. Paris: Nathan, 1986.

———. "Un 'Bel Artiste'?" Herschberg-Pierrot 135–44.

Monmonier, Mark. *How to Lie with Maps.* Chicago: U of Chicago P, 1991.

Montaigne, Michel de. "De l'expérience." *Œuvres complètes.* Ed. Maurice Rat. Paris: Gallimard-Pléiade, 1962. 1041–97.

———. "On Experience." *The Essays of Michel de Montaigne.* Trans. M. A. Screech. London: Allen Lane–Penguin, 1991. 1207–69.

Moretti, Franco. *Atlas of the European Novel, 1800–1900.* London: Verso, 1998.

———. *The Way of the World: The Bildungsroman in European Culture.* London: Verso, 1987.

Morgan, Cheryl. "Les Chiffons de la m(éd)use: Delphine Gay de Girardin, journaliste." *Romantisme* 85.3 (1994): 57–66.

Moss, Martha Niess. "The Metamorphosis of Vautrin in Balzac's *Comédie humaine.*" *Romance Notes* 20 (1979): 44–50.

Mozet, Nicole. *Balzac au pluriel.* Paris: PUF, 1990.

———. "La Description de la Maison Vauquer." *L'Année balzacienne* (1972): 97–130.

Nash, Suzanne. Introduction. *Home and Its Dislocations in Nineteenth-Century France.* Ed. Nash. Albany: State U of New York P, 1993. 1–21.

Nietzsche, Friedrich. *The Genealogy of Morals.* The Birth of Tragedy *and* The Genealogy of Morals. Trans. Francis Golffing. New York: Doubleday-Anchor, 1956. 147–299.

Paris, Jean. *Balzac.* Paris: Balland, 1986.

Perrot, Michelle, ed. *A History of Private Life.* Vol. 4. Cambridge: Harvard UP, 1990.

Petrey, Sandy. *Realism and Revolution: Balzac, Stendhal, Zola, and the Performances of*

History. Ithaca: Cornell UP, 1988.

Prendergast, Christopher. *Balzac: Fiction and Melodrama*. London: Arnold, 1978.

———. *Paris and the Nineteenth Century*. Oxford: Blackwell, 1992.

Przybos, Julia. *L'Entreprise mélodramatique*. Paris: Corti, 1987.

Pugh, Anthony R. *Balzac's Recurring Characters*. Toronto: U of Toronto P, 1974.

Reid, James H. *Narration and Description in the French Realist Novel: The Temporality of Lying and Forgetting*. Cambridge: Cambridge UP, 1993.

Reid, Roddey. *Families in Jeopardy: Regulating the Social Body in France, 1750–1910*. Stanford: Stanford UP, 1993.

Rignall, John. "Balzac: The Alienated Gaze." *Realist Fiction and the Strolling Spectator*. London: Routledge, 1992. 37–61.

Roques, Mario. "La Langue de Balzac." *Balzac: le livre du centenaire*. Ed. Jacques-Robert Duron et al. Paris: Flammarion, 1952. 246–57.

Rousset, Jean. *Le Lecteur intime: de Balzac au journal*. Paris: Corti, 1986.

Said, Edward W. *Beginnings: Intention and Method*. New York: Basic, 1975.

Sainte-Beuve, Charles Augustin. *Causeries du lundi*. 3rd ed. Vol. 2. Paris: Garnier, n.d.

———. "Madame Emile de Girardin." Sainte-Beuve, *Causeries* 384–406.

———. "M. de Balzac." Sainte-Beuve, *Causeries* 443–63.

Schehr, Lawrence R. "Homo-diégèse." Mahieu and Schuerewegen 135–41.

———. *Rendering French Realism*. Stanford: Stanford UP, 1997.

Schor, Naomi. *George Sand and Idealism*. New York: Columbia UP, 1993.

Schuerewegen, Franc. *Balzac contre Balzac: les cartes du lecteur*. Paris: SEDES; Toronto: Paratexte, 1990.

Schwartz, Vanessa. *Spectacular Realities: Early Mass Culture in* Fin-de-siècle *Paris*. Berkeley: U of California P, 1998.

Simmel, Georg. "The Metropolis and Mental Life." *On Individuality and Social Forms*. Ed. Donald N. Levine. Chicago: U of Chicago P, 1971. 324–39.

Stendhal. *Racine et Shakespeare: étude sur le romanticisme*. Ed. and introd. Roger Fayolle. Paris: Garnier-Flammarion, 1970.

———. *Romans*. Ed. Henri Martineau. Vol. 1. Paris: Bibliothèque de la Pléiade, 1952.

Storzer, Gerald H. "The Homosexual Paradigm in Balzac, Gide, and Genet." *Homosexualities and French Literature: Cultural Contexts / Critical Texts*. Ed. George Stambolian and Elaine Marks. Ithaca: Cornell UP, 1979. 186–209.

Suck, Titus T. "The Paternal Signifier: The Monetary Metaphor in Balzac's *Le Père Goriot*." *Romanic Review* 81 (1990): 25–44.

Sutcliffe, Anthony. *Paris: An Architectural History*. New Haven: Yale UP, 1993.

Terdiman, Richard. *Discourse/Counter-discourse*. Ithaca: Cornell UP, 1985.

Thibaudet, Albert. *Histoire de la littérature francaise de 1789 à nos jours*. Paris: Stock, 1936.

Vachon, Stéphane. *Les Travaux et les jours d'Honoré de Balzac: chronologie de la création balzacienne*. Paris: PU Vincennes; Montréal: PU Montréal, 1992.

van Rossum-Guyon, Françoise. "*Le Père Goriot* roman moderne." Balzac, *Le Père Goriot* [van Rossum-Guyon] ix–xxx.

———. "Texte et idéologie." *Degrés* 8 (1980–81): b1–b12.

Waggoner, Mark. *Bibliography of Balzac Criticism, 1930–1990.* Encinitas: French Research Pubs., 1990.

Walkowitz, Judith. *City of Dreadful Delight: Narratives of Sexual Danger in Late-Victorian London.* Chicago: U of Chicago P, 1992.

Waller, Margaret. "Disembodiment as a Masquerade: Fashion Journalists and Other 'Realist' Observers in Directory Paris." *L'Esprit Créateur* 37.1 (1997): 44–54.

———. *The Male Malady: Fictions of Impotence in the French Romantic Novel.* New Brunswick: Rutgers UP, 1993.

Watt, Ian. *The Rise of the Novel.* Berkeley: U of California P, 1957.

Weber, Samuel. *Unwrapping Balzac: A Reading of* La Peau de chagrin. Toronto: U of Toronto P, 1979.

Wilde, Oscar. *Intentions.* London: Unicorn, 1948.

Willms, Johannes. *Paris: Capital of Europe: From the Revolution to the Belle Epoque.* Trans. Eveline L. Kanes. New York: Holmes, 1997.

Wilson, Elizabeth. "The Invisible Flâneur." *New Left Review* 191 (1992): 90–110.

Wolff, Janet. "The Invisible Flâneuse: Women and the Literature of Modernity." *Feminine Sentences: Essays on Women and Culture.* Berkeley: U of California P, 1990. 34–50.

Wright, Gordon. *France in Modern Times: From the Enlightenment to the Present.* New York: Norton, 1981.

Index of Other Works by Balzac

Index of Names

Modern Language Association of America

Approaches to Teaching World Literature

Joseph Gibaldi, series editor

Achebe's Things Fall Apart. Ed. Bernth Lindfors. 1991.
Arthurian Tradition. Ed. Maureen Fries and Jeanie Watson. 1992.
Atwood's The Handmaid's Tale *and Other Works*. Ed. Sharon R. Wilson, Thomas B. Friedman, and Shannon Hengen. 1996.
Austen's Pride and Prejudice. Ed. Marcia McClintock Folsom. 1993.
Balzac's Old Goriot. Ed. Michal Peled Ginsburg. 2000.
Baudelaire's Flowers of Evil. Ed. Laurence M. Porter. 2000.
Beckett's Waiting for Godot. Ed. June Schlueter and Enoch Brater. 1991.
Beowulf. Ed. Jess B. Bessinger, Jr., and Robert F. Yeager. 1984.
Blake's Songs of Innocence and of Experience. Ed. Robert F. Gleckner and Mark L. Greenberg. 1989.
Boccaccio's Decameron. Ed. James H. McGregor. 2000.
British Women Poets of the Romantic Period. Ed. Stephen C. Behrendt and Harriet Kramer Linkin. 1997.
Brontë's Jane Eyre. Ed. Diane Long Hoeveler and Beth Lau. 1993.
Byron's Poetry. Ed. Frederick W. Shilstone. 1991.
Camus's The Plague. Ed. Steven G. Kellman. 1985.
Cather's My Ántonia. Ed. Susan J. Rosowski. 1989.
Cervantes' Don Quixote. Ed. Richard Bjornson. 1984.
Chaucer's Canterbury Tales. Ed. Joseph Gibaldi. 1980.
Chopin's The Awakening. Ed. Bernard Koloski. 1988.
Coleridge's Poetry and Prose. Ed. Richard E. Matlak. 1991.
Dante's Divine Comedy. Ed. Carole Slade. 1982.
Dickens' David Copperfield. Ed. Richard J. Dunn. 1984.
Dickinson's Poetry. Ed. Robin Riley Fast and Christine Mack Gordon. 1989.
Narrative of the Life of Frederick Douglass. Ed. James C. Hall. 1999.
Eliot's Middlemarch. Ed. Kathleen Blake. 1990.
Eliot's Poetry and Plays. Ed. Jewel Spears Brooker. 1988.
Ellison's Invisible Man. Ed. Susan Resneck Parr and Pancho Savery. 1989.
Faulkner's The Sound and the Fury. Ed. Stephen Hahn and Arthur F. Kinney. 1996.
Flaubert's Madame Bovary. Ed. Laurence M. Porter and Eugene F. Gray. 1995.
García Márquez's One Hundred Years of Solitude. Ed. María Elena de Valdés and Mario J. Valdés. 1990.
Goethe's Faust. Ed. Douglas J. McMillan. 1987.
Hebrew Bible as Literature in Translation. Ed. Barry N. Olshen and Yael S. Feldman. 1989.
Homer's Iliad *and* Odyssey. Ed. Kostas Myrsiades. 1987.
Ibsen's A Doll House. Ed. Yvonne Shafer. 1985.
Works of Samuel Johnson. Ed. David R. Anderson and Gwin J. Kolb. 1993.
Joyce's Ulysses. Ed. Kathleen McCormick and Erwin R. Steinberg. 1993.
Kafka's Short Fiction. Ed. Richard T. Gray. 1995.

Keats's Poetry. Ed. Walter H. Evert and Jack W. Rhodes. 1991.
Kingston's The Woman Warrior. Ed. Shirley Geok-lin Lim. 1991.
Lafayette's The Princess of Clèves. Ed. Faith E. Beasley and Katharine Ann Jensen. 1998.
Lessing's The Golden Notebook. Ed. Carey Kaplan and Ellen Cronan Rose. 1989.
Mann's Death in Venice *and Other Short Fiction*. Ed. Jeffrey B. Berlin. 1992.
Medieval English Drama. Ed. Richard K. Emmerson. 1990.
Melville's Moby-Dick. Ed. Martin Bickman. 1985.
Metaphysical Poets. Ed. Sidney Gottlieb. 1990.
Miller's Death of a Salesman. Ed. Matthew C. Roudané. 1995.
Milton's Paradise Lost. Ed. Galbraith M. Crump. 1986.
Molière's Tartuffe *and Other Plays*. Ed. James F. Gaines and Michael S. Koppisch. 1995.
Momaday's The Way to Rainy Mountain. Ed. Kenneth M. Roemer. 1988.
Montaigne's Essays. Ed. Patrick Henry. 1994.
Novels of Toni Morrison. Ed. Nellie Y. McKay and Kathryn Earle. 1997.
Murasaki Shikibu's The Tale of Genji. Ed. Edward Kamens. 1993.
Pope's Poetry. Ed. Wallace Jackson and R. Paul Yoder. 1993.
Shakespeare's King Lear. Ed. Robert H. Ray. 1986.
Shakespeare's Romeo and Juliet. Ed. Maurice Hunt. 2000.
Shakespeare's The Tempest *and Other Late Romances*. Ed. Maurice Hunt. 1992.
Shelley's Frankenstein. Ed. Stephen C. Behrendt. 1990.
Shelley's Poetry. Ed. Spencer Hall. 1990.
Shorter Elizabethan Poetry. Ed. Patrick Cheney and Anne Lake Prescott. 2000.
Sir Gawain and the Green Knight. Ed. Miriam Youngerman Miller and Jane Chance. 1986.
Spenser's Faerie Queene. Ed. David Lee Miller and Alexander Dunlop. 1994.
Stendhal's The Red and the Black. Ed. Dean de la Motte and Stirling Haig. 1999.
Sterne's Tristram Shandy. Ed. Melvyn New. 1989.
Stowe's Uncle Tom's Cabin. Ed. Elizabeth Ammons and Susan Belasco. 2000.
Swift's Gulliver's Travels. Ed. Edward J. Rielly. 1988.
Thoreau's Walden *and Other Works*. Ed. Richard J. Schneider. 1996.
Voltaire's Candide. Ed. Renée Waldinger. 1987.
Whitman's Leaves of Grass. Ed. Donald D. Kummings. 1990.
Wordsworth's Poetry. Ed. Spencer Hall, with Jonathan Ramsey. 1986.
Wright's Native Son. Ed. James A. Miller. 1997.